THE ONCE AND FUTURE MUSE

LATINO AND LATIN AMERICAN PROFILES

FREDERICK LUIS ALDAMA, EDITOR

the *Once* *and* *Future* *Muse*

THE POETRY AND POETICS OF RHINA P. ESPAILLAT

NANCY KANG AND SILVIO TORRES-SAILLANT

University of Pittsburgh Press

Published by the University of Pittsburgh Press, Pittsburgh, Pa., 15260
Copyright © 2018, University of Pittsburgh Press
All rights reserved
Manufactured in the United States of America
Printed on acid-free paper
10 9 8 7 6 5 4 3 2 1

Cataloging-in-Publication data is available from the Library of Congress

ISBN 13: 978-0-8229-6542-8

Cover photograph: Rhina P. Espaillat as a teen. Courtesy of Rhina P. Espaillat.
Cover design by Joel W. Coggins

To
Pyungja June Kang
(1943–2015)
Aapiji gi-zaagi'in

Aida Mercedes Torres Cruz
(1931–2018)
Gratitud infinita

Alfred Moskowitz
(1925–2016)
In Memoriam

CONTENTS

ACKNOWLEDGMENTS

A book is not brought about simply by the skills, efforts, and credentials of its authors. It typically depends on a constellation of supporters in the scholarly, institutional, familial, communal, and personal spheres without whom no academic undertaking could thrive. We owe a debt of gratitude to more people than an acknowledgements section can readily accommodate. At the very least we must mention those whose support has had the most direct impact on our work.

Nancy Kang wishes to acknowledge the generous support of summer research and conference grants from the University of Baltimore's Yale Gordon College of Arts and Sciences under the leadership of deans Laura Bryan and Christine Spencer. She is thankful for the mentorship of former division chair Cheryl Wilson at the Klein Family School of Communications Design. Associate dean Debbie Kohl and division chair Jane Delury have also been very supportive. She values generous mentors present and past, chief among them Linda Hutcheon, George Elliott Clarke, Paul Stevens, Nick Mount, and Naomi Morgenstern. Heartfelt gratitude is owed to her family and many inspiring friends and colleagues both near and far, especially Amy Huang, Elizabeth Underwood, Sarane Poon, Ashley and Adam Barkman, Dena Mandel, Ian Williams, Pari Kasotia, and Cherise Pollard.

Silvio Torres-Saillant deeply appreciates the benefit of a one-semester research leave that liberated him from classroom duties in fall 2014 in the English department of Syracuse University's College of Arts and Sciences, where colleagues, students, and staff have offered a stimulating environment for continuous intellectual growth. He feels particularly grateful to dean Karin Ruhlandt, associate dean Gerry Greenberg, and the personnel of the Syracuse University libraries, especially at Bird Library, who have invariably provided expert, cordial, and prompt assistance at nearly every step in the course of the research and writing of this book. As research assistant in 2012–2013 and at several points thereafter, Maxim A. Torres-Saillant contributed significantly to this project, compiling bibliographies, transcribing necessary materials, and verifying revisions to the final version of the manuscript.

The authors acknowledge the College of Arts and Sciences of Syracuse University for its generous support of their research and the production of this book. We also wish to express gratitude to the CUNY Dominican Studies Institute at City College of the City University of New York, especially for the invaluable archival research assistance of chief librarian Sarah Aponte and assistant librarian Jhensen Ortiz, who helped us locate key items documenting Espaillat's active involvement with the Poetry Society of America (PSA) and the *Ladies' Home Journal* since the late 1940s. Jhensen's findings in the main branch of the New York Public Library, which houses PSA archives, proved priceless. We also thank Nestor and Maria Teresa Montilla, leaders of the Dominican American National Roundtable (DANR), for the travel grant that allowed us to organize a productive panel on the work of Espaillat, featuring the scholar and fiction writer Roberta Fernández and the award-winning poet Alfred Nicol, along with Espaillat herself, who came accompanied by her beloved husband Alfred Moskowitz, during the Latin American Studies Association's 2013 Congress in Washington, DC.

At the University of Pittsburgh Press, we thank editorial director Sandy Crooms, who embraced our project since first hearing about it, and professor Frederick Luis Aldama, editor of the Latino and Latin American Profiles Series, for quickly endorsing the idea of our book and taking it under his wing as one of his titles. We appreciate the commitment of Joshua Shanholtzer, senior acquisitions editor, and the work of the production team for seeing our manuscript through to the final stages of publication. Nor can we overlook the invaluable suggestions for revision that we received from the outside peer reviewers.

Thanks to their feedback we have produced a more effective manuscript than we would have otherwise.

Finally, we owe the deepest debt of gratitude to Rhina P. Espaillat for the generosity and enthusiasm with which she approached every single one of our queries about biographical and textual matters and her willingness to read and respond to portions of our manuscript for specific details and factual verifications. The genteel hospitality that she and Alfred extended to us during our enormously pleasant visit to their home in Newburyport, Massachusetts, in early January 2013, when she granted us a two-day interview, enabled us to sharpen our sense of her life and work in incalculable ways. All the quotations and paraphrases of Espaillat's words that we identify with our initials in parenthetical references (NK/STS) throughout the volume came from the long interview we conducted at the poet's house in Newburyport. We only regret that our study did not emerge in time for Alfred to see it, as he passed away at home on February 27, 2016. An accomplished and prolific sculptor, a jovial host, and a sharp interlocutor, Alfred was one of his wife's most loyal fans. Since the couple moved to Newburyport, he seldom missed a chance to accompany her on readings and lectures, and he displayed genuine joy when he coined the title Poet Consort and Baggage Handler for himself. Espaillat agrees with us that he would have been thrilled to hold our book in his hands. *Requiescat in pace.*

We hope *The Once and Future Muse* may contribute to increasing the number of readers among students at various levels and in the general public who regard Rhina P. Espaillat among the indispensable poets of our times. Already widely acclaimed by peers in the poetry scene, Espaillat has a loyal following of readers from across the United States who treasure her art, her humane utterances, and the salutary model that she offers for junior writers. We hope our study will encourage other literary scholars to take up the poetry, poetics, trajectory, and legacy of Espaillat as the subject of their research, thereby further illuminating her significance for American literature writ large.

INTRODUCTION

THE POET'S VISION

*T*he Once and Future Muse: The Poetry and Poetics of Rhina P. Espaillat charts the literary trajectory, salient themes, aesthetic accomplishments, and critical reception of a major American poet whose work conveys a compelling message to our troubled world. The study also takes advantage of the chronology corresponding to the life of the poet to illustrate meaningful paradigmatic shifts in the production and consumption of literary texts in the United States after World War II that have indelibly marked the way subsequent generations would write, read, share, and discuss the art of literature.

We understand that our choice of title, one that hearkens back to *Le Morte Darthur* (1485), the fifteenth-century epic prose narrative by Thomas Malory (?–1471), may elicit a measure of perplexity. What connection could there be between the work of Malory, an English author active over five centuries ago, and the oeuvre of our contemporary Caribbean-descended American poet? Malory wrote his book while behind bars after a public life that started out with his receipt of knighthood before 1442 and service in the Parliament of 1445 but degraded into violence and crimes of various sorts to end his days in London's historic Newgate Prison (Baugh 305). On the other hand, Rhina P. Espaillat is a woman who has led a relatively quiet life. A brilliant and unassuming poet, she has spent her eighty-six years observing, reading, writing, teaching, looking after offspring and elders, building literary communities, and subtly conveying the gospel of poetry across the country. However, we trust that any perplexity prompted by the appearance of her name in the same paragraph as Malory may dissipate in the pages ahead.

With her feet firmly planted in the immediate reality of her historical moment while imaginatively claiming kinship with diverse members of the human tribe beyond it, Espaillat has an uncommon literary career that spans the 1940s through the second decade of the twenty-first century. Her voluminous poetic output reveals her to be a first-rate artist steeped in the intricacies of her craft, aware of the expressive possibilities of language, sensitive to the gamut of human yearnings, and trustful of the salutary role that art can play in bridging borders of difference within the fractious realm of social relations. Espaillat's verse exhibits a desire to observe her surroundings carefully, extracting meaning from the minutiae of ordinary existence. Her poems converse with artists or public figures from centuries ago and visualize the continuance of life after her own. Rooted in today, cognizant of the world that preceded her, and cautiously in awe of all that is to come, Espaillat stands out as a "timely" poet in all senses of the word. Her thematic range encompasses an array of broadly resonant foci: the power of nature and the mysteries of the cosmos; the complex fissures of the mind and soul; chance versus choice; and the temptation to quarrel with the divine in the face of widespread misery on earth.

Poems considered in this study will treat various salient topics. Espaillat often explores music and painting, plumbs the nuances of family life, and braids lived experience with Greco-Roman myths while dissecting her Dominican ancestry and Hispanic heritage. Love, misogyny, and the mysteries of life amid sickness, the nature of perception, the significance of place, and the precariousness of that which we might call fair play fall within her purview. Her foreign birth and Caribbean roots enter seamlessly into an inclusive US American identity. Similarly, an overarching desire to understand others comprises her ethics of compassion. Her veritable cornucopia of topics and themes blend into a striking harmony that resists homogenizing impulses and predictable outcomes.

Espaillat's compassion manifests itself as a willingness to empathize across time, space, race, culture, creed, and even species. Poet Roy Scheele comments upon "the breadth and depth" of her subject matter as well as her "unusual treatment" of it, which he illustrates by means of her poem "Retriever." In this text, the speaker unexpectedly assumes "the perspective of the dog instead of its master" (Scheele 36). Responding to Scheele's observations, Espaillat speaks of her tendency "to think [her]self into other heads whether the heads are those of animals or of other people," including "inanimate objects." She adds, "If I look at something long enough behaving as it behaves, whether it's an animal running or a tree blowing in the wind, I become it" (37). She sees poetry as well suited for that sort of self-transport into others insofar as it "allows you not only to move backward and forward through time but also through what's around you, with your imagination, so that you *become* things that you are not and can never possibly be" (37).

The transformative worldview that sustains this expansiveness, we would argue, hangs on Espaillat's freedom from deterministic narratives and all-encompassing paradigms of the kinds that normally split heritages, civilizations, branches of the human species, belief systems, aesthetic orientations, or literary practices into the garden-variety *us versus them*. In this dichotomy, the *us* is almost invariably representative of the supposedly superior option, the one more deserving of respect and admiration even at the wholesale expense of *them*. In the words of former president George W. Bush, spoken in July 2016 as he joined then president Barack Obama at a memorial for five police officers gunned down in Dallas, we tend "to judge other groups by their worst examples while judging ourselves by our best intentions" (Harris and Landler). Espaillat invites us to transcend such one-sided judgments through her practice of upholding a decentered view of human culture that envisions an empathic experience of the whole species and well beyond it.

Espaillat poignantly conveys her outlook on identity when answering a question about whether her poetry has benefited from bilingualism, that is, her having retained the Spanish language of her birthplace despite arriving in the United States as a toddler and receiving all her formal education in English. She suggests that the dual-language experience "severs an intimate"—though perhaps delusional—"connection we have with language" as monolinguals. We typically experience our one language as if it were "all there is," the rest seeming "mere translations of it" (Scheele 36). This response corresponds to Espaillat's critique of the nativist rhetoric that has long impugned immigrants and their ancestral languages. We witnessed, for instance, the anti-immigrant voices that expressed public indignation at marchers during a 2006 national Hispanic immigrant rally in Washington, DC, for "disrespecting" "The Star-Spangled Banner" by singing it in Spanish near the US Capitol. Such expressions of antipathy toward a second language have frequently recurred in US history. That singing the national anthem in Spanish should strike some patriotic citizens as disrespectful suggests that the fundamentalist view of American identity, with its abhorrence for cultural difference, has remained vibrant in some sectors of the population. By the same token, the obduracy of English-only ideologues has seldom failed to elicit ridicule from critics who ascribe to them the type of epistemic dysfunction illustrated by the remark, "If English was good enough for Jesus Christ, it ought to be good enough for the children of Texas"—attributed, perhaps apocryphally, to two-time Texas governor Miriam A. Ferguson (1875–1961) (Cárdenas; Zimmer).

Given the role of translation in spreading the Christian doctrine from one geographical realm or cultural context to another, it seems that the Lord has not cared much about the language spoken by those preaching the Word. King James I (1566–1625), who authorized the first English settlement of North America in 1607, sponsored the translators who worked from scriptures composed originally in various other languages to produce an English translation of the Bible. The king was free of the impediments encountered centuries earlier by the English theologian John Wycliffe (1330–1384), who had led the effort to produce an English translation. This infraction earned him much condemnation by church and political authorities alike even though his work had drawn from the Vulgate version (382 AD) of the Bible popularized by Saint Jerome (342–420 AD), itself a Latin translation of the Hebrew original, as well as the *Septuagint*, the version of the Old Testament available in Koiné Greek since the second century BC. The 1611 King James Version of the Bible would eventually become the standard source for Anglophone Christians to learn the word of the Lord.

Attributing to the advocates of monolingual public school education the claim that "English was good enough for Jesus Christ" bitingly mocks the idea that sacred national values (or even religious values) are diminished when expressed in a language other than English. Some see English as the only "real" language, with all others being, in Espaillat's words, "mere translations" of it. Espaillat harbors no metaphysics of language as it relates to identity or the sacred, appreciating it rather in accordance with its situational contingency. Convinced that the divine has no linguistic preference, Espaillat observes that a potential narrowness of perception may be deleterious to monolingual speakers. They take the words in their language as the "real" ones because in childhood they had "the illusion that when [they] say 'tree' [they] are naming something." Bilingualism thus "breaks" that Adamic illusion (Scheele 36). When we are able to step outside of a single linguistic framework, we become "undeceived of that, and [we] understand that all language is arbitrary, that there is no language that reality speaks—reality is mute" (36). "Each language," the poet maintains, "is as valid as all the others—and as useless, in the long run, because not one of them captures the whole of what we're looking for" (36).

Espaillat's bilingual upbringing has conferred upon her the capacity to enter on more equal terms a larger number of discursive spaces occupied by others who speak different languages. Likewise, whether connected to her view of language or not, her empathic imagination recognizes the multiple creative tools that poets have at their disposal. Not a poet to be pigeonholed into any one aesthetic or interpretive template circulating in literary criticism today, Espaillat advocates openness to all the manners of communication that language and the poetic art have allowed throughout the vastness of the world's expressive traditions. She asks of artistic communication only that it remain truthful, arguing that with so little time available "to communicate fully," it seems pointless to "waste a minute of it telling lies," especially since "you can't get those moments back" (Fox 137). She celebrates the truthfulness of Stanley Kunitz, whom she admires greatly for having deliberately turned to free verse after a stellar literary career as a formal poet. Kunitz engaged in the latter as devoutly and with similarly admirable results as when practicing the former. Espaillat dismisses as silly the idea that the working tools used to craft one's poems determine their social or political values. She contends further that one can find retrograde free verse practitioners and progressive formalists in equally bountiful numbers (Kang 181).

The Once and Future Muse plots a course through Espaillat's work from 1947 to the present. Significantly, the sequence of her books, as dated by year of publication, does not offer a reliable clue to her growth as an artist, the metamorphosis of her outlook from youth to maturity, or the evolution of her poetic thought over seven decades. She has, from early on, displayed a tendency toward thematic promiscuity in the sense of covering disparate subjects almost simultaneously. She has admitted that she does not sit down to write with the sole objective of producing book-length collections (Scheele 43). Given her copious productivity and the "lateness" of her decision to start publishing volumes of verse, she has had plenty of completed work to choose from when the occasion to compile another book has arisen. At those points, she has simply assembled "piles" of those poems "that seem to be speaking to each other as part of the same theme," with "no qualms about putting together the old and the new" (Scheele 43). However, even with the ostensibly accidental chronology of her collections, one might still discern something of a conceptual evolution. Her choosing texts that speak to one another around a particular theme results in distinct emphases for each of the volumes. In that sense, her choices communicate aspects of her existential disposition at the time of the assemblage irrespective of the composition date of the individual texts.

Whether or not one can consider the sequence of emphases a development or an evolution, they do correspond to meaningful states of mind that have prevailed in her work at various stages of her literary career. Espaillat herself would grant that in her early poems of the 1940s and 1950s, her gaze seemed focused on the present, one "full of personal observations of my own corner of the world," which she does not at all regret, since lyric poetry typically captures "the voice of the individual, after all" (Scheele 44). But in subsequent decades her writing "has had more to say about what we share, our common experiences, and it takes a longer view into the past and the future, as well as into other lives than mine." In her later work she has meditated at great length on the inevitability and trials of aging, along with its ultimate consequence: "Mortality has been on my mind, especially, because the last few years have brought the deaths of many old friends and members of my family and my husband's. When your generation begins to grow sparse all around you, you take stock of your situation and begin to imagine—or 'rehearse' the absence of those you still have, and eventually your own" (44).

The writer admits to this "elegiac thought" that permeates the later volumes, beginning most prominently with the collection *Rehearsing Absence* (2001). This volume features "a lot of reappraisal of what you thought was yours for good, a lot of leave-taking" (Scheele 44). But the acknowledgement of life's evanescence and contemplation of death—*thanatopsis*, as examined in our chapter six—has not diminished her "sorrow for those lives that are impoverished by the lack of so much that [we] think of as ordinary." While she feels it "impossible to be conscious at all without sorrow over huge 'unfixables,' both past and present," she remains resolutely aware of the inexorable continuance of life (44–45). Questioning the logic of physicians and other professionals who may prognosticate fixed limits to life, she has increased her engagement with the mysteries and potential of the future, one that belongs to generations to come. She believes that the future "doesn't need any of us specifically," hence her concomitant interest in all that will stay behind: "I am turning my attention to those things that will outlive me, and thinking of them with a pleasure and satisfaction that I can't explain even to myself" (45).

Espaillat also finds it necessary "to get that grateful acquiescence down on paper, that affection for unexceptional things that I hope will be part of the lives of my grandchildren's generation and beyond, as they were part of my grandparents' lives, and of mine, I mean the natural world, human creativity, thought, ordinary relationships, the common pleasures of the body and mind" (45). A signature poem expressing concern for the well-being of those future generations appears in her collection *Where Horizons Go* (1998), namely, "For My Great-Great Grandson, the Space Pioneer." In this piece, she "wanted to tell that mythical young man in the future that it's important to hold on to the earth, not to lose it, not to subvert it, not to corrupt it—to love it as it is, because it's like the body of an ancestor" (35–36). This strikingly conservationist ethos is gravely pertinent at a time when the United States, the leader of the capitalist world and the model that the countries within its sphere of influence eagerly emulate, finds itself at war with nature. This country, like other powerful industrialized nations, seems trapped in a scheme of economic advancement that requires the ongoing pollution of the Earth's soil, air, and water, the reengineering of flora to alter their natural reproductive capacities for the sake of accelerated growth controlled by corporations, the destruction of wildlife habitats such as rainforests and oceans, and the steady onslaught of greenhouse gases and other toxic emissions. Nearsightedness and shortcuts have become part and parcel of modern industrialized life, even as mighty corporate sectors, their allies in government, and their de facto spokespersons in the various legislatures apply themselves methodically to denying or underplaying negative outcomes, including climate change (Baxter). Espaillat's concern over whether future generations will have a planet on which to spend their lives comfortably while searching for meaning strikes a chord of utter and plangent urgency.

This poet's oeuvre imaginatively links the present, the future, and the past in ways that recall the legacy attributed to King Arthur by Malory. After the day of destiny arrives and the beloved monarch must meet his Maker, the narrator of *Le Morte Darthur* finds a way to relay the message that the exalted king remains among his subjects still. The engine of longevity runs on the faith of many throughout the kingdom who believe their magnanimous ruler will return: "Yet some men say in many parts of England that King Arthur is not dead, but had [been conveyed] by the will of our Lord Jesus into another place; and men say that he shall come again, and he shall win the Holy Cross. Yet I will not say that it shall be so, but rather I would say: here in this world he changed his life. And many men say that there is written upon the tomb thus: HIC IACET ARTHURUS, REX QUONDAM REXQUE FUTURUS" (Malory 873).[1] The inscription on Arthur's tomb,

---

1. We have modernized the spelling of English words in this quotation.

as rendered through hearsay by Malory's narrator, has become familiar in the abridged form used by T. H. White (1906–1964) in the title of his Arthurian novel *The Once and Future King* (1958).

Our title *The Once and Future Muse* intentionally echoes White's usage. We have meant *Muse* to denote not only Espaillat the person but also the composite ethos that has nourished her body of work, a creative corpus that convinces us of its enduring appeal. We take it that, the unexemplary course of his life notwithstanding, Malory wished for readers to see in the signified of the phrase "rex quondam rexque futurus" not a mere individual of flesh and bone but the legacy such an individual bequeathed to us, which would have to live on because of the humane values informing it. Espaillat's vision of humanity and her desire for the preservation of the Earth so that both human and nonhuman species may continue to flourish, is part of a timeless yearning that the fifteenth-century Britons conveyed in the desire to save Camelot from impending doom. The preteritness of *Le Morte Darthur* correlates with Espaillat's futurity in that it transports us to a time prior to rampant colonialism, the advent of capitalism as an economic system that holds almost nothing sacred, and the wholesale abuse of the natural environment for profit over the past five centuries.

Besides linking this Caribbean-born poet to the Arthurian legend, thereby associating her with the mythic domain of medieval Britain, our title also alludes to the first volume of Anglophone verse published by a resident of England's colonies on the Atlantic coast of North America. *The Tenth Muse Lately Sprung Up in America* (1650), penned in Massachusetts by Puritan immigrant poet Anne Bradstreet (1612–1672), herself a devoted wife and mother just like Espaillat, stands as a foundational text of American poetry. As Espaillat did in the twentieth century, Bradstreet in the seventeenth had endeavored to navigate the tension between her domestic duties and the demands of her art. She walked the delicate line between respecting tradition and asserting her aesthetic individuality; likewise, she resolved to embrace the new land as home even as she remained attached to affairs in her land of birth. We thought that a title with the semantic potential for drawing these historical parallels would seem appropriate for this book-length study of the poetic legacy of Espaillat.[2]

---

2. Espaillat does write prose in addition to her verse, but our study focuses on the poetry. We hereby acknowledge Leslie Monsour's *Rhina Espaillat: A Critical Introduction* (2013), a useful overview consisting of two critical essays, a short biography, an original interview, and a selected bibliography.

COVERAGE

Espaillat occupies an ambivalent place in American literature today. She has accrued numerous laurels for the humane vision of her work and her exceptional artistry, but she does not enjoy a national fame comparable to that of Richard Wilbur, Donald Hall, or Robert Pinsky, to name only three prominent American poets of her generation. Few would venture to claim that these better-known practitioners surpass Espaillat in terms of merit as a literary artist. Since her lesser centrality in the country's literary scene has to do primarily with events in her personal history, we have selected a "life and works" approach that seeks to provide as much of the poet's biography as is necessary to contextualize our critical assessment of her oeuvre.

We have thus undertaken a sustained study of the poetry and poetics of an artist whose work we admire, including her versatile translations as well as her experience teaching, mentoring, engaging with other wordsmiths, and winning new readers for the art. As the book will reveal, we have sought to maintain a balance between the social and the aesthetic. We have pursued this balance with the belief that the political intervention by a literary text convinces most readily when enabled by the artistic resources that sustain it and that, conversely, craft reaches its ultimate triumph when it succeeds at touching human beings in a salutary, illuminating way. As such, the reader will find in these pages a balance between a close reading of poetic texts and a scholarly effort to explain the contexts in which these selfsame texts achieve their immediate significance. We cover the poet's trajectory, focusing on details of her biography, family history, ancestral heritage, and literary education, in addition to tracing the artistic sensibility that could explain her early inclination to embracing classical English prosody as her chief arsenal of poetic modes. We have approached her poems with an eye on what they say as well as how they say it; in other words, we seek to dissect the complex partnership of content and form.

We begin this book with several chapters describing Espaillat's life and the trajectory of her career since her early years in the Dominican Republic and New York City. The first chapter offers an overview of her biography and pivotal moments of literary formation. It also identifies a wide range of salient features in her work so as to suggest a breadth of themes, topics, and registers appreciably greater than our book alone can cover. The second chapter charts the poet's rise as a young literary star in 1940s New York. The discussion visits her first encounters with poetry as a child and her auspicious educational beginnings in Manhattan. Chapter three explores sites of belonging that opened for Espaillat upon her return to literary visibility postretirement—among others, as a practitioner of her craft, as a writer in dialogue with literary traditions, and as a cultural broker via her translation work. Even as she asserted her Hispanic Caribbean ancestry, she became a builder of poetic communities among people of other ancestries in New York and Massachusetts, earning recognition from colleagues nationwide. Following this, chapter four outlines the ethnic compartmentalization of American literature that had taken place by the time Espaillat repositioned poetry at the center of her life. The discussion also examines her acquisition of the label "Latina" to locate her poetry in relation to ancestry, and the implications therein for how her legacy would be configured and acknowledged. Overall, using Espaillat's case as an example, the chapter tells the story of how social movements from the 1960s onward transformed the way Americans would read their country's letters.

The volume then shifts to a closer analysis of particular themes in Espaillat's oeuvre. Chapter five interrogates the poet's personal mode of feminist literary praxis. In doing so, it considers the gender implications of the thirty-year interruption in her literary career, a period when she privileged spousal, parental, and occupational responsibilities over active immersion in her craft. It then fleshes out the analysis by offering close readings of her Adam-and-Eve-themed pieces. These versatile texts provide the stage for the poet to dramatize the tension between artistic individuality and commitment to others. Chapter six undertakes a close reading of pertinent poems to explore the narrative contours of the aging body. Sickness serves as a thematic anchor for Espaillat's understanding of life, physical suffering, medical prognostications of death, and some more-than-human deviations from the reality of our mortal end.

The final two chapters take stock of Espaillat's critical legacy, reflecting both her own perspective and the reception of and engagement with her work by critics and peers. Chapter seven offers a compendium of responses to Espaillat's oeuvre broadly and to individual poems by critics, scholars, reviewers, editors, and fellow poets who have attested to the impact of her work. It also illustrates the remarkably varied facets of her vision by showcasing the multiple agendas that critics, scholars, anthologists, and editors have sought to advance through inclusion of her poetry, namely, celebrating distinct forms, exploring moral quandaries, revisiting classical myths, representing the spirit of particular regions, writing back to the great male poets, or simply advocating for the art of poetry, among others. Finally, chapter eight explores her poetic philosophy in the context of the "poetry wars," gauges her position relative to free verse and formalist factions, and analyzes her opinions on the failings and virtues of other bards.

Espaillat's richly inclusive messages about art, nature, empathy, compassion, and the future of our species prove particularly relevant to these turbulent times. Confident that her life and work will be of interest to nonacademic readers in the general public, we have made a sustained effort to explain cultural references and to locate authors, artists, or other historical figures in their corresponding chronologies and contexts. We have provided basic background information on poetic forms, styles, schools, social movements, literary histories, political events, and cultural debates relevant to the study of the poet. We hope to offer all that may be needed for any reader, whether seasoned or raw, to become acquainted with and proficient in the contributions of this major American poet. Concurrently, we anticipate fellow scholars will find in these pages enough enticements to teach the works of Rhina P. Espaillat to their students or to identify aspects and areas that we have left insufficiently examined that they might wish to take on as part of their own research endeavors.

THE ONCE AND FUTURE MUSE

1 | A FEELING, A BEAT, AND AN IMAGE

A CIRCUITOUS ROUTE

It is not hard to imagine how much it must have meant for Rhina P. Espaillat, the foreign-born daughter of working-class immigrant parents from the Dominican Republic and whose first language was not English, to travel to the august and proverbially Anglophone Longfellow House in Cambridge, Massachusetts, on September 24, 2006, to receive the May Sarton Award. She accepted the distinction from the board of directors of the New England Poetry Club, an organization founded in 1915 by Conrad Aiken, Robert Frost, and Amy Lowell, all three at the time having excelled as early masters of their craft. The board gives the distinction sporadically to an American "poet who has been influential to other poets," with the last recipient of the accolade before Espaillat being none other than Richard Wilbur. By then she had, indeed, shown her credentials as a devout citizen of the republic of letters, having served as workshop leader and mentor, interlocutor in the craft, and builder of poetic communities for the benefit of peers and younger practitioners.

During the 1980s, toward her last years in Queens, New York, where she and her husband, sculptor and industrial arts teacher Alfred Moskowitz, had raised three boys and worked in the public schools, Espaillat played a seminal role in the founding of the Fresh Meadows Poets group. Subsequently, when the couple relocated to Newburyport, Massachusetts, she helped organize the Powow River Poets, a literary association named after a tributary of the Merrimack River. Her use of traditional English prosody in a manner that avoids singsong rhymes or padded lines for the sake of meeting metrical demands has endeared her to American poets who believe that fixed forms can still speak compellingly to contemporary audiences. Her selection as keynote reader in 2010 at the West Chester Poetry Conference, a well-known hub of formalist poets, the year after Wilbur had received the honor and the year before Robert Pinsky, former United States poet laureate, would receive it also, demonstrates the extent to which Espaillat has earned inclusion as an important presence in the practice and promotion of poetry on the national scene.

Her eighty-six years of age at the time of this writing notwithstanding, we argue that Espaillat is a *new* American poet by dint of the vision discernible in her work, a vision that presages the future of the country's literary demographics. We contend that Anglophone American writers who were born outside the United States and who may not have spoken English as a first language will recur in the country's letters with increasing frequency in the decades ahead. The next great chapter of American literary history may very well be written by authors who in infancy did not lie down to sleep lulled by Anglophone songs and who, as adults, will have to travel abroad to visit grandparents.

Espaillat hails from the Caribbean and speaks Spanish as her first language; however, she never lived in a Hispanic ethnic enclave. A native of the Dominican Republic who received her education in New York during the 1940s, she won acclaim as an Anglophone poet in her teens and early twenties prior to the emergence of Latinos and Latinas as a self-differentiated ethnic component of the US population. Despite her success in the use of English, she never became disconnected from her ancestral culture or her mother tongue. Espaillat was transparent about her Hispanic and Dominican background even before she could imagine that Latino/a readers might take a special interest in her work. She remained proficient in the use of Spanish, a skill that she puts to use in translating English-language poetry into Spanish and Spanish-language verse into English. In this study of her poetry and poetics, we explore Espaillat's own understanding that her Dominican background, enriched by an early appreciation of her Hispanophone roots, may have prepared her ears for an easy sonic transition to the traditional forms of English prosody.

Born in 1932, Espaillat arrived in Washington, DC, as a toddler, following her father's appointment to the staff of the Dominican Legation in the US capital. A diplomatic list issued by the State Department in November 1935 identifies "Señor Don Homero Espaillat Brache, Second Secretary," accompanied by his wife, "Señora de Espaillat Brache," as a member of the staff since December 14, 1934 (*Diplomatic List* 51). His uncle, listed as "Señor Don Rafael Brache," headed the Legation (51). Don Homero sided with his uncle when the latter voiced his disapproval of the genocidal massacre of Haitian immigrant workers in 1937 perpetrated by the iron-fisted dictatorship of Rafael Leónidas Trujillo. This conscientious objection caused the family to sever their ties to their home country and seek exile in the United States.

After a two-year stay with relatives in the Dominican Republic separated from her parents, young Rhina settled with them in New York City in 1939. She soon began to feel comfortable with the English language and enthusiastically absorbed the world of knowledge made available by her primary education in the city's public schools. As early as high school, her poetic talents became apparent, coming to the attention of teachers who supported her artistic leanings and helped her publish her work. Espaillat went on to receive a baccalaureate degree in English from Hunter College of the City University of New York, find employment in the public school system as an English teacher, marry a fellow teacher who was of Jewish ancestry, and become the devoted mother of three sons.

Although she gained recognition in poetry circles and had her verse appear in literary magazines nationally from 1947 onward, Espaillat did not publish her first book until 1992, at the age of sixty. Her rise to visibility as a poet in the 1940s preceded the emergence of Latino/as as a panethnic segment of the American population as well as the Dominican subsection of that social formation. Before 1994, when an anthology edited by Chicana writer Roberta Fernández (*In Other Words: Literature by Latinas of the United States*) first claimed her as a Latina poet, Espaillat's work had primarily received the attention of Anglo commentators impressed by the poet's dexterity in handling the traditional poetic forms of the English language. They pointed to the emotional force of the texts and her ability to craft formal verse that felt "natural" to the reader's ear.

Espaillat came to traditional English prosody on her own; only after decades of practicing formal verse did she realize the existence of a large community of poets engaging in similar work. She has firmly held her belief since the 1940s in the value and relevance of formal verse as a means to communicate with and touch others without begrudging a similar potential to free verse. She probably did not need additional reassurance for her choice of poetic modes, but if she did, she would have felt much at home with the rise of formal verse among poets and literary scholars from the 1980s onward. Similarly, she spent years translating Anglophone poetry into Spanish and Hispanophone verse into English. In a prescient move, she included Spanish-language poems in her public readings even while addressing mostly English-speaking audiences. Only in the late 1990s did she discover the existence of a cohort of Dominican scholars who had begun to promote American writers of Dominican descent and to invoke her work as a milestone of their ethnically differentiated literary history (Torres-Saillant and Hernández, *Dominican Americans*; Torres-Saillant, "Espaillat"; Maríñez).

As a result of her distinct individual trajectory, well-recognized talent, and variegated heritage, Espaillat's verse occupies a unique place in the American poetic mainstream, the literary history of US writers of Hispanic descent, and the discretely Dominican portion of the Latino/a corpus. Presenting Espaillat as an American poet of the future may appear paradoxical given her advanced age—after all, the cult of the new and youthful prevails in the United States. Yet an examination of how the poet inhabits her social identities and her relationship with the human species as well as with the overall global ecosystem may mitigate the seeming paradox. A foreign-born artist whose first language is Spanish but who developed a prodigious command of English as a child, Espaillat oscillates easily between acquired and native languages. She writes about contemporary topics in traditional poetic forms, including villanelles, sestinas, haikus, and sonnets. While rooted in tradition aesthetically and socially, she consistently subverts the conservative assumptions associated with the received forms by forging expansiveness out of structures that many might regard as sources of poetic and ideological constraint.

Espaillat's oeuvre lends itself to a great variety of critical and scholarly treatments, emphases, and approaches. Given that her fame, albeit growing, has not yet become commensurate with her literary accomplishments, we find it necessary to document some of the esteem that Espaillat has earned as a convincing practitioner of primarily formal verse, someone who draws on a wide range of options from classical prosody but often with a signal difference. This facet of her profile merits attention because of the rarity in American literature for a poet of Hispanic descent to gain recognition in the areas of prosody and linguistic dexterity. However, we underscore as well Espaillat's commitment to an expansive openness to all poetic modes.

Espaillat's work also invites consideration among American women poets broadly or the ethnically differentiated segments within them. As a native of the

Dominican Republic, a country located historically at the center of the Caribbean experience, Espaillat provides substantial material to fuel reflections on the interrelationship between the fields of "American" and "Caribbean" studies. Meanwhile, the speculation by one of our students that a US author who also writes in a language other than English may be perceived as "less" American may have some merit. The "English-only" cultural ideology certainly still has a hold on the national imaginary at the time of this writing. Thus, irrespective of its inherent virtues, it is an open question whether Espaillat's bilingualism has served to enhance or hamper the acclaim accorded her by critics and the reading public.

Emanating from her keen interest in the work of others and a sense of herself as an artistic bridge-builder, Espaillat has actively promoted cross-lingual communication through the craft of translation. She has garnered several translation prizes, beginning with the Der-Hovanessian Translation Prize in 2001 (Maríñez 68). Espaillat has produced English versions of key poems by the sixteenth-century Spanish devotional poet San Juan de la Cruz (Saint John of the Cross) as well as other poetry from early modern Spain, colonial Latin America, and Iberian American verse through the twentieth century. In addition to translating Spanish into English, Espaillat has also produced Spanish versions of the work of poets from England and the United States. In 2005, for instance, the magazine *Literary Imagination* published three of the many poems by Robert Frost that she has rendered into Spanish. Likewise in late 2006, a collection of her works that was issued by the Dominican Republic's Ministry of Culture carried Spanish versions of poems by fellow Powow River Poet members Alfred Nicol and Len Krisak (Espaillat, *Agua*).

Espaillat's poem "Translation" presents the linguistic and cultural difficulties that face newcomers as they endeavor to understand the structure of everyday life in the alien setting of the United States. Practicing one's English for the cousins who have recently migrated over from the Old Country involves hearing them "picking out what they can, slippery vowels / queasy in their ears, stiff consonants / bristling like Saxon spears too tightly massed / for the leisurely tongues of my home town" (*Shadow* 34). Languages, of course, harbor within them ideological orientations, historical memories, and inherited demeanors that shape diverse ways of knowing for a range of users. Thus, the cousins wonder

if I can think in this
difficult noise, how well I remember

the quiet music our grandmother spoke
in her tin-roofed kitchen, how love can work
in a language without diminutives. (35)

By helping her cousins with their English, the speaker recognizes her role as a mediator of difference, a bridge of good will forming between divergences in lived experience, and in view of a larger human imperative to communicate empathetically as well as effectively:

I want to tell them the goodness of people
who seldom touch, who bring covered dishes
to the bereaved in embarrassed silence,
who teach me daily that all dialogue
is reverie, is hearsay, is translation. (35–36)

Espaillat notes, "The real 'translation' taking place in the poem is reciprocal and …involves reading body language, understanding gestures, seeing beyond behavior to the motive behind it, so as not to misinterpret socially-conditioned reserve as coldness, indifference or hostility." She adds a note of advice: "That [process] takes time, patience and good will, and is learned through long experience, just as the love of a new landscape, new language, new folkways and neighbors, is learned through association and close attention" (Qtd. in Cruz-Hacker 20).

Another poem on the same theme, "Translating," draws on the metaphor of marriage to speak about the challenges involved in transporting meaning from one language to another. The speaker considers the parallel and announces, finally, "no, this is harder, this is love in action, / not contemplation; this is live dissection / cobbling the monster into breathing fiction, / discarding this, salvaging that" (*Her Place* 79). The enterprise involves "one wish," which is ideal, and "one fruition," which is real. Both come together to explain "how the face, the phrase, / through long devotion manages to fuse— / not sum, not seamless—into compromise" (79).

Translation in Espaillat's view presents serious hermeneutic and stylistic challenges, and often all the translator can hope for is an approximation that will do some justice to the original. She has no sympathy for those who opt to resolve the problems they encounter by resorting to drastically altering the form of the original, replacing it with a version that comes more naturally to them. She dismisses the practice as not only wrong but also unethical (Scheele 34). Amid such unique difficulties, the task of translation also offers significant rewards given the degree of concentration it demands and its implications for one's writing in the long run. Since a translator is expressing someone else's feelings rather than his or her own, Espaillat observes that the ability to focus on "the how, rather than the what" comes to the fore; what results is the aggregate sense that when "you go back to your own work, you have more under your belt" (33).

On the whole, Espaillat's output forwards more border crossings and thematic intersections than would be fruitful to enumerate here, including ethical orientations and subject positions discernible from many of the thematic emphases found in her writing. Her poems are keen to tackle the randomness of life. They also grapple with ecological concerns, the quest for social justice, the vicissitudes of family life, the complexities of gender relations, the mysteries of religious faith, the imperatives of intergenerational and intercultural communication, and the place of art in people's lives, inter alia. Espaillat affirmed her ethnic difference vis-à-vis the Anglo mainstream before the stance of self-affirmation had become the expected behavior of racialized ethnic minorities in the United States, and she did so, remarkably, without compromising her artistic individuality. She has refrained from jumping onto the easy bandwagons that some writers may settle for as they respond to a literary market all too hungry for performances of ethnic identity and representations of the groups to which they belong. Her stance in that respect brings us closer to understanding the complexity of our humanity irrespective of our social identity, although it does not seem clear to us whether her independence of thought and artistic individuality may contribute to or detract from her enjoying a greater national visibility.

In an endorsement for *Landscapes with Women* (1999), a collection featuring Espaillat's work, Dana Gioia, a poet and former chair of the National Endowment for the Arts, decried Espaillat's "underrated" status in the country's literary scene at the time. Since then, her reputation has grown, and she has received a number of notable awards and accolades, particularly from other poets. Other recognition has followed since her return to poetry in the 1990s. She was, for example, one of eighty writers from across the country invited to participate in the National Book Festival in October 2003. Gioia, as editor of an anthology that aims to outline the development of English-language poetry by selecting one hundred "great poets" whose works constitute "high points of . . . artistic achievement" over the twelve centuries that run from *Beowulf* to the present, included Espaillat among the eleven living poets on the list (Gioia, *100* xxi, xxiii).

CRAFT AND CHARACTER

The poems in Espaillat's first published collection, *Lapsing to Grace* (1992), announce the central concerns and the stylistic profile that would characterize her overall oeuvre for years to come. The collection begins with a villanelle, "Highway Apple Trees," which meditates on the tenacity of trees that thrive in the most inhospitable terrains, namely on the side of the road and in regular contact with the poisonous emissions of heavy traffic: "These apples may be sweet. Nobody knows / What future orchards live in cores one throws / from glossy limousines or battered vans. / Nobody seeds this harvest; it just grows" (1).

The meditative tone dominates the majority of the poems, nature often providing the focal point for personalized inquiry into the place of our species in the vastness of creation. The speaker sees her future as inextricable from the planet's as a whole, as we read in "Unison": "Past all horizons, wind and dark, / all life grows hushed as if by sign: / there is no grief in me but Earth's, / there is no grief on Earth but mine" (2). Similarly, in "Framed Stars," a piece that evokes the underacknowledged history of death submerged under the lapping waves of Cape Cod, the speaker enunciates our need to downsize the firmament and frame the stars, because unframed, "they swell the sky" impossibly "beyond a human roof" (5). The poem "Pig" mourns a departing summer, combining this natural phenomenon of cycles with reflections on the slaughter of the fattened animal for Christmas dinner (13).

The volume also includes "Bodega," which, through the tastes, smells, and imagery of tropical meals and snacks, summons forth the speaker's "childhood and another place," with memory being the chief filament that weaves her identity together in the metropolis (18). "You Call Me by Old Names" recalls the speaker's resentment at hearing cherished family names "mangled" by native English speakers, triggering her refusal to accept the marginalization that ensues from mispronunciations (16).

Espaillat also explores the limits of faith in poems whose vision exudes a deistic texture as they retain the commitment to belief while acknowledging the banality of consolation when one loses, for instance, one's "bedbound mate." The speaker in "Recollection" regrets not having understood the depth of a bereaved person's despair: "I offer calm and reason, feeling wise, / dismiss her helpless rage with a smooth word, / not having learned how hard a thing it is / to pray against the wind and go unheard" (20). "Eucharist," "Gutter Preacher,"

"Slum Church," and "Church Whispers" offer similarly textured and ambiguous expressions of devotion.

Several of the poems cultivate the memory of the speaker's father and the deforming malady of her mother when Dulce María contracted Alzheimer's disease. The speaker in "Visiting Day" wonders whether her own existence depends on her mother's vanishing memory: "She called me out of nothing, and I came. / Will I still be when she forgets my name?" (38). She comes to terms with the corrosive force of her mother's condition, finding it pointless to deny "this sullen woman wearing Mama's eyes," since the gentler face of her parent is "gone beyond recall." The daughter confronts the present imperative: "I must love you so, or not at all" (36).

In the poem "Encounter," meeting her father who has been "dead these fourteen years," the speaker deludes herself into thinking the occasion suitable for remedying "the hurt of life gone wrong over small failures," but finds that words have little retrospective power against the injuries of the past. The specter vanishes, leaving her "with everything and nothing yet to say, / nothing to do but live and walk away" (*Lapsing* 33). The exorcising of regrets must remain the province of the living, an understanding evinced by the speaker in "Learning Bones," a poem applauded, among others, by fellow poet Joseph S. Salemi ("Poetry"). The text reminisces about the speaker's arguments with her father, who insisted on calling bones by their proper Latin names. *Sternum* would thus replace *breastbone* (34). She undertakes to learn the Latin names "to please my father's ghost," but understands the irony that the knowledge that had conferred such intellectual affirmation upon him proved useless against the ailment corroding his own bones. She consoles herself, therefore, with her own sense of reconciliation with the idea that, sound in the sleep of death, "we make amends in any way we can" and in whatever language is available (35).

Lapsing to Grace asks readers to consider everyday moments as the impetus for lifelong meditations on the nature of art, human emotion, and the value of intimacy. In the poem "Calculus," for example, the speaker recalls an evening conversation with her son, at the time a graduate student in physics. She found that his worldview and hers were not so different, even though their respective disciplines—the arts and sciences—seem oppositional at the outset (58). Reflecting on the real-life circumstances that prompted her to compose the piece, the poet notes, "The pleasure of that quiet conversation, the affectionate humor of my son's attempt to help me understand a difficult mathematical concept by means of visual imagery, became, for me, a metaphor for the nature of love, which reaches so tenaciously across distances of all kinds" (Espaillat, *Greatest Hits* 8).

The volume is also metapoetic in its capacity to reflect upon craft and the fleeting nature of fame. "Being the Ant," for instance, alludes to Aesop's fable of the industrious ant and the carefree grasshopper. What Espaillat's poem emphasizes is not so much the didactic angle—that idlers should be punished for their leisure or alternatively applauded for their carpe diem life philosophy—but rather the need for self-possession and focus on the tasks at hand. The ant reminds itself that everyone is endowed with strengths and talents, and it is wasted time to obsess about what one does not have. Sometimes practicality and focus are key, and working hard can also be another form of gratification, even if rewards are long delayed. The ant thus concludes, "To tell the truth, although I like his voice / I have no time for envy, having much / to do storing the nest against harsh days / from which sweet singers think themselves exempt" (22).

Elsewhere, musing on the windward flight of skilled hang gliders, the speaker's awe gradually turns into a realization of the common fate that awaits all great performers:

> But time will teach us that, since every craft
> slips from its own command at last to tremble
> free, as in the giddy wind of love
> and undertow of loss we stumble
> into wisdom, lapse to grace, give,
> flow on the breath that speaks us, cease to know,
> forget ourselves, become ourselves, let go. (28)

The speaker in "Avant Garde" invokes her friendly disagreements with Mario, a sculptor friend who "likes to hide / one of his curious figures in another / made of white wax." The sculptor does so to stress the point that the artist, no less than the physicist, operates within time and must consider change, freshness, and surprise among the resources of his trade (54). Firm at first on her stance that good art is "forever, like pure gold, whether it's dance or pigment, stone or song" and withstands all that is fleeting, she finds herself moved to considering this craftsman's view. In light of what experience shows, she admits, "I am resigned, / almost, to Mario's way of making art / a kind of dress rehearsal for the heart" (55).

Espaillat has evidently pondered the artist's relationship to peers and the diversity of outlooks, resources, and talents represented in the larger community of creators. When the notions of envy of and competition with other poets have surfaced in conversation, Espaillat has insisted, "You compete with yourself." She adds that if an artist has sufficient self-knowledge and self-confidence, what matters most is whether the work accomplished the day before was "as good as you could have made it" (Scheele 46).

LANGUAGE AND HERITAGE

Lapsing to Grace includes "Nosotros" (17), "Resignación" (21), "Quise olvidarte, Dios" (44), and "No le entristece al ruiseñor su suerte" (50), four Spanish-language poems unaccompanied by corresponding English equivalents. Perhaps the poet included them to give monolingual speakers of English cause for pause and reflection. Having never lived in a Spanish-speaking ethnic enclave such as Washington Heights or Spanish Harlem, she was not buoyed up by a sense of community behind her work, nor could she expect a large bilingual following at the time. Nevertheless, her commitment to adding to her ancestral store of knowledge in Spanish was pivotal in her mission to treat "the language well," an injunction passed down from her father (Espaillat, Letter).

As an only child to parents who were avid readers of literature and who harbored a deep appreciation for the role of arts in their Hispanic heritage, Espaillat came of age in a linguistically rich environment. As a young child under the care of aunts and grandmothers in the Dominican city of La Vega, she enjoyed the benefit of having an extended family of elders with artistic interests who hosted readings and impromptu recitals. She thus had an early exposure to the use of words and sounds for creative purposes. She remembers composing poetry in Spanish before she had even learned how to write. Her grandmother indulgently jotted the words down for her. Espaillat's family never faltered in its appreciation of Spanish. Hispanophone authors stood shoulder-to-shoulder with the Anglophone greats in Don Homero's estimation.

Her home abided by a language policy that Don Homero enforced with orthodox strictness. While encouraging her immersion in English at school to ensure her mastery of the new language, he prohibited its use at home. Because he viewed English as "the medium of the outer world, the world beyond the door," he inculcated in his daughter the idea that Spanish was the portal to the inside, the familial and domestic universe. Not only was it the *only* language permitted, it "had to be pure, grammatical, unadulterated Spanish," not intermingled with

English catchphrases or the slang of the day (Espaillat, *Where Horizons Go* 67). Espaillat recalls that the "words in his own language were the 'true' names for things in the world," and that "if it could be said at all, it could be said best in the language of those authors whose words were the core of his education" (69, 67). Although less linguistically rigid than her father, Espaillat has continued to endorse mastery of both languages separately as a means of optimizing one's intellectual power and imaginative reach: "I mean by bilingualism . . . what my father meant by it: the complete mastery of two languages, with no need to supplement either one by injecting into it words from the other, either orally or in writing" (Cruz-Hacker 25).

In the United States, a country populated by speakers of numerous languages, one can hardly escape opinions about the relationship between dominant languages, political power, and differential access to a sense of national belonging. In her second collection of verse, *Where Horizons Go* (1998), Espaillat broaches the language question in two memorable texts written in different genres while sharing a common title, namely "Bilingual/Bilingüe." One is a verse evocation of the poet's relationship with her father mediated by his resolve to maintain Spanish as the language of the home even as she developed a passion for Anglophone poetry. The other, an essay that stands as the afterword, examines the pain and the recompense that came from the language policy that prevailed in her childhood home. A third piece, titled "An Imaginary Dialogue," published separately, wrestles with the same issues as it places father and daughter in conversation about the nature of language. This text's genesis was Espaillat's coming upon a Spanglish dictionary and "wondering what could be the need for such a book, and what might result from it" (Espaillat, *Agua* 104). In keeping with Don Homero's view, Espaillat contends that speakers of Spanglish are intellectually impoverished; instead of deriving the best of both languages, the hybridization leads to dilution. She asks readers to envision what happens when "words in one [language] . . . drive out perfectly good equivalent words in the other. The habitual speaker of such a mix ends by speaking not two, or even one complete language, but fragments of two that are no longer capable of standing alone" (*Where Horizons Go* 68). As Espaillat summarizes, "The language of Cervantes, of Neruda, of Darío and Borges and Sor Juana, and yes, of Don Pedro Mir, deserves better treatment; and so does the language of Shakespeare, and Walt Whitman, Emily Dickinson and Robert Frost" (Kang and Torres-Saillant 186).

This dismissive view of Spanglish sounds more conservative than we will find Espaillat to be in any other aspect of her aesthetic or linguistic philosophy. In interviews, she admits to the key role of lexical, phonological, and syntactical borrowings as well as linguistic hybridization generally in the cultural histories that led to the emergence of both Spanish and English as the seminal languages they are today. We also know of her admiration for a poet like Brooklyn-born Puerto Rican Martín Espada, whose verse occasionally lapses into code-switching for particular effects such as a sense of solidarity and insidership. We regard Espaillat's closed view of linguistic intermixture as stemming more from affect than ideology, a loving allegiance to her father whose strict language policy indeed had the salutary effect of enabling her to preserve the mother tongue and through it, to retain a deep appreciation of her ancestral heritage.

That Spanish is in every respect the equal of English and that it has as impressive a literary history to substantiate it is probably a key factor that motivated Espaillat to include the four Spanish-language poems in *Lapsing to Grace*, thereby also expressing filial piety by paying tribute to the language that Don Homero loved best. No less important, perhaps the poet saw the inclusion of poems in her native tongue as a way to assert her mixed cultural identity, a testament of her bilingualism that she could not omit without repudiating and silencing an important part of herself. Finally, including poems in a language that the expected Anglophone readership of her volume would lack the proficiency to read may have been prompted by her almost transcendental view of poetry as an inherently communicative code. She offers the story of the poetry reading she ended by reciting a poem in Spanish, a choice that greatly moved an English-speaking member of the audience. The listener approached her, and Espaillat soon learned that the woman did not understand Spanish but had reacted to something else: "What I understood was the music of what you read" (*Where Horizons Go* 69).

Espaillat draws on examples like this to substantiate her belief that poetry contains an element that supersedes specificities of language, making it possible "for transplanted people" like her to recognize, identify with, and fully understand "the songs of the Other" (70). Clearly, the poet's belief that linguistic differences will not necessarily preclude a reader's understanding at some level connects with Espaillat's broader thinking about the sonic nature of the verse-making craft. The anecdote of the reading as well as the poet's more explicit theoretical formulations point to an aural ingredient that crosses boundaries of communication: "the music, the formal elements of poetry that do travel from language to language, as the formal music of classic Spanish poetry my father loved followed me into English and draws me, to this day, to poems that are patterned and rich and playful" (69–70).

Given the capacity to move a monolingual speaker of another language by virtue of the music emanating from the formal elements of verse, Espaillat makes an important aesthetic declaration, one that sheds light on the stylistic features of the work included in her first published volume and that she would build upon in her subsequent books. While she was still an undergraduate student, she recognized that she had a preference for poems that were "formal, metrical and consciously musical" (Gale Database). She recalls that meter and rhyme "came naturally" to her from quite early on, and that in her childhood she actually thought she had invented prosody (Scheele 30). Espaillat recognizes the Elizabethans, the Metaphysical poets, Emily Dickinson, Thomas Hardy, A. E. Housman, Charlotte Mew, Robert Frost, W. B. Yeats, W. H. Auden, Edna St. Vincent Millay, Sara Teasdale, Elinor Wylie, and Stanley Kunitz as formative influences.

Lapsing to Grace did not make a great splash when it was published by Bennett and Kitchel, a small press in East Lansing, Michigan. Commentary on it mostly took the form of short reviews, typically two or three sentences in the "new books" pages of periodicals. Her second volume appeared under more auspicious circumstances: *Where Horizons Go* garnered the 1998 T. S. Eliot Prize for Poetry, an annual award given to "the best unpublished collection of poetry in English" sponsored by Truman State University Press "in honor of native Missourian T. S. Eliot's considerable intellectual and artistic legacy." X. J. Kennedy, the judge who chose Espaillat's work, described the collection as one "likely to persuade readers who think they don't like poetry that they do, after all." Reviewing the volume for *Poetry* magazine, Bill Christophersen focused on some of the ways in which contemporary practitioners of metrical poetry differ from their predecessors. Alluding to the resignation with which Espaillat's speaker meditates on life's inevitable end in such poems as "Last Day" and "Review," Christophersen stresses how "unsentimental empathy plus a willingness to deal with issues of mortality candidly set her poetry apart. This is formalist verse at its most resourceful, accessible, and startling" (345–51).

In addition to meditating on life and death, many of the poems in *Where Horizons Go* convey a dispassionate view of nature, recognizing the self-sustaining logic of its cycles and its quiet indifference regarding the human presence in its midst. The short poem "Solstice" evokes the unconcerned aloofness with which the seasons pass:

Now in our maple a dove is whooing;
caught in the branches, the wind is warm;
somewhere heaven is plotting storm
and the bird's undoing.
Now in the flames of its petals burning,
sunflower praises the gift of sun;
elsewhere petals are all undone,
and the leaves are turning. (12)

The overall tone of the volume seems to be dominated by the sedate recognition of our relative insignificance in the overall scheme of things, nature's uncompromising configuration of space, and the cosmic structure of time. But the observing mind does not, as a result, surrender to the seduction of the existentialist's anguish. Rather, it affirms the opportunistic wisdom to derive whatever joy the fleeting moment may offer. Looking at the ways in which nature makes and remakes her "quarter-acre in the sun," the speaker resigns herself to the small pleasures that change and adaptation afford:

I would not dress it otherwise
than seasons in their turn have done,
but do give thanks that sultry weather
of much to feel and less to know
gives way, after a time, to this
clear view of where horizons go. (8)

Ultimately, the role of art in Espaillat's view seems to be the key that enables humans to forge a haven of self-realization within the enormity of nature's unpredictability. The poem "Song," cast deliberately in the "playful" and "highly musical" form of the villanelle, records the poet's observation of her mother's "slow loss of selfhood and memory" as a victim of Alzheimer's (Espaillat, *Greatest Hits* 9). The use of alliteration, repetition, and other sound devices hauntingly contrasts the corrosive silence to which the patient was reduced as her ability to coordinate ideas and find the right words to express them painfully ebbed:

She settles in a thoughtful pose
as if she understood her fate,

her face, her gaze, her ghost. She goes
downstream relentlessly, she flows
where dark forgiving waters wait.
From hair to horse to house to rose,
Her gaze, her guise, her ghost she goes. (*Where Horizons Go* 26)

Perhaps more militantly than any other, this poem intends to convey Espaillat's conviction that "the arts succeed and triumph over the griefs they record by deliberately making beauty out of them, turning into 'song' whatever in our lives wants to emerge as a cry" (*Greatest Hits* 10).

The Spanish language makes an appearance in *Where Horizons Go* in a markedly different manner from the way it does in *Lapsing to Grace*. Apart from the words inserted parenthetically in "Bilingual/Bilingüe," Spanish figures in the titles of "Agua" (*Where Horizons Go* 27), a poem about the mother's obsession with water during one of the stages of dementia, and of "Grávida" (42), a sonnet in which the speaker voices her identification with a pregnant woman she sees passing in the midst of the wind, sleet, and traffic of an inclement December night. The collection includes only one poem with title and text entirely in Spanish, namely "Para mi tátaranieto el astropionero," which is followed by "For My Great-Great Grandson, the Space Pioneer," its English translation (30–31). The poem appears first in Spanish because, as she has explained, it constitutes one of those instances in which a poem came to her first in her native language (Scheele 35).

The poem illustrates a feature of Espaillat's verse that recurs throughout her oeuvre in diverse ways, namely the tendency to step outside the speaker's historical time to converse with an interlocutor of the future or the past. The text enacts a pep talk and lesson addressed to a descendent in the future ("down the byways of my blood") to instill in him a sense of appreciation for the less scientifically stable forms of knowledge and the skills for living that do not have a clear exchange value on the market: "Watch that you don't run short of butterflies; / learn the colors of the hours; / and here, in this little case of bones / I've left you the perfume of the seas" (31). Thinking herself "into the future," Espaillat cherishes the imaginative possibilities that poetry affords, essentially allowing her to "cheat time" (Scheele 35).

Another way of cheating time in her poems involves bringing an interlocutor from the remote past into the present, as in "Six of One," in which the contemporary speaker questions Columbus about whether his voyages can truly be considered successful (*Where Horizons Go* 23). Likewise, "If You Ask Me," the piece that opens the collection, travels to the beginning of Judeo-Christian mythic time. Dwelling on the moment prior to the tasting of the forbidden fruit in the Garden of Eden, the work imagines what may have gone through the snake's head when it decided to proceed with the task of temptation: "Now I'm not blind: / I see her fidget with her hair and cough / That nervous cough; she's bored out of her mind" (1).

Often, in the collections that follow, Espaillat's speakers display humor and compassion when presenting readers with commentaries from the perspective of a nonhuman participant. This tactic occurs in the poem "Retriever," from her third book, *Rehearsing Absence* (2001). A loyal dog explains the motivation behind its constantly returning the objects that the master tosses into the air (11–12). We could note another key implication of the poet's propensity to transport herself to the heads of nonhuman entities (usually animals), which relates also to her dynamic engagement with nature. Her disposition consistently embraces an ecocentric vision by questioning anthropocentrism, "the parallax engendered by human-centered vision, particularly in the modern age of print culture and technology." Such long-held assumptions constitute a major impediment to reinvigorating the currently feeble health of our planet (Buell, *Environmental* 20).

By the end of the 1990s Espaillat had come into herself also as a poet with a deep sense of her artistic self, namely the nature of her poetic voice, her particular approach to the craft, and the choices she had hitherto made in her literary career. The poems in *Landscapes with Women: Four American Poets* (1999) seem to constitute a statement of self-definition. They reflect on the salient concerns that pervade her overall oeuvre: our relationship to the dead ("Cutting Bait," "Happening"), the trials that inhere in marital relationships ("Framing the View," "A Love Poem, Off Center"), the meaning inscribed in the places we live ("Moving Away," "Ousting the Murphys"), the march of time, philosophical meditations about ironic circumstances, and the resilience of faith. The poem "Their Only Child" reflects on the accidental nature of birth, while "Where Childhood Lives" recreates the landscape of the speaker's Caribbean birthplace with the affection that is built into the very texture of the natural environment: "And morning takes the never road / down to the bank where childhood lives, / where stones and water know my name / and stroke me with diminutives" (White 66).

Also included in the collection, the Shakespearean sonnet "Salve Regina" features a speaker overtaken by the "unlabored music" made by the voices of men and women in a choral performance. The speaker muses mischievously (and perhaps a bit sacrilegiously) that the singers sound the way angels would if they existed. The text unabashedly privileges the work of artists over the abstract forces of divine goodness, arguing, "If any song is sweet, / they sweeten it, inventing the unfound / serenity of heaven, to rejoice, / shaming God to compassion with one voice" (63). In that meditation resides the affirmation that art perseveres as a preeminent human activity. In "Metrics," a companion piece, we encounter an avowedly classical demand for artistic expression to show itself through figurative language. Let the "clattering of hoof" signal "horse" that the art may bear its "nature's imprint to the end," the speaker advises. She reveals her creed as follows: "Under soul's music, the eternal tone, / I like mortality to play the bass; / Love and the dancer's gestures must be grace / Wrested from bone" (54).

But perhaps no other text in the volume forwards as emphatic a poetic *prise de parole*—or *ars poetica*—than "Prosody," which upholds the preponderance of music in her conception of poetry as an art form. More recently, Espaillat has identified three elements that make a poem possible for her: "a feeling, a beat, and an image" (Gross 18). The speaker in "Prosody" gives center stage to just one: "The words are what I know, / but they are no comfort. / The comfort is in the music / That says what I cannot know." The closing stanza tilts the balance even more steeply against the primacy of words: "The words are a name / for the shadow I dress in. / The radiance that wears me / Answers only to the music" (White 61).

CAREER AND COMMUNITY

The favorable reception of *Where Horizons Go* came at a time when Espaillat was actively participating in poetry contests. Her receipt of the Howard Nemerov Sonnet Award, the *Sparrow* Sonnet Prize, and several first prizes in national competitions sponsored by the Poetry Society of America date from that period. Her energetic involvement in the competitive side of the poetry scene exudes a sense of joy at having returned to her art in full force. The young poet's stardom in New York had lasted until approximately 1953, when her attention turned away from poetry to marital, parental, and professional concerns (Monsour, *Rhina Espaillat* 29). For nearly thirty years, she had occupied herself primarily with family and her teaching career. She would need to finish raising her boys, the two younger ones eventually earning doctorates in physics from MIT and the older one an accomplished photographer, before renewing her old ties to the poetry scene. When she returned to the craft upon retirement, she admits that she was "glad to discover that the ability to write is as enduring as the desire" (*Greatest Hits* 8). She wrote copiously and submitted work with equal vigor, largely to literary venues that had shown a taste for rhyme and meter such as *Sparrow*, the *Formalist*, *Orbis*, *Blue Unicorn*, the *Lyric*, the *American Scholar*, and *Plains Poetry Journal*, among others.

The unusual way in which Espaillat has navigated her path in literature merits attention. The literary space as we know it breaks down not so much into novels, short stories, plays, and poems as it does into literary careers. The poetry or fiction that a person writes is seldom valued as a finite contribution to the tradition by one individual talent; rather, an industrial imagination prevails that construes individual texts as promising signals that the individual may accrue enough of the same for an eventually outstanding career. A sheaf of superbly crafted poems, a first collection of brilliant short stories, or an impressive debut novel will not only elicit satisfaction in the writer's contribution but also trigger impatient curiosity about the writer's ability to repeat or surpass the accomplishment the next time around. Not publishing a second book that at least matches the caliber of the first within a reasonable period of time becomes a source of pressure that can weigh heavily on a writer's credibility. We might recall the disquiet that informs the scholarship on *Invisible Man* (1952) over the novels that Ralph Ellison did *not* write, or the media craze surrounding Harper Lee's novel *Go Set a Watchman* (2015), fifty-five years after the publication of her classic *To Kill a Mockingbird*. Overall, the focus on careers rather than on texts has a detrimental effect on the recognition of literary figures whose output does not follow a regular progression from an initial break into print to a steady and ongoing crescendo of accomplishments.

Excessive focus on the literary endeavor as a career that one continuously builds rather than on the discrete contributions made by aesthetically successful works can encourage an atmosphere in which writers feel compelled to devote themselves entirely to the demands of the craft. Life, in the most extreme of cases, may be regarded as an impediment that blocks the progression of the work. Alienation from relationships and social involvement then becomes an ideal to which a writer may—somewhat perversely—aspire. For instance, seven years after his separation from the English actress Claire Bloom, novelist Philip Roth, living alone, boasted of having reached that ostensible ideal. With "no one else to be responsible for or to, or to spend time with," he began to exercise total control over his schedule, as we read in the in-depth profile of Roth penned by the *New Yorker*'s David Remnick. "Usually I write all day," the novelist proclaims, "but if I want to go back to the studio, after dinner, I don't have to sit in the living room because someone else has been alone all day. I don't have to sit there and be entertaining or amusing. I go back out and work for two or three more hours" (Remnick 79).

In contrast to this solipsistic view of writing, Espaillat's understanding of the communal nature of artistic creation would seem to preclude any ruling out of extratextual reality for the sake of an isolating commitment to work. Discussing the road she took in her dedication to rearing three sons, Espaillat has dismissed the possibility of regret: "Of course raising them took time, but it was time well spent and worth any number of poems. I think that the things a woman does that keep her from writing may frustrate her in the short run, but in the long run they contribute to the poems that she may write eventually" (Espaillat, Letter).

This perspective is most evident in her poem "Workshop," which juxtaposes the demands of the craft and the exigencies of all else in a person's life. The poem, she muses, was "a reexamination of my life, and an assessment of the relationship between any creative pursuit and the time-consuming daily human experience out of which, after all, art is made" (*Greatest Hits* 9). The text pivots on the query, "Where have you been and what have you been doing?" posed by a poet-friend who remembered her work from decades earlier. In an easy, conversational tone, the speaker accounts for a few of the tasks that have kept her busy: "Well, I've been coring apples, layering them / in raisins and brown sugar; I've been finding / what's always lost, mending and brushing, / pruning houseplants, remembering birthdays" (*Rehearsing* 34). The closing of the poem seamlessly connects daily living with the task of writing; the extraliterary aspects of life make up a sort of "workshop" and site of essential literary training. The speaker declares resolutely, "I've been putting a life together, like / supper, like a poem, with what I have" (*Rehearsing* 34). Espaillat has also realized the wisdom of creating a sense of community as a way to enrich poetic activity through the synergy of close collaboration and mutual support. This is a point that one can glean from her words of gratitude to organizations and individuals in her first book. Among them are the Fresh Meadows Poets, the group that Espaillat had cofounded in Queens, New York, in 1986 (*Lapsing* ii). The organization's readings and workshops helped increase her contacts with fellow wordsmiths in the area (Maríñez 68). By the time *Lapsing to Grace* appeared in print, however, Espaillat had already relocated to Newburyport, Massachusetts. There, she started an organization with the mission "to unite local poets and provide a supportive environment for them" (Gross 18). The Powow River Poets convened, among other gatherings and workshops, a monthly reading series as well as a poetry competition in collaboration with the Newburyport Art Association. In her adopted state of Massachusetts, Espaillat also found the Spanish-speaking enclaves that had been largely unavailable to her during her thirty-eight years as a resident of Flushing in Queens (Sklar and Barbato 217). In 2001 she published the chapbook *Mundo y palabra/The World and the Word*, a sampling of fifteen of her poems, four of which are accompanied by their corresponding Spanish versions. The Spanish conspicuously in the title marks her increasing engagement with the language as part of her core imaginative practice—a shift that probably results from her new engagement with Hispanophone communities. Espaillat's pivotal move to Massachusetts, her literary activism, community building, and legitimate record of accomplishments contributed to enhancing her reputation among circles of poets nationwide. Speaking about Espaillat's influence on the Powow River Poets, Kennedy has characterized her as the "spark plug of the group, a kind of bardic queen bee or aesthetic den-mother, a teacher by vocation and by nature and, as many fellow poets will attest, a generous friend" (xii). It came as no surprise that when the group published *The Powow River Anthology*, a collection grouping twenty-four of the poets who had participated in its activities over the first fifteen years of its existence, the volume bore a dedication to Espaillat (Gross 17). The high value that this artist-mentor places on the invigorating interaction with fellow members of the group may be discerned from her own dedication of her second volume of poems to "the members of the Powow River Poets, with many thanks for their encouragement and good company" (v).

AT THE FOREFRONT OF FORM

Espaillat's insistence on the legitimacy of choices she has made as a literary practitioner accords with her clarity about her aesthetic sensibilities in general. She has spoken in plain language about the stylistic practice required to earn a place among the country's foremost formalist poets. By the mid-1990s, with *Lapsing to Grace* under her belt in addition to nearly three hundred poems published in journals and select anthologies, Espaillat had begun to occupy a firmer place in the literary community as a full-fledged formalist (Finch, *Formal Feeling* 297). She explained her process as one characterized by tension and adaptation: "I feel at home in the apparent constraints of formal verse, as I've never felt at home in the apparent freedom of free verse. Formal verse more accurately parallels the way I live, working inside the rules but straining away from them, getting away with as much disruption as I can without actually destroying the pattern, thumbing my nose while looking respectful, actually *being* respectful of the idea of order while seeming to thumb my nose" (Espaillat, "Why I Like to Dance" 64).

Espaillat's affirmation of prosodic identity, which merely conceptualized a practice she had sustained since she began publishing verse in the 1940s, coincided with a peak moment in the movement that we now know as New Formalism in American poetry. Gioia, a leading proponent of traditional prosody, described the beginning of the 1990s as the time of "a major revival of formal verse among young poets" in the United States, offering a stark contrast to the scenario of twenty years earlier when "it was a truth universally acknowledged that a young poet in possession of a good ear would want to write free verse" (Gioia, *Can Poetry* 31). He contends that from about 1960 onward, free verse became the norm in the US poetry scene, predicated largely on the charge that meter and rhyme, insofar as they may curtail expressive freedom, represented authoritative, retrograde, right-wing values. Dismissing such a charge, he points out that poetic techniques cannot be assigned inherent moral or political values (32). In contrast, he argues, the hegemony of free verse may instead have arrested the development of the English language to a degree, as no new forms entered the mainstream of American poetry during that time, except for two miniature forms: the double dactyl and the ghazal (32, 37).

Since Gioia blames free verse for poetry's loss of popularity with nonspecialized audiences since the 1960s and the seclusion of the art within the echoing halls of academia, it follows that he should celebrate the rise of the New Formalists, who have put free verse poets in the ironic position of occupying the status quo (40). The New Formalists, he assures us, reject the existing split between their art and its traditional audience and frown on the arrangement whereby one finds only poets reading contemporary poetry. He believes these poets are superbly poised to reconnect with the ostensibly vulgar vitality of popular tradition, making poetry matter again as it once did (40).

An advocate of traditional prosody who disavows aesthetic militancy, Espaillat does not accept the charge by free verse polemicists that strict form hampers communication. She contends that, if approached irresponsibly, all poetic modes lead to bad results (Scheele 42). Looking at the vigorous proliferation of rhyme and meter in American poetry since the 1980s, Espaillat has welcomed the rebirth of "formal verse as one of the legitimate choices available to the poet" (Gale Database). She believes that instead of stymying the flow of language, "formal constraints" stimulate the imagination, liberating it from the commonplace by means of a "tension that charges and enriches it" (Gale Database). She advises aspiring poets to read a great deal from across the centuries and to "write for the ear as well as for the mind," further stressing her understanding of music as inextricable from poetic communication. She thus encourages a self-liberation from the unwritten rule that often inhibits a contemporary poet from identifying with the voices and eras considered outmoded or otherwise unworthy of revisiting.

Espaillat prefers not to be considered a New Formalist poet, since her use of formal verse predates the advent of the movement by several decades, but her aesthetic kinship with that coterie of peers has no doubt evolved into a productive working relationship. Recruited by Gioia, she conducted poetry workshops since 2000 at the West Chester Poetry Conference, an event regarded as "New Formalism's premier proselytizing forum," held annually at West Chester University in Pennsylvania (Krisak 82). As a result of that association and her steady commitment to promoting the power of meter and rhyme, Espaillat ended up at "the forefront of a movement she never had to 'join'" (Krisak 79).

LIFE'S HARSHNESS, POETRY'S PROMISE

Espaillat won the 2001 Richard Wilbur Poetry Award for *Rehearsing Absence*, a slender volume that comes to terms with death by asking how to bring life's ledger to a quiet close without the folly of regret. Robert B. Shaw, who reviewed the book for *Poetry*, praises the collection using a number of examples that highlight the extent to which "her confidence is well aware of life's stubborn negatives" (Shaw 353). Crediting Espaillat with having composed "some of the best written sonnets in recent decades" and noting her skill at crafting pantoums, sestinas, and villanelles, Shaw claims that her "prosodic dexterity would mean little if it were not twinned with a mastery of tone" (353). The reviewer goes on to credit the artist's powers of observation as well: "She notices what we typically overlook, and she delineates it with lucid intelligence, tolerance, and good humor. Hers is a voice of experience, but it is neither jaded nor pedantic. She speaks not from some cramped corner but from somewhere close to the center of life" (352).

Espaillat observes that with old age, "you take stock of your situation and begin to imagine—or 'rehearse'—the absence of those you still have" (Scheele

40). That realization of an approaching finale marks one's state of mind, since mortality provides a sort of prism through which to examine what has been, what will be, and what will remain behind. Placed in this contemplative state of mind, one feels compelled to read the ovillejo "In Stone," the shortest and most lapidary poem in the collection, as a possible epitaph:

> Learn, as you read me, stranger,
> How danger
> Surrounds every delight,
> How night
> From which none can wake you
> Will take you
> And memory forsake you,
> As you, just now, are turning
> From old inscriptions, learning
> How danger, how night, will take you. (*Rehearsing* 74)

Some of the poems in the collection have a distinctly teleological heaviness while addressing this subject matter, as is the case with the sonnet "Moods." The piece traces the evolution of a person's lifespan in terms of verbal moods: "I'm learning the subjunctive, mood of choice / once the indicative has stripped away / that seemed to say it all at once." The work concludes with the question of "how to acquire a taste for the impure / provisional, that's what I need to know, / before the last imperative says 'Go'" (17). It is a striking reminder that language simultaneously ushers in consciousness of aging and death while undergoing in real time a panoply of continuous, often irretrievable changes itself.

The maturity and twilight consciousness that characterized Espaillat's earlier books reappears in this volume, albeit accented with wry humor that works to mitigate the saddening finale of death. We can think here of "For the Lady in the Black Raincoat Who Slept through an Entire Poetry Reading," a text in which the bemused speaker addresses a member of the audience who, as the title implies, has committed herself fully to slumber. Devoid of resentment and aware that some poems really are beneath the dignity of wakeful attention, the poet meets the woman halfway in the concluding stanza: "Truce, then: you promise not to snore, / I'll whisper to preserve your sleeping. / Let's wish each other nothing more / Than dreams worth keeping" (33).

Espaillat's books published in the new century have garnered considerable acclaim, with two of them—*The Shadow I Dress In* (2004) and *Playing at Stillness* (2005)—winning, respectively, the Stanzas Prize and the National Poetry Award sponsored by Salmon Run Press. In his evaluation of *Playing at Stillness*, the poet Peter Makuck lauds Espaillat's command of "surfaces and depths," a skill that enables her to deliver a formal poem in a way that makes "you forget, say, that you've just read a sonnet" (Makuck 505–6). Overall, the collection has a pervasively meditative tone, treading an often thorny spiritual ground that leads to humorous resignation, stoic understanding, or somewhere in between. The opening piece, "Weeping Fig," features a monologue in which the speaker, identifying with the tree, explains petty human hang-ups out loud:

> We name you, as we
> name, through the
> glass of our obsessions,
> careless galaxies,
> and post there
> a legendary guard
> circling our fortunes,
> our orbits. (Espaillat, *Playing* 3)

Displaying similar philosophical preoccupations, the speaker in "Maudslay Park" seizes on a riverbank and the surrounding scenery to contemplate humanity's puny dimensions in the face of the vastness of Creation:

> But at this moment, caught in a web of motion
> we play at stillness, imagine ourselves
> imagining the sun, the riverbank
> and its reflection, behind us the cries
> of gulls and children, the voices of friends. (*Playing* 23)

Her poem "People in Home Movies" ruminates upon the persistence of memory, the passage of time, and the echoing effects of regret in a conversational tone not unlike the memorable phrasing of Eliot's "The Love Song of J. Alfred Prufrock" (1915), whose line "And would it have been worth it after all" she reproduces nearly verbatim in her seventh stanza.

> And would it be worth it, after all,
> out of a moment's regret, to run toward them
> and buy them back at the price of ourselves, moving
> weightless out of ourselves into heart's ground,
> the future discarded like old clothes full of patches,
> and the child in us naked, dancing and turning? (47)

"Answering to Rilke" addresses the difficulty of parting with the past, "tossing out" anything that evokes a meaningful memory (59). "On the Avenue" dares to go head to head with God on matters of fairness, justice, and compassion. The speaker airs grievances about whether His is the right way "to run a universe" (70). As might be expected, the poems that deal with death remain prominent, whether pondering the speaker's own fears or the losses grieved by others. "November Music" dwells on the contents of the speaker's home in order to contemplate the simultaneously exhausting and yet revitalizing joys of past time. The body, comfortable and sentient for the moment, is but a temporary home for the speaker and a warm chamber for thoughts, memories, and fleeting connections:

> This house contains
> me, as my weathered
> flesh cradles the loves I breathe.
> . . .
> home here like rain, and sons I mothered
> mirror this place, this life, this man, this mouth. (87)

Espaillat's third chapbook, *The Story-Teller's Hour* (2004), is a bleak publication consisting of seven thematically intertwined sonnets and five additional pieces in varying forms that imagine legendary or historical events in hypothetical terms. The text conveys an overall balance between the wheels of misfortune, irony, and wishful thinking. Narratively rich and thus consistent with the concentrated idea of storytelling announced in the title, the seven sonnets that make up the first part share a dark, subtly macabre quality. The rhymes' fluidity places in stark relief the harshness of the incidents recounted, and the tense remains in the present indicative throughout. On the whole, *The Story-Teller's Hour* contributes additional features to Espaillat's fund of stylistic registers and expands on several of her latent thematic concerns that may not have fit easily with the tone and vision of the other collections.

The first sonnet speaks of adoring parents who wrestle successfully with life's vicissitudes to raise their nine-year-old son, only to have him slip "through the rings of waves" (2) and drown on a fateful summer outing. The second recounts a visit by a man who comes bearing a pretty gift—"a floral candle in a dish"—to console the friend who has learned "she has six months to live." Unfortunately, that gift causes her bed to go up in flames, leading to his own sad demise in an adjacent room (3). The third piece introduces us to a woman "married too young" who, overwhelmed by the discovery that "her husband keeps a woman," attempts suicide. Ill-aimed, the bullet she shoots into her skull only blinds her. She is not even afforded the pleasure of seeing her son's face (4). The fourth deals with a homeless man who dwells amiably and peacefully in the town square. When invited over for dinner by a well-meaning neighbor, he rushes through his meal at the abundant table, choking to death on the bounty. Sonnet five narrates the plight of a young widow who, married anew, loses her second spouse. Her lasting inheritance and burden is bringing up seven children alone. The sixth poem features a man at a party searching for a young woman who has disappeared into the crowd after he has taken an immediate liking to her. His search concludes when he finds her photograph resting on the piano. He learns that she is the host's "daughter, dead these eighteen years" (7). The final sonnet presents us with a speaker recalling a moment of her childhood when she envisioned the sea as a monster wrestling with her father. The man endeavored, successfully, to rescue her from drowning, thereby giving her life not once, but twice.

This diverse sonnet sequence, on the whole, explores the precarious and ironic nature of human life. Mortals find themselves caught between joyful ideals and devastating realities, good intentions and unfortunate outcomes. Perhaps the lasting takeaway is the Aristotelian combination of pity and fear so easily recognizable in classical tragedy as cathartic. Bearing witness to these small tragedies proves perversely joyful for the observer who has the luxury of putting the book down and walking resolutely—if sadly—away.

The Shadow I Dress In (2004), Espaillat's fourth book-length volume, seems to bring together many of the questions that have occupied her mind since her return to the craft in the 1980s. Poems that revisit moments in the lives of her revered parents, including those chronicling their physical decline, recur in the volume, as do other signature subjects already mentioned: animals, gardening, the seasons, domestic life, and natural landscapes. Two poems on photography ("Snapshots in an Album" and "To Make a Photo Wall"), a subject Espaillat so often uses to ponder the metaphysics of time, broach the inevitability of change and our desire to recuperate swiftly receding memories. The photography poems obliquely treat the question of aging, a theme to which the volume returns by means of a wide range of perspectives. The joyful piece "Canticle of Her Coming and Going" celebrates a child's body, unmarred by careless use or the harsh self-judgment—not to mention outside scrutiny—that women's aging usually engenders. The speaker affirms, "I sing Ilana as she comes, / thighs firm and tight as little drums, / a silky down just barely there, / the same fine gold as brows and hair" (53). The prayerful "Passage" appeals to Memory, a relentless goddess, to slow her course and exit so that the speaker may "salvage whatever clings to / brittle branches, gather the last, most stubborn / harvest there where blackbird alone can pluck it / earlier than frost will" (123).

Connected to the question of aging, many segments of the text tackle the corollary subject of death, whether expressed as "dying," the "shadow of dying" (9), or as defiant declaration that she will resist death by embracing all that life has on offer. Thus, in "My Cluttered House Accuses Me of Greed," the speaker avers:

> No, I mean to fall,
> heavy with sound and color, dense as clay,
> into the rose and satin of old wood,
> the kiss of wine still on my lip to say
> this much I tasted once, and it was good.
> Afterward, let my shadow find its way
> to who knows what austere new neighborhood. (*Shadow* 15)

The carpe diem motif reappears in the "Ballade of the After-Dinner Thinker," which has the sharper tone and warning textures of a manifesto: "Loosen your belt, remember we're / built for small pleasures here below. / But what's this whisper in your ear? / 'Much less awaits you than you know!'" (16).

Espaillat extends her engagement with the carpe diem theme in the poems that look to poetry, music, dance, and the arts broadly as the ultimate affirmation of humanity's passage through this brief life. Such revelries make up the most sustained thematic focus of *The Shadow I Dress In*. Evoking an encounter in a New York City train with a man as interested in avoiding contact with her as she with him, the speaker construes the missed opportunity for contact as an inability to find the "poem" that the experience might have contained (55). "Idle Talk" likewise stages a conversation among Van Gogh, Caesar, and Mozart about the point of living, the problematic nature of legacies, and the whims of nameless posterity, with artistic creation and political participation implicitly compared. "Poet in Summer Garden" summons up a live performance by a particularly compelling poet—one would assume the late Leslie Mellichamp, from the dedication to him—with the speaker recalling the experience with earnest awe: "He lifts his body's load / of bird in transit, and the music drifts / over the trellised green, women and men / waiting to let this happen once again" (76). The text presents us with a speaker contrasting the physically challenging craft of dancers (who "work by forgetting: they let go of what / leads us by the mind, / follow a bolder syntax") with her own verbal instruments, the mind and tongue. These often clumsy tools seem less suited to "meticulous abandon" than the dancers' bodies. So "when the house lights undo / the night's miracles," the speaker confesses, "I blink and stagger / home on my words like crutches" (81–82).

The poem "God Contemplates the Imminent Arrival of Emily Dickinson" attributes so much power to the verse of the reclusive poet from Amherst, Massachusetts, that it imagines God trembling at the prospect of such a woman's presence in heaven. Poetry is itself the speaker in the self-reflective "The Author Begins Work"; it tells us of the changes in the poet's perceptions as she sets out to compose her texts. The alphabetically versified, cleverly experimental "All of It" recreates the genesis of a poem in a way that parallels the act of starting a busy day:

> A poem
> begins with the
> casual and
> daily:
> eggs
> frying,
> gulped coffee. (*Shadow* 92)

Similarly, the persona presented in "Baked Goods" describes her trip to the market in the company of her poem, personified as a companion who "sat down / among the produce" and who "found its calling" through a conversation with "the wafers / in their stiff little cups" (98).

In "Warning," the speaker advises herself against harboring the vain hope that her creation will wholly satisfy anybody's needs. Living "on hunger," a poem cannot "feed you"; because it remains "naked as the sun / since the day it was born," it will not clothe a person either (100). Nor does it seek any special comforts for itself because "it likes best to loaf outside / back doors and miss the main event," as we are reminded in "What the Poem Wants" (102). In "Shop Talk," which tells of "a poet friend" who "hates / enjambment" and then uses that poetic technique to develop a whole poem, Espaillat simply basks in the joys, versatility, and paradoxes of the craft (107). Finally, "Theme and Variations" celebrates summer, whose light triggers an unseen element that makes "Something that never hopes, something whose name / unlocks secret doors, is blessing us with music." The poem closes on a note of aesthetic mystery: "Leave it alone; it needs no name; / it wants to be light, it wants to be music" (106). This lyrical sestina reaffirms the key role Espaillat assigns to music as she writes for the ear as well as for the mind and heart.

EXPANSIVE AMERICANNESS

One feature that distinctly sets *The Shadow I Dress In* apart from Espaillat's other volumes is the strength of its meditation on cultural differences. Two interconnected geographical poems flesh out the complexities of reconciling—or at least acknowledging—the impact of such differences. In the first, "Circling Boston," the speaker describes a game she plays to help reconcile herself to the absence of her sons, both of whom are away in graduate school in another state: "an idle game I play with maps, / as Earth is played at by cartography / and mocked by the close travels of the heart / circling their days as Boston circles me" (30). The second poem, "Cartography," continues describing the practice of a kind of emotional spreading, now in terms of her grandchildren whom she imagines being "at the kitchen table / while they drink their milk and prepare for bed" (31). The playful lesson encompasses the town "beside the Merrimack," where the family lives, and its history as suggested by its street names: "Atkinson, Howard, Butler, Boardman, Caldwell." Likewise, public monuments allude to traders and soldiers who subsequently "climbed out of steerage / to commerce, farming, learning, the slave trade" (31–32). What dawns on the speaker is the realization that her dead ancestors are "sleeping elsewhere" and hence do not figure "on this map." Their names preside over another geographic domain "where my grandfather's cows / sought shade from tropic sun" (32). She thinks of her Dominican grandfather's diverse forebears ("Spaniards, Africans, Frenchmen, nameless Arawaks") as well as those of her husband's family ("blessed in Hebrew, beside Rumanian rivers"). The text muses on the "remembering[s]," the "crossings," and the many "doorways left vacant" (32–33). The map before them, therefore, offers a site for planting roots, not just for unearthing and reclaiming them. She evokes her now-married sons, whose wives "show us the tartans of their clans," all becoming ancestors to future generations of people with richly heterogeneous backgrounds. The closing stanza captures the hybrid tapestry that results from the fusion of races, histories, cultures, and ethnic traumas in the United States:

> Children, asleep, breathe stillness, but in their bones
> an endless knitting takes place, a long forgiveness:
> slaver and slave, Jew, Christian, stranger and stranger,
> soldier and slain lie down in this one bed,
> persuade us from the piecemeal we were born of
> into the wide unfolding of the sea. (33)

This poem consolidates the broadly historical with the intensely personal, illustrating how such large phenomena as cultural hybridity and ethnic admixture take place in a discrete family unit. It also constitutes the most explicit expression of the identitarian implications of her bilingual upbringing, cross-cultural experience, and interethnic marriage that the poet has thus far formulated. As we have seen, self-assured in the legitimacy of her ancestral culture and her native tongue from very early on, Espaillat has long promoted communication between English- and Spanish-speaking constituencies. Significantly, the recognition of difference—her own as well as that of others—has never caused her to doubt her belonging in American society. She exhibits little, if any, anxiety, insecurity, or dividedness over her constituent parts.

Arguably, Espaillat, more than many, represents "the new American" projected by J. Hector St. John de Crèvecoeur (1735–1813). After settling in the State of New York in 1759, Crèvecoeur lived off the land and wrote his *Letters from an American Farmer* (1782), in which he offered some hypotheses about what renders someone "an American": a combination of crossings, heritages, and bodies of knowledge. Over two hundred years since his time, Espaillat returns to the conundrum of American identity. She regards herself as a "typical" American, by which she means the following:

> A person with a foreign background who grew up speaking English and some
> other 'mother tongue,' who has relatives elsewhere and profound emotional
> ties to some other place, but who is mostly wholly 'home' in the United States,

in its language and ideals. I grew up in New York City among such people, from 1939 and through the 40s and 50s, and we all knew that we had someone at home who spoke only Polish or Yiddish, Spanish or Chinese or Italian or Greek. (Cruz-Hacker 7)

Although self-identifying as quintessentially American, Espaillat did not have to endure the cultural abuse prompted by the fundamentalist "Americanization" campaigns during her formative years that enthroned monolinguality as a virtue and rendered bilingualism (alongside multiculturalism) suspect, if not also downright unpatriotic. Reports abound of Eastern European and Italian immigrant children who suffered punishments in school for displaying their ethnic or linguistic differences vis-à-vis the Anglo-American majority. Probably because of personal circumstances, such as coming from an immigrant group that at the time enjoyed no distinct recognition as an enclave by virtue of its small size, or perhaps given the speed with which she took to the English language, Espaillat escaped the cultural policing as it existed in many schools. Conceivably, she may also have profited from the immigrant presence among the faculty of the New York City public schools, where during the late 1940s and the 1950s many teachers themselves came from households with foreign parents or grandparents. As a result, she was able to retain Spanish, value her ancestral heritage, and succeed at bridging English- and Spanish-speaking constituencies even while striving to carve a space for herself among poets of the English language.

During her keynote address at a conference on May 12, 2006, at Hostos Community College of the City University of New York, Espaillat encouraged the audience to think of identity "not as something we have, but as something that happens" ("Migration"). Ironically, the etymology of the word notwithstanding, our identities change in proportion to what happens in our lived reality. Where ethnicity is concerned, then, Espaillat thinks that "more is better," because the larger the group into which we feel we belong, the smaller the number of those we can marginalize through exclusionary othering. She adds, "I think that overemphasis on physical ethnicity, and exclusive loyalty to those with whom we have traceable blood ties can be a dangerous thing as well as a source of comfort" (Cruz-Hacker 8). Comfort comes from conferring an immediate sense of belonging to a collective; danger arises from our tendency to exclude those we regard as "not ours . . . therefore not our responsibility, and perhaps even the enemy somehow" (8).

Espaillat harbors a capacious, humane view of identity that respects difference, embraces inclusion, and guards itself from the consuming vortex of homogeneity. Nor is it insignificant that, as this chapter's survey of her writings suggests, she arrived at that view of her own accord, prior to the advent of diversity as a value embraced by this country's ever-shifting ideological climate. Her democratically minded avant-gardism parallels her attraction to (and mastery of) the techniques of formal verse prior to the revival of formalism in American poetry writ large. An artist in harmony with her cross-national reality, Espaillat is also attuned to what literary scholar and ecoactivist Lawrence Buell terms the "environmental unconscious" (Buell, "Ecocritical" 699; Buell, *Writing* 25–26). She endorses the understanding that the wellbeing of the Earth—possibly "the twenty-first century's most pressing problem"—remains our shared responsibility, a crucially inclusive sensibility at a time when the human species has begun to suffer the devastating consequences of climate change and other environmental terrors. Although Rhina Polonia Espaillat published her first book at the unconventional age of sixty, we argue it would be difficult to find a younger poet more deserving of the title "a poet of the future."

2 GENEALOGIES OF SENSIBILITY

STARDOM OF A NEW YORK TEEN POET

At fifteen, Rhina P. Espaillat was a fifth-term student at Julia Richman High School, at East 67th Street and Second Avenue in Manhattan, New York. Given that her poems had appeared in the school's publications, she already enjoyed a measure of literary visibility among teachers and peers. But her local acclaim grew in November 1947 when that month's issue of *Ladies' Home Journal*, featuring three of her poems, hit the newsstands. This was hardly a negligible feat given that this periodical, founded in 1883, had become the first magazine in the United States to reach one million subscribers by 1903. By the 1940s its circulation had exceeded four million (Yellin 25). Until 1961 *Ladies' Home Journal* enjoyed the greatest circulation among the group of magazines known as "the seven sisters," the top-selling serial publications that competed for the loyalty of the country's female readership. As its subtitle at the time read, it was the "magazine women believe in." The *Journal* became "one of the most trusted venues" during WWII for the federal government to convey war-related information to women, usually via advertisements or targeted articles (Yellin 25). With her poems featured here, Espaillat's reputation had clearly transcended the confines of her high school, transporting her into the limelight at the national and—to some extent—international level.

Preceded by a photograph of the fifteen-year-old Rhina striking a pose that exudes self-confidence and aplomb, her three poems appeared on page 298. The biographical note underneath the picture explains that the student's interests "are divided between poetry and art." She aspired to pursue the study of "art in Europe at some future date." As for poetry, she had already composed a "collection of some four hundred poems." Indeed, after her debut, her work would appear "regularly" in that magazine, as reported in the *New York Herald Tribune* ("Julia Richman Senior" 12). The media exposure would lead to her selling "a number of poems to British women's magazines" and to her accruing "fan letters" that attested to "the pleasure and confidence she instills in her readers" (12).

Over seven decades later, Espaillat would self-effacingly describe her earliest publications as "exactly what you would expect from a fifteen-year-old: sappy love poems based on no personal experience whatsoever, dripping with half-digested Millay, Teasdale, and E. B. Browning. But metrically and prosodically competent" (Monsour, *Rhina Espaillat* 57). However, the three poems published in the *Ladies' Home Journal* in 1947, "There is Nothing of You Not Worshipped," "On Waiting," and "Answer," stand out for their sophisticated diction and mature management of affect. A two-stanza poem, the first recreates the voice of a speaker aware that her feelings for the beloved dwarf any he could possibly harbor for her:

> There is no part of your spirit,
> Vast as it is, and free,
> No note of its song not cherished
> More than you'll ever cherish
> The whole of the song in me. (Espaillat, "There is Nothing" 298)

The second, with a pithy terseness reminiscent of Emily Dickinson's verse, impersonates a voice of experience meditating on the need to wait things out during anxious times:

> I thought a day too much
> Not long ago;

> But neither days nor years are long,
> I've come to know.
> Perhaps there'll be a time,
> Some distant date,
> When I shall think eternity
> Not long to wait. ("There is Nothing" 298)

The third poem, "Answer," deploys clever metaphors of the kind known as conceits for the ungraspable lover, a person the speaker can neither contain nor liberate from her consciousness. She proclaims, "Lose you? I shall not lose you: / You are gardens after the rain; / How would I lose the warmth of the sun, / Or the dawn when it's spring again?" Later, she remarks with a combined tone of awe and resignation, "Hold you? I cannot hold you: / You are snow on a starlit night; / You are a sea gull calling, calling—/ How would I keep the snow from falling? / The bird from flight?" (Espaillat, "Answer" 298). Espaillat's early knack for the use of these often ingenious comparisons foreshadows the use of conceits as a trademark of her craft. In later years she would exhibit a predilection for applying witticisms to ordinary, even mundane subjects. This early attraction for unexpected formulations illustrates the extent to which she had already imbibed the style and content of the Metaphysical poets, especially George Herbert (1593–1633), whose devotional messages and poignant imagery, paired with superior craftsmanship, would serve as a pivotal model.

In addition to her prosodic skill, this imaginative verve may have been behind her repeated acceptances to the *Ladies' Home Journal* over the next few years. An August 1948 piece titled "À Minuit" (At midnight) finds the young poet venturing into the rather adult field of the erotic, complete with a French title:

> Something brought me back from
> slumber:
> Subtle touch of finger tips,
> Hands, familiar, dear, insistent—
> Sudden warmth upon my lips.
> ...
> Darkness could not hide your
> presence,
> Straight to me your love came
> winging,

And over all the bitter ocean,
I heard you singing. ("À Minuit" 48)

Since at age sixteen, as she would confess later, Espaillat did not know "which side of a guy was up," the poem attests to her mimetic capacity to reproduce adult sentiment and convincingly perform maturity in her verse (NK/STS).[1]

Two years after her first professional publication, Espaillat shared with the press a letter from Shabani, Southern Rhodesia (present-day Zimbabwe), by an author who had translated one of her poems into Afrikaans and was asking for permission to reprint the text as part of the foreword of a book she had written about South Africa ("Julia Richman Senior" 12). Espaillat could produce similar fan letters from Manila, Berlin, Rio de Janeiro, and London, in addition to correspondence from various US residents, such as one written by a high school girl from Kansas. The admirer praised Espaillat's "great contribution . . . in an era in which our generation is so nearly unaware of life's challenges" (12). A year later, in a 1950 interview with the *New York Sun*, Espaillat shared an encounter with another young American girl who had written to her from Germany. The letter writer's father served there as part of the Occupation forces. Having read some of Espaillat's work in a magazine and found it very moving, she contacted the poet, and the two became pen pals, leading to a close and enduring friendship ("Teen-age Poet"). This early visibility afforded Espaillat the unique experience of providing mentorship and inspiration for her readers while still a minor. In addition to testifying to the widespread appeal of her poems at so early a stage in her career, this precocious leadership prefigures a pattern that throughout her life would manifest itself in a frequent advisory role to individuals and literary communities, among them the Fresh Meadows Poets and the Powow River Poets. Her openness to assisting fellow practitioners is an aspect of her literary persona that has earned her recognition in the form of the May Sarton Award, among other notable honors from fellow poets.

Equally illustrative of the demand for Espaillat's poetry from abroad is the June 1948 publication of her poem "Read Between the Lines" in the *Lethbridge Herald*, a newspaper based in southern Alberta, Canada. The poem appeared in the *Herald*'s "Page for Women," a section that included recipes, a calendar of

---

1. We will use NK/STS (Nancy Kang/Silvio Torres-Saillant) to identify all statements and information we collected in the course of our extended interview with Espaillat on January 4–5, 2013.

local events, announcements of weddings and engagements, and coverage of accomplishments by women in the city and throughout the province. There was also advice on home and health matters, alongside advertisements for consumer products that targeted women readers. In the midst of the topical medley that crammed the page was a subsection titled "Our Poetry Corner," which in this edition was devoted to showcasing a poem by Espaillat. Spoken as a postscript to a love letter, the text recreates the emotional turmoil of a speaker who grieves the loss of her sweetheart yet remains stubbornly resolved to conceal her grief. Consisting of two quatrains in iambic pentameter, the poem in its entirety reads as follows:

> In this last letter you will never find
> One word of pain; I meant it to be gay—
> But read between the lines, and you will know
> How many things I thought and couldn't say.
>
> It seems to mean that all is quite forgotten.
> And all I felt for you no longer real—
> But read between the lines, and understand
> How much I miss you, dear, how lost I feel. (Espaillat, "Read" n.p.)

Given the attribution at the bottom of the poem, "By Rhina P. Espaillat," devoid of any biographical detail, one wonders whether the *Lethbridge Herald* readers— or even the section editors—had the slightest inkling that the speaker in those world-weary lines came from the pen of a sixteen-year-old. Tempered feeling and emotional restraint do not typically describe the mental disposition of the very young, especially when discussing romance. As conventionally represented in literature, the stages of a person's psychological development tend to evolve from restlessness and wild passion to serenity and self-control. The *New York Herald Tribune* article of January 1949 stressed precisely this point: "Expressing mature depth and understanding in her verses, Rhina expresses the longing and regret that is usually felt only by older people. She says she is very grateful that her appeal is universal and hopes that, some day, she may make a real contribution to the establishment of world peace" ("Julia Richman" 12).

In the memorable "Lines Composed A Few Miles above Tintern Abbey, on Revisiting the Banks of the Wye During a Tour. July 13, 1798," the English Romantic poet William Wordsworth (1770–1850) evocatively captured an understanding of his psychological evolution. This poem is included in *Lyrical Ballads, with a Few Other Poems* (1798), a volume that is still regarded as both a landmark in English poetry and a foundational pronouncement of the Romantic era. "Tintern Abbey" evokes the bracing sensations and remembrances prompted by an older man's return to a familiar site of his youth. Having approached the banks of the river, the speaker recalls the time

> when first
> I came among these hills; when like a roe
> I bounded over the mountains, by the sides
> Of the deep rivers, and the lonely streams,
> Wherever nature led. (Wordsworth, *Complete* 261)

The speaker associates his "boyish days" with "coarser pleasures" and "glad animal movements"; just as the "sounding cataract" haunted him "like a passion," the provocation of the landscape elicited in him intense emotion that he terms "an appetite, a feeling, and a love" (261). On the speaker's return to the River Wye, mature and free from the compulsions of "thoughtless youth," he can now hear the "still, sad music of humanity" with its "ample power / To chasten and subdue" (261).

Unlike Wordsworth's journeyer, Espaillat's speaker in "Read Between the Lines" makes no reference to previous stages of maturation that might account for the aged tone of her discourse, yet she exudes the deep understanding of someone who has already reached a stage of psychological growth wherein emotions can be harnessed and enunciated rationally, as well as adjusted, perhaps, to the dictates of social norms. The speaker's sadness at the absence of the lover, including its ensuing graduation to a sense of resigned loss ("How much I miss you, dear, how lost I feel") must remain concealed in a letter originally meant "to be gay."

Formally, the quatrains in "Read between the Lines" follow an irregular rhyme scheme (*abcb*; *defe*). This rhyme scheme (though not the meter) resembles quatrains of the kind found in Dickinson's poem 712, which starts with the much-recognized lines, "Because I could not stop for death— / He kindly stopped for me—" (Dickinson, *Complete* 350). In Dickinson's poem the penultimate quatrain—or stanza number five—rhymes the second and fourth lines, leaving the first and the third unrhymed. With similar irregularity, Espaillat's poem dramatizes a tension between obedience to and rebellion against the constraints of prosodic formulae, perhaps foreshadowing the poet's lifelong habit of working within the august tradition of classical English prosody while adding her individual accent throughout.

Decades later, as a seasoned poet, she would describe this inclination through the metaphor of "dancing in a box" (Finch, *Formal Feeling* 64–65). We often hear the clichéd praise for people who can "think outside the box," meaning that they achieve creativity by stepping out of the comfort offered by established and habitual practices. Espaillat's metaphor points to a different avenue to creativity, a combination—recalling the title of T. S. Eliot's iconic essay "Tradition and the Individual Talent"—which acknowledges the individual artist's necessity to speak with his or her own voice amid a requisite awareness of literary precedents. Robert Frost (1874–1963), who would become Espaillat's most admired poetic ancestor, had spoken of meter and rhyme as basic necessities. A resolutely formal poet, Frost believed that sound makes sense in poetry, going as far as to claim that "sound often says more than the words. It may even, as in irony, convey a meaning opposite to the words" (Frost, *Selected Letters* 113). Frost explicitly urged poets to "learn to get cadences by skillfully breaking the sound of sense ... across the regular beat of the meter" (80). The poet's "emphasis on the interaction of meter and rhythm explains a lifelong suspicion of free verse," a poetic method that, devoid of "a grid on which to measure its rhythms," becomes, "as one of Frost's most famous aphorisms has it—akin to playing tennis with the net down" (Kendall 8).

From the outset, Espaillat willingly embraced both the limits and possibilities that the elements of prosody have afforded poets across generations. The traditional poetic devices of rhyme, meter, stanzaic divisions, metaphor, personification, and the like, in addition to witticisms, triggers of emotion, or meditative states of mind have traditionally enabled successful versifiers to have their artful combinations attain literariness with readers and listeners. But, especially after the Romantic period with the revolution spearheaded by Wordsworth and Coleridge, poets seem to have generally focused on making "room for individual work by forgetting or suppressing the devices that represent the institution of literature" (Wesling 19). A scholar of poetic form, Donald Wesling contends that "prosodic avant-gardism" confronts the inevitable failure of its project to abolish style. The project "must fail because its means are themselves stylistic: abandoning form in the name of form" (19).

Perhaps no single text in the Western literary tradition has enacted the aspiration that Espaillat evinces in the "dancing in a box" metaphor more cleverly than a sonnet by the English Romantic poet John Keats (1795–1821) titled "On the Sonnet." The text was part of a series of experimental works written in the spring of 1819 when Keats was wrestling with the problem of verse composition. An entry in his journal on April 15 suggests his ongoing unease about his practice: "I am still at a stand in versifying—I cannot do it yet with pleasure" (qtd. in Ward 272).

Written in the same week as when he composed his famous "Ode to Psyche," Keats's work "takes as its theme the pattern-making faculty that gives a poem form" (Ward 279). "On the Sonnet" demonstrates the tension between the dictates of received forms and the desire for unencumbered expression in the overall execution of the poem. The opening lines thus feature the speaker complaining about prosodic constraints ("by dull rhymes our English must be chain'd"), which leaves the sweet sonnet, like the mythical Andromeda, "fettered in spite of pained loveliness" (qtd. in Bate 497). Scholars have detected here a burning desire to liberate the sonnet from "the elegiac monotony" of the "regular pendulum-like swing of the lines" as Keats would have practiced abundantly by that time (497).

Readers of Keats's poem will notice that he metapoetically bemoans the prosodic fixity of the genre while using the occasion to demonstrate how to subvert its guidelines even while abiding by them. Written in iambic pentameter and setting out with an *abab* rhyme scheme, as one would expect from a typical English (or Shakespearean) sonnet, Keats's poem loosens the fetters of the "dull rhymes" by altering the scheme in the third line and again in the sixth line, producing the less familiar structure *abca bdca*. In addition to altering the typical *abab cdcd efef gg* rhyme scheme, the poem offers an enjambment interlacing three lines that point to sonic elements, which run without a sense of pause at the end of each line (lines 7–9). However, the poet succumbs to expected regularity as he closes the text with a *dede* scheme and allows the classical "turn" to remain where one traditionally expects to find it.

Following in this tradition, Espaillat's early poetic practice suggests that by age sixteen, whether through cognition, artistic intuition, or sheer mimesis, she was already attuned to this age-old predicament of her craft. When interviewed by the *New York Sun*, the young poet would declare that she did not "believe in poet's license," an early invocation of an aesthetic philosophy that in her mature years she would refine by declaring a preference for meter and rhyme, which offered her the paradoxical mix of freedom within received structures and forms. Espaillat's rapport with form would continually evolve into a restless duality that casts her as anxious to master received poetic structures while simultaneously aiming to reconfigure them just enough to assert a distinct sound.

MATURITY AND SENSE

The aforementioned *New York Herald Tribune* article captured Espaillat at the pivotal moment of her senior year, when she was on the verge of receiving her diploma. The article features a large photograph of Espaillat working at a table with an art project before her; the accompanying caption describes her as putting "finishing touches on a new drawing." In addition to her poetic gifts, Espaillat had distinguished herself as a visual artist, having "made many posters for school affairs" and "helped to paint scenery for class plays." She would not pursue her interest in drawing with as much assiduity as she took to her verse because the "pull" of poetry was simply much greater (12). The article reproduces a poem, "Looking Backward," which, we are told, illustrates the young woman's "hopes and desires":

> I hid my love and my lament
> Behind a face of passive stone:
> A little late I spoke your name,
> And wept alone.
>
> How many hearts grow dry and brittle
> And end with life before they live
> Because they never learned to whisper
> "Forgive, forgive!" ("Julia Richman" 12).

Appearing on the seventeenth birthday of the talented "verse-maker," "Looking Backward" again adopts the discursive demeanor more often associated with older people than with carefree teenagers.

Julia Richman High School seemed an ideal place for the young poet in the 1940s. In our January 2013 interview, Espaillat remembered the institution—not coed until 1967, and named after the first woman district superintendent of schools in New York City—as a "huge school, an enormous school," although she only attended a moderately sized section of it called the "honors school" or alternatively, the "country school" (NK/STS). Espaillat's admittedly insufficient strength in mathematics had caused her to fail the admissions test for the then all-girls Hunter College High School. But she later gained admission to Richman's honors program, a space teeming with "girls who liked writing, painting, and so forth," putting her in the company of a select group of achievement-oriented, dynamic, and artistically inclined peers. She recalls that as students, they "were *supposed* to do interesting things." Therefore, while the celebrity she gained after she began to publish in major venues earned her much appreciation at school, it placed her on no special pedestal with peers or teachers, since her program fostered the pursuit of creative excellence in everyone. Espaillat remembers the faculty fondly, as "sensitive, imaginative, and generous," and who would do their best to support student interests once they "fished out that you had any talent at all" (NK/STS).

Facing the culmination of her high school life, Espaillat had to entertain serious thoughts about the future. She wanted to attend college but, as the *Herald Tribune* divulged, "family responsibilities" compelled her "to seek work immediately" ("Julia Richman Senior" 12). Given her limited financial means, she adopted a characteristically mature outlook, even displaying a sense of humor about her economic condition. She remarked to her interviewer, "I am paid four dollars a line. That is good, but my poems are always short, so I'm looking for a beginning job as a secretary." She explained further, with what the journalist called "a smile of understanding wisdom," that realism and imagination must always coexist for her: "You see, one part of my mind translates my dreams into poems, but the other side of my thinking is very practical—I shall always write poetry, but if someone will give me a chance to prove myself in business I will work very hard" (12).

What the *Herald Tribune* writer euphemistically termed "family responsibilities" refers to the modest parental income that was maintaining the Espaillat household. Looking back at those slim years, the poet has characterized the financial situation at home as being precarious but sufficient: "We never lacked the essentials. We had everything we needed, but there were no luxuries like vacations or anything fancy. . . . We always managed but there was nothing left over. So I appreciated being allowed to finish school." Her attitude relays an awareness of filial responsibility tempered with a deep love and respect for her elders: "I know they were sacrificing for me. I know they didn't have a lot of money. . . . I was all right with going to work right away because I never wanted to cost them anything" (NK/STS). Despite the material constraints, Espaillat's parents insisted on her going to college—not "away to college" (that is, to one of the non–New York City schools that had offered her tuition scholarships)—but to college nonetheless. She passed the admissions test to Hunter College of the City University of New York and subsequently enrolled. Calling her postsecondary experience "the biggest bargain in the world," she counts herself fortunate to have attended when public higher education in the city was still tuition-free. She declares, "The greatest gift I've ever received was the free education that New York City gave me at Hunter" (NK/STS).

When Espaillat attracted the attention of the *New York Sun* in June 1950, she was already a college student majoring in English with an eye on pursuing "a career as a high school teacher in the New York City public school system" ("Teen-age Poet"). Her previous career indecision had evidently fallen to the wayside. At the age of sixteen, she had become the youngest member ever to enter the oldest poetry organization in the United States, the Poetry Society of America. The article quotes Espaillat describing the induction as "a wonderful honor" that "surprised and thrilled" her. While focused on pursuing a career path, the "serious-minded," "dark-eyed" young woman vowed to "keep writing poetry." The young writer spoke of carrying her "quick inspiration book" wherever she went to jot down observations and verses when hit by powerful impressions. She added, "Usually I finish the poem right there. I don't revise too much." This self-assurance would undergo a transformation as she grew up, with an older Espaillat theorizing that inspiration only offers material for a first draft. In many respects a consummate New Yorker, the teen also spoke of writing many of her poems on the subway. A train ride home from school, for instance, served as occasion for her to think of the pigeon's nest on the windowsill of her home, on 8 West 65th Street in Manhattan, leading her to pen the short piece "The Pigeons," which also appeared in the *Sun* article:

> A lady, proud in poverty,
> Refined but underfed,
> With wary and disdainful eye
> Scans my gift of bread.
>
> A cautious hop from sill to sill,
> A peck, a warning note—
> Love draws the lady back to fill
> Two small and raucous throats. ("Teen-age Poet" n.p.)

Impressive in its haiku-like concision, the text is richly evocative of the plight of the urban poor who strive to preserve their dignity amid the diminishments and cravings of poverty. It is also a sensitive study of a creature that is both ubiquitous and maligned in the city streets.

Describing Espaillat as a seventeen-year-old who came to the United States while very young and who took to poetry in English with great eagerness, the *Sun* article frames its coverage primarily as an immigrant success story. A full-body photograph of an elegantly dressed Espaillat accompanies the piece. The centerpiece of the article is Espaillat's recently received invitation to share her work at the Poetry Society of America. Also mentioned are the checks that came in the mail "from several well-known periodicals, here and abroad, and from New York quarterlies of verse that published her poems." The article attests to the young poet's success at touching the lives of readers through her craft, and allows her to offer a broad conception of the genre as a form of art that fundamentally connects people across planes of difference. She also endorses the use of ordinary language rather than that which "sounds dead and peculiar," so that the insights emanating from the poems may be personal to the poet yet accessible to everyone.

FAMILY AND SADNESS

To trace the genealogy of Espaillat's aesthetic philosophy, it may be useful to consider the environment that surrounded her as a student, her precocious attraction to language, and the family background that encouraged her creativity. Espaillat's good fortune to have had supportive teachers actually preceded her high school years. These earlier experiences may have equipped her with the wherewithal to take full advantage of the guidance and mentoring opportunities she would find at Julia Richman High.

Her run of luck with caring instructors began at P.S. 94, a Manhattan elementary school that went up to the sixth grade. There, she first entered into direct contact with the power of poetry; she learned that the genre touched readers and listeners alike by provoking their imaginations, prompting them to forge emotional connections between what they heard or read and their own life experiences. To this day she remembers the class—"either in fifth or sixth grade"—in which she was reduced to tears in front of all her classmates by the teacher's moving rendition of "Little Boy Blue," a well-loved 1888 poem by Eugene Field (1850–1895), the American writer best known for his children's verse and humorous prose. The poem evokes the orderly faithfulness of toys left behind by a child who has passed away. The first stanza details the time warp in which the items seem to stand suspended: "The little toy dog is covered with dust, / But sturdy and staunch he stands; / And the little toy soldier is red with rust, / And his musket molds in his hands." Of course, the gathering of dust alludes not only to the particles that collect on unmoved objects over time but also to the mortal powder into which the boy has been reduced since his death. As Field's speaker explains, "Time was when the little toy dog was new / And the soldier was passing fair, / And that was the time when our Little Boy Blue / Kissed them and put them there" (Field).

The boy's death and the constancy of "the little toy friends" who remain "true" to his instructions that they not move until he returns transported the young Espaillat to yet an earlier stage of her own childhood. Hearing Field's melancholic lines sent her back to 1939, the year she left La Vega, Dominican Republic, where she had spent from ages five to seven living with doting grandmothers and other relatives until her parents felt stable enough to send for her. She had parted with her kinfolk, still vividly remembering and missing the sounds and the smells of the native land. Coming from a large, tight-knit group of relatives in that small, traditional town, she reveals that she could simply leave the house and "go either direction [to] visit family" (NK/STS). While fully immersed in the metropolitan maze of New York City, to which she had acclimated quickly, she still missed her paternal and maternal grandmothers, as well as her namesake, her vivacious Aunt Rhina. The imagery in "Little Boy Blue" that describes the playthings waiting "in the same old place" for the touch of their owner's hands resurrected the tender memory of her paternal grandmother who, at the moment of their parting, assured the seven-year-old Rhina that when she returned to La Vega, she would find everything exactly as she had left it. "Everything will always be preserved here for you," Espaillat recalls the elder promising with utmost confidence. Reconstructing the scene seventy-four years later in Newburyport, herself now a grandmother, she understood—again tearfully— that poetic language had the capacity to stir the emotions, to recreate feelings, and to elevate the poignancy of life with sound, sense, and profoundly personal meaning.

It was in elementary school, then, that Espaillat experienced the epiphany that to a large extent gave her the motivation to embrace her poetic calling. She had spent the earlier years of her childhood, at least from age five onward, sur-rounded by the sounds of poetry. The only child of parents who were avid readers of literature and history in their native Spanish, she enjoyed regular exposure to "language manipulated for the ear," a phrase that would come to encapsulate the core of her definition of poetry (NK/STS). Her father would often recite poems around the house, invoking works that ran the gamut of Spanish-language verse from Spain's Golden Age to the major poets of modern Latin America. She recalls his routinely declaiming lines by the mystic Saint Teresa of Avila (1515–1582), also known as Saint Teresa of Jesus. The opening lines of one of this Carmelite nun's best-known poems ring with particular clarity in her mind: "Vivo sin vivir en mí / y de tal manera espero / que muero porque no muero" [I live, yet no true life I know, / And, living thus expectantly, / I die because I do not die] (Teresa 277).[2]

Her father also recited verses by another notable mystic from sixteenth-century Spain, Saint John of the Cross (1542–1591). In particular, the rousing "Noche oscura" (Dark Night), featuring the soul as speaker telling of its joyful departure from the flesh in pursuit of perfect union with God, was a favorite. The opening stanza reads, "En una noche oscura, / con ansias, en amores inflamada, / ¡oh dichosa ventura! / salí sin ser notada, / estando ya mi casa sosegada" [On a dark night, / Anxious, by love inflamed, / O joyous chance! / I left not seen or discovered, / My house at last completely quiet] (John 102–3). Saint John of the Cross would reappear in Espaillat's life during the period when, in her late six-ties, translation became an increasingly important part of her expanded literary repertoire. This holy man's works would figure prominently among the Span-ish and Latin American poets whom she would translate into English. Her own version of the above stanza reads: "One darkest night I went / aflame with love's devouring eager burning— / O delirious event!— / no witnesses discerning, / the house now still from which my steps were turning" (Espaillat, "Spanish" 51).

Latin American poems from among her father's favorites that linger in Espaillat's memory include samples from the defiant Sor Juana Inés de la Cruz (1651–1695), the Hieronymite nun from New Spain who fought suffocating sexist barriers to assert herself as a poet and scholar, as well as the intense Peruvian poet José Santos Chocano (1875–1934), a member of the *modernista* school of poetry. She recalls hearing Sor Juana's feisty retort—in octosyllabic quatrains with an *abba* rhyme scheme—to the hypocritical dictates of colonial society

---

2. Here and throughout this volume, we use existing translations attributed in the bibliography unless otherwise indicated.

that rendered women the objects of male desire while expecting them to remain chaste and virtuous:

> Hombres necios que acusáis
> a la mujer sin razón,
> sin ver que sois la ocasión
> de lo mismo que culpáis:
> sin con ansia sin igual
> solicitáis su desdén,
> ¿por qué queréis que obren bien
> si la incitáis al mal? (Sor Juana 148–49)

> [*Misguided men, who will chastise | a woman when no blame is due, | oblivious that it is you | who prompted what you criticize; | if your passions are so strong | that you elicit their disdain, | how can you wish that they refrain | when you incite them to their wrong?*]

Equally memorable to Espaillat are lines from Chocano's "Los caballos de los conquistadores," perhaps the best-known single text from the 1906 collection *Alma América: Poemas indo-españoles*, whose first stanza sings mellifluously to the majesty of the horses that came to the so-called New World during the Spanish expeditions of conquest:

> ¡Los caballos eran fuertes!
> ¡Los caballos eran ágiles!
> Sus pescuezos eran finos y sus ancas
> relucientes y sus cascos musicales.
> ¡Los caballos eran fuertes!
> ¡Los caballos eran ágiles! (Chocano 41)

An English version of these lines from the poem, translated by Edna W. Underwood under the title "The Arab Steeds of the Conquerors," appears in Phyllis Rodríguez-Peralta's study of the life and works of Chocano. It reads: "Oh! The battle-steeds were mighty! / Oh! The battle-steeds were nimble! / Their haughty necks were slender / And their broad breasts silken, shining! / Oh! The battle-steeds were mighty! / Oh! The battle-steeds were nimble! (Rodríguez-Peralta 68–69). Written from a perspective of sympathetic identification with the excitement that the conquest must have triggered in the hearts of the Spanish, the poem undertakes to replicate the nature of the enterprise through sound. Rodríguez-Peralta's study of Chocano noted decades ago the formal features whereby the poem conveys the stridency of the "heroic" endeavor undertaken by the conquerors: "The surging, insistent rhythm marks the clatter and pawing of the horses' hoofs as they traverse mountains and valleys—manes flying and heads erect" (67–69).

Espaillat traces her poetic genealogy, then, to the cadences, rhythms, and overall sonic potency that she heard grown-ups sharing in Spanish verse around her during a part of her childhood when she could not have possibly understood the semantic contents of the words being uttered. She had the privilege of a family environment shaped by parents who enjoyed the arts and a gregarious, educated paternal grandmother—affectionately called Mama Pincha—who, back in La Vega, periodically convened writers, musicians, and visual artists to share their works with one another at her home. Consequently, the young Rhina had imprinted the sense that "things were metrical . . . , that one could play with language" without being limited to producing "drumbeats," and could achieve complex and subtle types of musicality in manifold ways. She learned early on to recognize language as capable of giving "that kind of [sensory] pleasure that nothing else in the world could give" (NK/STS).

SOUND, SENSE, AND UNTERMEYER

Well beyond her initial awareness of the poetic capacities of Spanish while living in La Vega, Espaillat's immersion in English via New York City life catalyzed a conscious awareness of the sound-sense connection in poetry. Espaillat's earliest extant poem, composed after three years of linguistic exposure to New York, contrasts nature's summer frenzy with its winter pallor, revealing an early knack for the logic and the rhythms of English. Written at age ten, with the title "The First Snowfall," the piece demonstrates the young poet's disposition to make meaning out of quotidian surroundings:

Fell on the first snowfall
flowers from the skies,
Burying under heaps of snow
The place where summer lies.

> And in that same tomb lies my heart,
> Dead with summer's gladness,
> Harried by the autumn winds,
> Prey to winter's sadness. (Espaillat, *Greatest Hits* 7)

Espaillat recalls that she had recently acquired the words *harried* and *prey* from "a story about hunting in colonial days and the hardships endured by the Puritans," and that she quickly seized on them with delight as she would do habitually throughout her life, grabbing "newly-learned words" for immediate use in some context of her own devising (7).

Alexander Pope (1688–1744) articulated the sound-sense connection in his *Essay on Criticism* (1711), an influential didactic poem written in heroic couplets. Pope scoffed at versifiers solely occupied with communicating ideas and erudite thoughts, poets whose "style is excellent" but whose "sense, they take upon content" (Pope 65). The Englishman dismisses with equal disdain the "tuneful fools" who admire only the "voice" of "the bright muse," working only to "please their ear, / Not mend their minds; as some to church repair, / Not for the doctrine but the music there" (66). Pope required of poetry to harmonize the content and the form so that both worked together like a marriage of equals: "'Tis not enough no harshness gives offence, / The sound must seem an echo to the sense" (67). The enduring impact that Pope's poetic thought would have on future generations in the English language may be gleaned from the recurring use of the "sound and sense" pairing in the critical lexicon of modern poets. Equally meaningful in this regard is the esteem among teachers for *Sound and Sense: An Introduction to Poetry* (1956), an anthology of verse in English designed for introductory courses, edited by Lawrence Perrine (1915–1995). A posthumous edition, the fourteenth published in 2014, now titled *Perrine's Sound and Sense* and coedited by Greg Johnson and Thomas A. Arp, vouches for the continued appeal of an anthology over six decades since it first appeared in print (Johnson, Arp, and Perrine).

Though she would not issue a lengthy, didactic statement on the art of poetry, Espaillat's engagement with the legacy of poetic thought bequeathed by practitioners throughout the Western tradition would become easily discernible in her practice. She would develop a vocabulary of her own as illustrated by such characteristic catchphrases as "dancing in a box," "language manipulated for the ear," or the link between "the how and the what" to personalize her poetic principles. Additionally, she would devote numerous poems to meditating in verse about diverse aspects of the craft, as suggested by such titles as "Metrics," "Prosody," "What the Poem Wants," and "Shop Talk."

During her time at P.S. 94, Espaillat became an avid reader. By a stroke of luck, right next to the school was a bountiful library that she would often visit during her lunch periods, being "less crazy about lunch" than she was impatient to read (NK/STS). Children her age normally had to stay on the ground floor, but when librarians realized that she was a serious reader who treated books with care, they allowed her special access to the regular shelving areas upstairs. That guided trespass into the part of the library reserved for use by adult readers proved crucial for the young Rhina; there, she chanced upon a poetry anthology that would become her veritable bible during those formative years. She came into contact with the mammoth collection *A Treasury of Great Poems English and American* (1942), edited by the prolific American poet, anthologist, critic, and translator Louis Untermeyer (1885–1977).

Untermeyer, who would go on to become the poet laureate of the United States in 1961, aimed to account for poetic creativity throughout the entire lifespan of the English language. The volume starts with sections from the Bible as one of the key tributaries to the "foundations of the English spirit," in the words of the text's subtitle. It then proceeds to the unknown bards of the tenth century, and subsequently reaches the Middle English period when Geoffrey Chaucer (1343–1400) predominates. The volume moves on to the major eras that include the Elizabethan period (1558–1603), with its requisite selections from William Shakespeare (1564–1616), the Metaphysical poets, the eighteenth century, the Romantic period, and then the nineteenth century. In this period, American poets increasingly infiltrate the pages heretofore dominated by their British counterparts. The volume offers a sampling of the first decades of the twentieth century and concludes with a selection of poems by Stephen Spender (1909–1995). Overall, the compendium's goal was to "suggest the vastness of the poets' imagination and the variety of their multiple worlds" (Untermeyer, *Treasury* 1).

The anthology's coverage fascinated Rhina, who read voraciously from the pages of the rather forbidding volume, thereby setting the stage for the evolution of her poetic consciousness. Though she knew about its existence and its value as a "holy" book, she had never read the Bible before, and it amazed her to no end to find portions of it included in a book of poetry (NK/STS). The selections from the popular ballads of the medieval era also proved fascinating. When she perused "horrible" stories that featured "dead people, violent loves, [and] illicit relationships," she found them "terrific" for their complexity and daring. She took to Chaucer with zest and imbibed verses by Edmund Spenser (1553–1599) and Sir Philip Sidney (1554–1586), eventually arriving in her own century with Wilfred Owen (1893–1918) and Hart Crane (1899–1932) as favorites. The more she read the thick assemblage "from page to page to page," the more she felt a passion to keep reading. But she had only limited access to the book given the time constraints posed by the lunch period. She tried to check the book out to prolong her time with it, but the library would not allow a child to borrow books from the adult section. Given her level of motivation, however, she would not give up, resorting instead to asking her parents to purchase a copy of the volume for her home use.

The young Espaillat made a powerful endorsement of the anthology as something that she "needed." Delighted by their daughter's passion for a compilation of poems rather than dolls or dresses, her parents hoped to oblige. But when they looked up the price of the volume, they found its cost prohibitive. An appraisal of Untermeyer's anthology by the poet William Rose Benét (1886–1950) that appeared in the *Saturday Review* the year of the book's publication lists the price as US$3.75 (Benét n.p.). A conversion of that amount, factoring in inflation from 1942 to 2016, yields an equivalent price in present value of roughly US$57.42, an amount that an immigrant couple earning just over minimum wage in New York City today would most likely find challenging ("Calculators/Inflation"). But the price was only a temporary setback for Espaillat's parents. They asked for the intercession of better-off relatives, namely her great-uncle and godfather Rafael Brache, who, together with his wife, affectionately called Mama Lola, purchased the anthology and gave it to the girl as a Christmas gift in 1943 (NK/STS).

Her love for the book was, at its heart, paradoxical; she muses, "I misunderstood most of it, I'm sure. I must have misread 90 percent of the book, but I didn't care because it all sounded so good. I used to read it aloud, and I read a lot of it to my mother while she worked at the sewing machine" (NK/STS). The seamstress, bewildered by the arcane words sounded out by her daughter so enthusiastically, would ask her what they meant, and the girl would do her best to translate. Not only that, she would offer explications of the hidden nuances, imagery, and turns of phrase. This scenario epitomizes the child's role as a kind of cultural-*cum*-linguistic broker for her immigrant parents, foreshadowing perhaps her future role as a teacher of literature and language arts. Whether she realized it at the time or not, it seems that in moving about the apartment reciting poems, Espaillat was reproducing her father's habit of sharing the sounds of poetry, doing in English what she had so often seen him do in Spanish. Decades later, the Untermeyer compilation still remains among her cherished possessions. In June 2014, she would still brandish the tome, which she described in an email message as "bandaged with tape but miraculously in one piece and still at work, like a brave old veteran" (Espaillat, "Re: Following Up").

Through Espaillat's relationship with this anthology, the passion with which she tackled its intricacies, and the family support that enabled her acquisition of the book, she had accrued the poetic literacy for taking full advantage of the creative environment awaiting her in the honors program at P.S. 118 after graduation from P.S. 94. This school, also known as Joan of Arc Junior High School, was a magnet for high-achieving sixth graders previously selected by their teachers from all over Manhattan. A "rigorous, wonderful school with a no-nonsense faculty," Joan of Arc offered enriched arts and crafts classes, home economics, foreign-language instruction, a nature room, and occasional field trips (NK/STS). Part of a group called "Rapid Advance," whose program aimed to enable students to enter high school early by skipping one semester, Espaillat recalls a class trip to the Shakespeare Theater in Stratford, Connecticut, to attend a performance of *The Tempest* starring the African American actor Canada Lee (1907–1952).

Through her early exposure to poetry, Espaillat had been initiated to the mysteries of aesthetic experience, the artistically induced states of mind in which the percipient's pleasure may have its roots in inexpressible sadness, as the encounter with Field's "Little Boy Blue" had demonstrated. It was such a profound feeling of identification that, in making young Rhina weep, the poem attracted her to—rather than pushed her away from—the art. No less important, through the rapport with and modeling provided by the Untermeyer anthology, she had attained a consciousness of literary creativity as something with a long history. A poet in the here and now could fruitfully engage in a conversation with a counterpart who wrote centuries earlier. Espaillat had thus equipped herself with a sense of intertextual tradition, of the grand design to which she could contribute. Perhaps this depth of perception was the germinal principle behind the "maturity" that commentators from the New York press discerned during the 1940s following the appearance of her verse in professional venues and her early stardom as a teen poet.

INTUITION OF DIFFERENCE

Espaillat's youth and relatively sheltered life in a close-knit, protective family made it unlikely for her to have developed the keenly sensitive political awareness necessary to discern patterns of exclusion based on class, gender, race, ethnicity, sexuality, and nationality, and how these might affect literary canon formation. For instance, enamored with the Untermeyer anthology, she likely had no way of grasping the meaning of exclusions implicit in his mapping of the poetic tradition. The gaps and fissures would be more apparent to those coming to the text after learning about the struggles for inclusion that occurred, for instance, during the Civil Rights Movement and the rise of second-wave feminism in the 1960s.

Untermeyer devoted only 70 out of his nearly 1,300 pages to poetry by women, even if his sympathetic commentary on the gender-inflected self-assertiveness of British modernist Anna Wickham (pen name of Edith Alice Mary Harper, 1883–1947) seems conceptually devoid of literary misogyny (Untermeyer, *Treasury* 1117–20). Nor did the meager representation of women poets in the anthology seem odd to the literary establishment at the time. We can deduce that much from the review of the compilation published by the aforementioned Benét, recipient of the Pulitzer Prize for poetry for his book *The Dust Which Is God* (1942). In fact, Benét praises the anthologist for his democratic choices, noting that Untermeyer had "even managed the inclusion of some light and nonsense verse, American folk songs, and certain Negro spirituals." Clearly such a reading of inclusiveness would seem severely limited and problematic today.

From the standpoint of the post–Civil Rights era, the reference to "Negro spirituals," with the purpose of illustrating the compiler's inclusiveness, would most likely draw attention to an important area of exclusion. Contemporary readers might wonder about Untermeyer's failure to consider any of the then well-known African American poets among the authors of great English-language poems. Paul Laurence Dunbar (1872–1906), for example, had already gained distinction in the US literary scene; further, Untermeyer's literary career overlapped with the constellation of poetic talents that aligned in New York City during the 1920s, with Harlem Renaissance poets such as James Weldon Johnson (1871–1938), Claude McKay (1889–1948), Arna Bontemps (1902–1973), Countee Cullen (1903–1946), and Langston Hughes (1902–1967), to name only a handful.

Her high school teachers introduced Espaillat to the poetry of women, giving her occasion to identify gender particularities in literary production. As she grew older, her sense of solidarity emerged more organically: "The poetry of women in particular touched me because it was about relationships, about losses, about people lost or left behind, about things I could understand from the gut." She admits that she "imitated [these women] consciously" and "loved Edna St. Vincent Millay and still do. Elizabeth Barrett Browning as well. Sara Teasdale I loved. In high school Millay was a tremendous influence because they gave us poems she had written when she was very young, probably our age" (NK/STS). Lines from "Renascence," the title poem in Millay's 1917 collection *Renascence and Other Poems*, comes quickly to Espaillat's memory as offering a paradigm for the worldview of the artist:

All I could see from where I stood
Was three long mountains and a wood;
I turned and looked the other way,
And saw three islands in a bay.
So with my eyes I traced the line
Of the horizon thin and fine,
Straight around till I was come
Back to where I'd started from. (Millay 1)

This recursive momentum, dependent upon natural imagery, conveys "the idea of the poetic eye turning 360 degrees looking at the landscape" and subsequently inward. The text's distinct meditation, geometric simplicity, and precision helped to convey "what life is good for, what consciousness is good for" (NK/STS). The young Espaillat gathered from women poets the sonic and tonal resources with which to begin to create her own voice. She found them "musical, like the poetry I remembered in Spanish." She credits Millay, Browning, H.D. (Hilda Doolittle), and Teasdale, among others, with lending her the sound of "sophistication" and "pretended" passion that allowed her poems to convey a depth of insight that she had not lived long enough to possess. Without understanding fully their adult issues and more finely wrought attitudes toward the complexity of life, she at least gleaned from their diverse offerings the ambition to imitate and the will to become.

Given her parents' position as immigrants and exiles, the young Espaillat was not unaware of areas related to politics and enduring social concern. Her previously quoted poem "The Pigeons," with its metaphorical commentary on the stress that poverty may exert on a person's dignity, and her declaration to the *New York Herald Tribune* that she would need to work to fulfill "family obligations," leave little doubt of her understanding that social class was a major determinant of success. Political implications might be ascribed to Espaillat's self-assertiveness in terms of the value she eventually assigned to her dual Hispanic and Caribbean heritage, and to her having first spoken a language other than English. When she came of age, the ideology of assimilation, namely the expectation that one should *overcome* any non-British ancestral origins, still held sway as a prerequisite to entering the sphere of genuine Americanness.

During the early decades of the twentieth century, state-funded programs existed with the purpose of making "an American people out of the vast army of immigrants who have come from every nation of the world to seek homes in the United States" ("Americanization" n.p.). Informed by what was then called "the science of race assimilation," Americanization often equated becoming an American with shedding the trappings of difference that one's family may have brought from elsewhere. While many related programs mobilized following the proclamation of July 4, 1915, as "Americanization Day," its ideological beginnings date back to the 1890s. In the first and second decades of the twentieth century, voices from the highest levels of political power could be heard decrying bilingualism and condemning multiculturalism. Harvard-educated former president Theodore Roosevelt would categorically affirm in a 1916 speech that the country's "crucible" ought to turn "our people out as Americans, of American nationality and not as dwellers of a polyglot boarding house, and we have room for but one loyalty and that is a loyalty to the American people." Two years later, Woodrow Wilson would prevail upon his party's platform to take a position against ethnic associations, contending that "any man who carries a hyphen about him carries a dagger that he is ready to plunge into the vitals of the Republic" (Dicker 35; McClymer 98).

It was in this climate of obligatory homogenization and intolerance toward ethnic and linguistic difference that some prescient, isolated voices began to offer alternative views. They argued for an "Americanization" that did not require the obliteration of the immigrant's cultural background or ancestral memory. Radical thinker Randolph Bourne's 1916 essay "Trans-National America" sets forth a vision that would only gain widespread acceptance with the rise of post–Civil Rights multiculturalism five decades later (Bourne 249). We do not know how much exposure Espaillat had to the larger public discourses on cultural difference, national identity, and Americanness during her high school years. Whatever the case, her younger self seems not to have felt any hesitation in recognizing and valuing the duality of her background, nor to have viewed her native Spanish or her Dominican ancestry as representing impediments to her evolving sense of Americanness.

TACKLING DUAL HERITAGES

Untermeyer's influential anthology included at least three authors of dual heritage who may have proven useful to Espaillat in situating herself culturally as an American literary artist. Given the paucity of women in her beloved anthology, she may have had occasion to consider the singularity of Marya Zaturenska (1902–1982), a native of Kiev, Russia, who came to the United States at the age of eight, one year older than Espaillat was when she settled in New York. Zaturenska had a hard life, struggling to make a living and to secure an education, but in the end she thrived, cultivating her poetic talent and writing eight volumes of poetry, including *Cold Morning Sky* (1937), which made her the first foreign-born person to receive the Pulitzer Prize in Poetry. The second poet, William Carlos Williams (1883–1963), was born in Rutherford, New Jersey, the city where he also died. The son of an English-descended father and a Puerto Rican mother who boasted Basque and Dutch Jewish ancestry, Williams became a poet of note among the generation associated with Imagism, the aesthetic movement spearheaded by Ezra Pound (1885–1972) and Amy Lowell (1874–1925).

Williams matters in a discussion of Espaillat's development because of the way his approach to dual heritage contrasts with hers. Clear differences between the poets include his mixed Hispanic and non-Hispanic identity and the fact that he was not an immigrant. In terms of literary attitude, however, he did not assign equal value to each of his ancestral sides, appearing instead to subordinate one to the other. Speaking in a section of his autobiography, Williams characterized his mother's native language this way: "Spanish is not, in the sense to which I refer, a literary language" (Williams 349). He continues: "There is a noteworthy body of verse for us to work upon. It isn't as rich as English in the multiplicity of its achievements, but there are lyrics in the Romancero of distinguished beauty" (349). Williams did do considerable "work upon" Spanish verse. Many of his translations from that language appear in the collection *By Word of Mouth* (2011), though critics such as Julio Marzán and T. Urayoán Noel point to mistranslations and a difficult rapport with Spanish and Caribbean culture. The contrast with the experience of dual heritage epitomized by Espaillat, whose embrace of English stemmed from the realization that it contained resources that matched and complemented those she had learned to love in Spanish, could not be any starker.

The other poet from Untermeyer's anthology whom we can regard as bearing meaningful resemblance to Espaillat in terms of ancestral complexity is George Santayana (1863–1952), a native of Madrid, Spain. Santayana came to Boston at age nine. As a professor of philosophy at Harvard, he had an influence on students who would go on to become major literary figures, including T. S. Eliot (1888–1965) and Conrad Aiken (1889–1973). Espaillat's idol Robert Frost also studied under Santayana. Along with William James (1842–1910) and Josiah Royce (1855–1916), Santayana formed the great triad of American Pragmatic philosophers, but it was his poetry that earned him a space in Untermeyer's compilation.

The consideration of Santayana resonates with Espaillat's experience because of his approach to Spanish, his first language; he did not regard English as natural to him. In the preface to his 1923 volume *Poems*, he offers a meek apology: "Even if my temperament had been naturally warmer, the fact that the English language (and I can write no other with assurance) was not my mother tongue would of itself preclude any inspired use of it on my part; its roots do not reach my center. I never drank in my childhood the homely cadences and ditties which in pure spontaneous poetry set the essential key" (vii–viii). Though he never returned to Spain, Santayana maintained the ancestral ties that linked him to it. During the Spanish-American War, he responded to the US destruction of the Spanish fleet in the Battle of Santiago (1898) with the poem "Spain in America," in which he wrestles with the moral difficulty presented by a war between the two countries closest to him. As someone who would eventually reconcile herself with being severed from an original homeland, Espaillat would have found much to consider in Santayana's view of exile as freedom even if the outlook of the exile did not become a defining feature of her identity.

VERSIONS OF BELONGING

The cultural grounding and self-confidence of Espaillat's parents must have played a role in her development of an ample sense of self. Had Espaillat needed any, the examples of Zaturenska, Williams, and Santayana could have provided assurance that a dual cultural background need not be odd or burdensome, nor was it necessarily a boon. It was up to the individual to negotiate a relationship or not, circumstances permitting. It seems that Russian literature did not form part of Zaturenska's everyday life following her immigration. Williams did not have occasion to develop enough of a respectful rapport with his mother's native language to even consider it capable of spurring a literary corpus comparable with that of English. Santayana was too cultivated a mind to be ignorant of the greatness of his ancestral culture, but he decided to adopt English as his primary literary language and carve a place for himself in the intellectual community of the United States without becoming a nationalist advocate for either his ancestral or his adopted country. This choice was symbolized best by his leaving the United States forever upon his early retirement from Harvard, and spending the last decades of his life in Italy, where he expressed the wish to be buried in a Spanish cemetery in Rome. This could have been his way of upholding exile as his ultimate identity space while paying respect to the inexorable fact that everybody has an origin. Espaillat seemed to simply embrace her double cultural heritage without torturous inner conflict or self-questioning.

Commentators in the New York press who covered her early stardom generally failed to make reference to her writing in a second language. Their biographical notes did make passing mention of her birth and early childhood in the Dominican Republic, but not of the different language that people spoke there. Perhaps the omission of references to the young woman's literary language as different from her native tongue stems from a widespread, unspoken consensus that the phenomenon does not merit much examination. Children, the thinking goes, have an inherent ability to move across linguistic codes without impediment. Nor can we tell with any precision at what point Espaillat became aware of herself as a speaker crossing the boundary from one language into another, ascertaining the significance of her command of the newly acquired tongue. The novelist and poet Julia Alvarez has evoked a moment in her childhood when she did not know languages existed as differentiated entities. Born in New York, Alvarez spent her earliest years in the Dominican Republic in a bilingual home where Spanish functioned as a lingua franca while English served the communication needs of the adults, especially at times when they had to exchange information unfit for the ears of children. Realizing she understood less when the grown-ups changed to the other linguistic code, the young Alvarez came to regard English not as "a different language but just another and harder version of Spanish" (Alvarez, *Something* 22; "My English" 24).

Espaillat has been unable to discard memories of times when linguistic matters resulted in marred social interactions, but not necessarily because of prejudice. Two powerful examples date from experiences at the very first school she attended in New York, namely Sacred Heart of Jesus School, on 456 West 52nd Street in Manhattan. Her parents had enrolled her in the Catholic elementary school with the expectation that it would be smaller, less frightening, and more welcoming than a public institution. But she "hated every bit of it." On Rhina's first day of classes, the Mother Superior ushered her into the homeroom, putting her arm around the small girl to explain her status to the class. Espaillat did not understand any of the introductory remarks: "I suppose it meant something like: 'Be nice to this young girl because she doesn't understand, and now she is your peer.'" Because she had learned from her parents that it was only good manners to reciprocate well-meaning words and gestures—especially to adults—she responded in kind: "So I put an arm around her, but because she was tall, what I put my arm around was her backside—her tush. She immediately, looking stern, held me by both shoulders and pushed me backwards" (NK/STS). The adult Espaillat, analyzing the incident with a bitter smile, affirms that the harshness of the Mother Superior's reaction did not stem from any negative attitude about racial difference or xenophobia, but an aversion to the unexpected nature of the touch. This strong reproach was certainly a contrast to the girl's experiences with nuns back in the Dominican Republic, where she remembered being able to climb onto their laps and cling to their hands. Because she lacked access to the proper language, she was unable to explain her misconstrued actions. The incident and sense of helplessness were seared with painful acuity into her mind (NK/STS).

Another unpleasant memory from the Catholic school relates to classroom prayer. She comments, "They stopped to pray several times a day, and I resented prayer in a language I did not understand. . . . I felt completely left out because I was the only one who was different. Everyone else understood" (NK/STS). Espaillat knew about prayer, understanding it to be something intimate, sacred, and loving that she had performed beside her grandmother in Spanish before an image of the Señora de la Altagracia back in La Vega. She could not fathom how the robotic gestures of rising when instructed, lowering her head, closing her eyes, and repeating words the teacher uttered could be the same thing. At one level, the crises of understanding at Sacred Heart had to do less with language— the semiotic system with a lexicon, a grammar, syntax, and so on—than with a level of comfort and capacity to communicate generally. The teachers, to their credit, did everything possible to make her feel included: "They lent me pencils, they told me where to hang my coat. I can't say that I was made to suffer or that I was victimized in any way, but I have never in my life been as lonely as I was in that school." Fortunately, within six months, a sea change occurred: "We moved, and I went to P.S. 94 where everyone was Japanese, and Greek, and Italian, and Russian, and I felt great. It was heavenly because we were all peculiar" (NK/STS).

As she looks back across the decades, Espaillat has accrued her share of moments involving prejudiced incomprehension or cultural mistranslations, but she feels she has received abundant recompense in many equally telling moments of inclusion across language and ethnicity. Even so, her awareness of the precarious position of the foreigner or "alien" in the nativist imaginary has sharpened her sensitivity toward those sharing varying degrees of otherness, a sensitivity reflected in the poetics of inclusion that would become a trademark of her work. Her occasion to feel most discriminated against as an adult, an instance of prejudice that endangered her chance to pursue her chosen profession as an educator, was oddly related to the notion of an "ethnic" language. It came when she had to take the licensing exam for teaching. By this time, Espaillat had married Moskowitz, and while she kept her maiden name, she used her married name for all legal transactions and documents. The proctor saw her surname and, possibly swayed by anti-Semitic feelings, heard a "Jewish" intonation in the voice of a Hispanic (NK/STS). One part of the test involved an oral exam, and the proctor, who had the power to decide unilaterally whether she passed or not, gave her a hesitant pass. He qualified his reservations with the following recommendation: "You should really work on losing your Jewish intonation."

Venturing into broader communities of poets after her induction into the Poetry Society of America at age sixteen—and meeting with acceptance there—overshadows all other crossings for Espaillat. As a member, she began to enjoy the privilege of occasionally sharing the stage with renowned poets whose works she had read with admiration. Espaillat's contact with the Poetry Society continued through her postsecondary years, including readings, awards, and other sponsorship opportunities. Receiving a degree from the English department at Hunter College infused her with further self-confidence and enthusiasm, especially in light of her contact with Professor Marion Winnifred Witt, a specialist in the works of William Butler Yeats (1865–1939). Espaillat remembers Witt fondly as a brilliant and dynamic teacher "who made every poem she discussed feel as if it had just been written that moment, specifically for us" (NK/STS). Witt's talent as an explicator of literary texts with the power to elicit her students' enthusiasm about poetry has been corroborated by retired professor Milton McC. Gatch, a nephew of Katherine Haynes Gatch, the Hunter College colleague with whom Witt shared residences until the latter's death in 1978. He, like Espaillat, remembers her as an inspirational teacher who could make poems come alive in the classroom ("Yeats Collection").

Witt encouraged Espaillat, then in her senior year, to enter a poetry competition for college and university students from New York City sponsored by Riverside Church. Three major poets whom the young woman greatly admired, formed the panel of judges: W. H. Auden (1907–1973), Marianne Moore (1887–1972), and Karl Shapiro (1913–2000). From the hundreds of poems submitted by applicants, the panel selected forty, including four by Espaillat. The winning entries subsequently formed the anthology *Riverside Poetry, 1953*, edited by the panel, with an introduction by the notable religion scholar Stanley Romaine Hopper (1907–1991), who mentions Espaillat's works specifically in his remarks.

Beyond the celebrity she enjoyed as a teen poet in the 1940s, her welcome embrace by the more seasoned practitioners in the Poetry Society of America, and the fan letters received from readers at home and abroad, the limelight accorded to her work in *Riverside Poetry* served as a definite milestone in Espaillat's development as an artist. She had exhibited the psychological depth, verbal talent, formal proficiency, and acuity of vision necessary to regard herself as a poet and as such, to seek her way forward in the world through words. Poetry could potentially have served as her principal location of identity, but the idea of viewing the craft as a profession did not seem available to her in 1953 any more than it had in 1949 when she reflected in the *New York Herald Tribune* that, although she would "always write poetry," she still faced a material reality that required for her to be "practical" ("Julia Richman" 12).

PORTRAIT OF THE ARTIST AS AN ADULT WOMAN

After her graduation from Hunter College, Espaillat's dedication to writing would wane significantly, which many would regard as an unusual turn in light of the celebrity she had already accrued. From that point onward, she would depend on the mentorship of the poet, critic, and scholar Alfred Dorn (1929–2014) as her primary link to the poetry scene. A man of letters known for his generosity with colleagues as well as junior practitioners, Dorn merits special consideration here. Not long after receiving his doctorate from New York University with a dissertation on Christopher Marlowe, Edmund Spenser, and John Donne, Dorn became very active in the Poetry Society of America. As vice president of the society, he very early on recognized the talent of Sylvia Plath (1932–1963), just as he would recognize that of Espaillat ("Alfred Dorn"; Salemi, "In Memoriam"). As founding director of the World Order of Narrative and Formalist Poets, Dorn later became one of the major figures behind the rise of New Formalism.

Espaillat credits the Poetry Society of America for much of her awareness of how effective community building can be for artists. Even though she was among adults much older than she, she says that they "paid attention, but I knew I was a kid writing. . . . They used to have monthly meetings that all members could attend. They also had monthly contests, and they chose maybe three or four [poems] to read aloud at the meetings, and I got to do that a couple of times. It was encouraging. It gave you the sense of being in the right company" (NK/STS). The society, along with Dorn's guidance, gave Espaillat the sense of belonging in "a writing community," and she remained "very faithful to it" during her Manhattan years (NK/STS).

With her marriage in 1952 and relocation to Queens to start a family, Espaillat discontinued her frequent contact with the society largely because of the scheduling of events there: "It was all at night, and I couldn't travel back and forth by myself. So that was gone." However, the society, embodied by the generosity of Dorn, whom she did not get to meet during her visits there, kept the bond going. A "magnificent human being," Dorn would take the trouble to write to her, as he did with "a lot of other young people," with tips and encouraging messages such as "you are very good," and point to poetry contests in which she might participate. When she finally had a chance to meet him, she thought of him as an old friend: "It was as if I had known him for years" (NK/STS). Espaillat's correspondence with Dorn, only three years her senior, remained her contact with the literary community of Manhattan and other poets generally.

When the Poetry Society of America celebrated its fiftieth anniversary in 1960 by publishing *The Golden Year*, a volume of selected verse written by its members over the preceding five decades, the editors chose poems based on a selection committee's "unanimous or two-thirds vote." They included Espaillat's work among that of such major twentieth-century poets as Robert Frost, Carl Sandburg, May Sarton, Anne Sexton, Sylvia Plath, Marianne Moore, Robinson Jeffers, and Ted Hughes (Cane, Farrar, and Nicholl v). For the commemorative volume, the editors chose Espaillat's "From the Rain Down," a meditative poem whose speaker observes the evocative presence of a tree to ponder our ultimate oneness with the natural world. The closing stanza drives the point home with stark clarity:

Through death uncasual, season's range,
From rain to flower to fruit we go,
No more miraculous or strange
Than stars above or stones below
Or seed before, or past all change,
The starry blossoming of snow. (88–89)

In addition to the poem, *The Golden Year* sets forth a biographical sketch outlining the "practical" realities of Espaillat's adult life at the time: "Espaillat, Rhina P. (Mrs. Alfred Moskowitz) was born in the Dominican Republic in 1932. She received her B.A. from Hunter College (1953) and is currently working for her M.A. at Queens College. Her poems have appeared in *Voices*, *Ladies' Home Journal*, and elsewhere" (Cane, Farrar, and Nicholl 320). Understanding that she already had a name that many readers (as well as peers) in the literary community recognized, Rhina and Alfred agreed to keep her maiden surname for literary endeavors, and use her married surname for legally binding matters such as official documents. The placement of the married name in parentheses alongside, rather than instead of, her family surname points to an abiding attachment to her poetic identity. By the same token, the married name underscores the poet's allegiance to a wider set of social obligations, including marital duties and child-rearing. The mention of her degree programs gestures to a professional path extending well beyond creative writing. All of these paths would occupy central roles in Espaillat's life for the decades to come.

3 | LOCATIONS OF IDENTITY
CRAFT, ETHNICITY, AND AMERICANNESS

By the time *Riverside Poetry* came out in 1953, Espaillat had already held a job as a substitute English and social studies teacher at P.S. 26 in Queens, New York, and had both domestic and professional duties to attend to concurrently. Having wedded industrial arts teacher Alfred Moskowitz in 1952, the twenty-one-year-old was no longer just a precocious poet who had impressed so many in New York City and elsewhere. Sharing her life with a Jewish man who brought to the household a fund of Yiddish culture no less enriching than her Hispanic roots would variegate her rapidly expanding and integrative worldview. A veteran of the Battle of the Bulge in the Ardennes, where he experienced his first combat at the end of December 1944 as a nineteen-year-old rifleman with the rank of PFC, Moskowitz brought to the household a sense of stark realism as experienced by US military personnel during World War II. This was a time when many young Americans took to the front with a profound desire to fight for freedom and justice against regimes that endorsed tyranny and oppression (Moskowitz 13).

The newlyweds settled into an apartment in an area of Flushing, Queens, that had been farmland, staying there until the birth of their first child. They then relocated to another section of Flushing that had two blocks' worth of compact and inexpensive houses. They lived primarily among African Americans, mostly middle-class professionals. Espaillat recalls being met by neighbors who would knock on the door holding flowers with long stems and roots still attached. These offerings were to be planted in the garden for lasting enjoyment. She reveals, "I had a sense of having come home because of the welcome we received." While surrounded by such hospitable community members, the couple could look out from their door to other sections of the neighborhood populated by still more ethnic groups, especially Asians, who at the time were arriving in Queens in large numbers. The new family lived among "everybody" in "the most multicultural, polyglot county in the United States" (NK/STS).

Seeing herself as Hispanic and being viewed that way ("which is what I am, meaning a mixture of everything"), Espaillat rejoiced in the ethnoracial and cultural diversity that pervaded the borough. The editor and freelance writer Joseph Barbato, a resident of Jackson Heights, who assembled a collection titled *Patchwork of Dreams* (1996), observes that no other city or county in the United States has "the extraordinary mix of people now found in the two-million popu-lation outer-borough called Queens." He proudly asserts that "people from 120 nations who live in Astoria, Sunnyside, Woodside, Jackson Heights, Elmhurst, Flushing, and other Queens neighborhoods are writing the latest chapter in the American story" (Barbato 9). Barbato's coeditor, the poet Morty Sklar, himself a native of Sunnyside, grew up in Elmhurst before settling in Jackson Heights, following which he lived for eighteen years in Iowa City, Iowa, the site at the time of an ethnically homogeneous population of fifty thousand. Upon returning to Jackson Heights in 1989, Sklar admits that he finally understood what his mother had meant when, during their Iowa City years, she had exclaimed, "I feel like I'm living in a foreign country" (Sklar 5).

Espaillat figures among the contributors to *Patchwork of Dreams* with two poems that resemble sides of the same coin. "Purim Parade" pays tribute to many forms of diversity in Queens, stressing the porosity that cultural forms tend to experience in a climate hospitable to difference. The work refers to a carnival that began in Tel Aviv in 1912 as part of the Jewish holiday Purim. In Israel the annual revelry, also called Adloyada, has maintained much of its national focus and often abides by state-prescribed guidelines of propriety vis-à-vis endorsing a specific national image. In contrast, when celebrated in Queens, the Jewish holiday allows for costumes, floats, and other creative flourishes that defy the more rigid expectations of the foreign original. Espaillat's poem captures the mosaic nature of the celebration in lines that juxtapose "Queen Esther in tinsel wig" with "sheiks on skate boards." She pairs "witches shrieking in Spanish" with enthusiastic Jewish teens representing the Temple Youth Group. The poem ends with "the Emerald Band / elegant in kilts, bagpipes / skirling Hatikvah" (Sklar and Barbato 120).

In contrast to such carnivalesque exuberance, the second poem, titled "Replay," steeps readers in the melancholia associated with living in a world stripped of the tolerance for difference that Espaillat so admired in Queens. An autobiographical piece, its four stanzas recreate the scene of three seven-year-old girls joyfully "jumping an old clothesline" in a "dusty courtyard." The location ("inner city") points to Manhattan, and the date (Sunday 1939) places the action in the year of Espaillat's permanent settlement in New York. A yarmulke-wearing boy approaches the trio, hoping to play too. Cathy—the owner of the rope, hence the leader—reveals a rather stark policy: "We're not supposed to play with Jews." The speaker, "foreign-born," does not "know what Jews are," but the effect of the hard edict on the child ("the sudden aging of his eyes") leaves little room for doubt: something horrible has just happened. Dorothy, the third girl, "scans the ground" while the speaker fidgets, wondering whether she should speak. The spurned stranger simply recedes, "goes away," but the speaker's memory of the experience never fades, as the closing lines attest: "In my dreams we always call him back / to say the words that heal our common exile / and switch the looming future from its track" (Sklar and Barbato 119).

During her Queens years, Espaillat was neither unaware of nor indifferent to the country's track record of injustice toward minorities. She hailed from a family that had chosen exile over collaboration with a repressive regime, and she married a Jew who was the child of leftist parents. Alfred was already an active labor organizer with the teacher's union. The couple identified fervently with the Civil Rights Movement, which Espaillat describes as "one of the most significant events of the twentieth century—and an ultimately positive one, for a change, even though its goals have not yet been wholly achieved." She recalls that the borough offered "a lively political environment" and that it was "in the center of things" (Espaillat, "Re: Some Answers"). The couple shared interests with neighbors who were active liberals or progressive to the core, and they "went together to rallies and marches, signed petitions, donated, wrote to legislators, and distributed flyers in support of school and housing desegregation and voting rights, among other civil rights issues of the day." Espaillat recalls that those issues "mattered, not only because racism was a long-unresolved injustice, but also because, as teachers in our own very mixed neighborhood, we lived among, and taught the children of, the very people who had endured that injustice in their own lives." She did not conceive of African American victims of violence as statistics enumerated in the nightly news, but rather as neighbors, "many of whom had come up from the South and had worked and struggled hard to achieve an education against powerful odds" (NK/STS).

No less important was what she called "the anti–Vietnam War" movement. The agitation formed part of Espaillat's daily concerns during the Queens years because, as a high school teacher, she faced classes full of young people who knew that they, "their brothers or cousins or boyfriends—would soon be receiving ominous invitations from Uncle Sam." While some seemed "ready, even eager" to enlist, most of the young people in her memory "appeared angry and bitter over the prospect of interrupting their education—and possibly giving their lives—to fight a war they didn't understand in a place they had never heard of" (Espaillat, "Re: Some Answers"). She recollects the heartbreak of learning from colleagues or from older students that former classmates had already received the summons and been sent off to Asia.

Espaillat acutely recalls the challenge this conflict presented to those laboring in the public school classroom. They found it hard persuading some of their students that learning was still worthwhile and that "they had a future in which they would use their knowledge." The pervasive unease among the student body "created alienation in a few of them and a desire to act out and rebel against the school, which they began to see as an arm of 'the system.'" Despite this testiness, many teachers were entirely sympathetic. Espaillat reasons that this was "not least because we had sons of our own approaching draft age, like our students; the anti-war movement occupied our thoughts and our efforts to a high degree."

In addition to the racial struggles at home and the geopolitical strife abroad, Espaillat and her husband participated actively in the class activism that the unionization of teaching entailed in "those hectic decades." She summarizes their union involvement as follows:

> Alfred was a very active Chapter Chairman in his school and helped to organize the faculty when the [United Federation of Teachers] was being created. I was still at home with young children at that time, but when they were old enough and I returned to the classroom, I too became a chapter officer at my school, and both of us eventually became union delegates from our districts, and attended the delegate assemblies that deliberated and voted on union issues, including

strikes. Our house was strike headquarters in our district more than once. The experience left both of us feeling strongly loyal to the labor movement everywhere, to workers in every field and across racial, ethnic, gender, and all other lines, as necessary to justice and the protection of workers' rights. (Espaillat, "Re: Some Answers")

With so much at stake at home and abroad, Espaillat sums up the 1960s and 1970s as "very stressful decades." However, in retrospect, she feels content that those turbulent years gave the couple "opportunities to serve" students as well as fellow working people, which proved gratifying.

One could argue that Espaillat underestimates the impact that the social struggles of the Civil Rights era had on her writing. She concedes that the period exerted an "indirect and subtle" influence, "filtered through the personal, rather than ideologically overt" given that she claims to "have no gift at all for literary polemics" (Espaillat, "Re: Some Answers"). Nor does she lack grounds for her claim. The social consciousness discernible in her verse predates the Civil Rights Movement. Her poem "The Pigeons," published by the *New York Sun* in June 1950, is a case in point. Meanwhile, her 1953 poem "You Call Me by Old Names" makes it plain that her seeking to assert the dignity of the ethnoracial other vis-à-vis Anglo-Americans predates the struggle of disenfranchised minorities to claim their rightful space in the narrative of the nation. Yet one is hard-pressed to see such works as "Two Cameos," published in the guest folio section of *Post Road Magazine* in 2012, evoking the figures of Rita Hayworth (1918–1987) and Hattie McDaniel (1895–1952), as unrelated to the social justice struggles of the 1960s.

The first "cameo" resurrects the "daughter of Spanish dancers" Margarita Carmen Cansino, whom the film industry renamed Rita Hayworth. Her father, the Spanish dancer Eduardo Cansino, and her mother Volga Hayworth, an entertainer of Irish-English descent, may have frowned upon the renaming since in the Hispanic tradition carrying the maternal surname only identifies a person as born out of wedlock. But the legitimate Hispanic name of the actress would most likely not "play in Centerville" as easily as an Anglo revision would. Cansino's identity, like her ancestral culture, did not much matter to the executives and star makers, as Espaillat muses:

Entertain,
that was the mission: and to fill the bill

you needed looks to please the businessmen
who made the films. And talent—but again,
beauty came first, and glamour that could thrill
the glamour-starved at once with the first scene. (Espaillat, "Two Cameos" n.p.)

In the second "cameo," a tribute to "the first Black winner of an Oscar," the speaker takes sides with McDaniel against those among her coethnics who "resented her role, her *dis* and *dat*, / the humbling of her gifts; they felt betrayed / by her portrayal of the race." The talented actress "laughed at symbols," happily asserting her choice to play "the part on the screen" for the royal sum of "seven hundred a day" instead of "earning seven as a real live maid." Insults about selling out were undoubtedly countered by praise for buying in. After her Academy Award acceptance speech, McDaniel still had to go sit in "the Negro section." The poem ends by weighing "how far we've come," inviting readers to consider the price paid by those women whose sacrifices and indignities brought "us here" to a place of progress as well as unresolved anxiety about sexism and racism in Hollywood and other sites of concentrated public perception.

Suggestive of the intersections of gender and ethnoracial exclusion, the poem is a paean to the legacy of those ancestors who, working within their respective constraints, did what was necessary to assert their human dignity. Espaillat salutes them and their often Pyrrhic victories for contributing to the degree of justice and equality that many of us enjoy today. There is little doubt, as we will see in the chapters that follow, that Espaillat inhabits the world as a socially engaged individual whose solidarity falls invariably on the side of those who have suffered dismissal and disappointment for factors largely outside their control, including the accidents of birth and ancestral origins.

RETURNING TO THE REPUBLIC OF LETTERS

Even during the years of Espaillat's diminished literary output, Alfred Dorn, her mentor from the Poetry Society of America, continued his long-distance commitment to her work. A typical letter from him, such as one dated May 3, 1983, would applaud the poems he had seen published by her, recommend other venues she might wish to consider, and encourage her to participate in upcoming readings. Dorn had seen her verse included in *Modern Lyrics Anthology* (1982), and he wrote to inform her of his review of the book: "I cited your work, as well as that of four other poets in section I, for special commendation" (Dorn, Letter, 3 May 1983). In the same letter, he directed her attention to *Manhattan Poetry Review*, a magazine founded in 1982. Prognosticating that the publication had "a great future," he urged her to submit some of her work to the editor and volunteered special advice should she wish to follow through. Dorn enclosed in the letter an announcement about an upcoming poetry reading on May 14 at the Queens Botanical Gardens sponsored by the Shelley Society, suggesting that she might wish to appear on the program. He encouraged her to contact Annette Feldmann, the society's head, stating that he had already put in a good word for Espaillat by describing the young woman as "a distinguished Queens poet."

The collection that Dorn had reviewed, *Modern Lyrics Anthology*, edited by poet Angelo Aaron Schmuller, had published four of Espaillat's poems: "Kite Flying," "Calculus," "Learning to Ride," and "Retrospect." The four pieces draw on ordinary situations to contemplate existential questions. Two of them—"Kite Flying" and "Calculus"—deal with a mother's rapport with her offspring. In the former, she looks at her children flying a kite, which they let go "up so far" and then predictably "reel in by and by" with the string looped around their small hands. The symbolically potent sight prompts the mother to consider the invisible string that links the children to her, questioning whether she will be prepared to loosen her grasp on them when she can no longer reel them in: "When at my loving's tether / They pull and fling, / Where shall I find the courage / to pay out string?" (Schmuller 14). "Calculus" recreates an instance in which the mother finds herself receiving simplified instructions from her adult son about the branch of mathematics that studies change. The latter explains: "think of it as a line / Looped back and forth to bridge an open space / Unbridgeable at last." The metaphor employed in his lesson compels her to think about love, which fails, "As it must / to seize the flying prize." The affective synthesis emerges in the closing couplet: "think of it as a line / Weaving between your orbiting and mine" (14–15).

The third poem included in the anthology, "Learning to Ride," reconstructs the speaker's experience of climbing on a bicycle at the age of fifty, swallowing the fears that had kept her from mastering the "perverse machine" in earlier years. The closing stanza connects the small personal victory to a larger sense of connectedness with family and with the assurance of a loved one's approval: "I fly above the wind who never ran / And round and round the speeding streets go past, / Circling my fifty years, the careful man / Whose watching eyes tether me home at last" (14). The fourth, "Retrospect," has a looking glass act as a stand from which to reflect upon the reliability of memory and our relationship to change. The mirror throws a likeness back at us, but the poem questions the seeming flatness and transparency of that rendition. It notes that when tilted at a certain angle, the mirror can "let us see / Behind us," assigning to the term "behind" a temporal rather than merely spatial connotation. The speaker comments, "The glass held high before us lets us see / Things never were the way they used to be" (15).

After receding from the poetry scene for nearly three decades, Espaillat had come back to reclaim her spot among her peers, and it did not take long before the poetic community began to recognize her and grant her a new place of belonging. Remarkably, by the time Espaillat published her first book-length poetry collection, *Lapsing to Grace* (1992), she had nurtured a literary life with meaningful impact on the lives of others. As a result, she reentered the American poetry scene as an elder, not so much because of having reached the age of sixty, but because of a record of literary practice that preceded her and attested to artistic—rather than merely biological—seniority.

An important factor behind Espaillat's relatively rapid return to public recognition after publishing her first poetry volumes may have been her role as a literary activist, promoting the craft and generously devoting her efforts to creating poetic networks. The Fresh Meadows Poets, which Espaillat led while she lived in Queens, emerged out of her resolve to build community with fellow literary artists from the surrounding area. An anthology resulting from that experience, edited by fellow poet Emily Wolf and titled *Fresh: Poetry Collection for Young People* (1998), features seven poems by Espaillat even though it appeared in print long after she had moved away (Wolf). The collection's title, *Fresh*, pays tribute to the neighborhood that nurtured the creativity of the collective, while its subtitle conveys a sense of social concern (and continuing hope) for youth in the community who might become both inspired and empowered by exposure to good word-art. At the end of the 1980s, having retired from teaching, Espaillat and Alfred moved to Newburyport, a small coastal city in Essex County, Massachusetts, lured by suitable nursing homes for her Alzheimer's-afflicted mother who needed around-the-clock care. The new location also offered a greater proximity to their sons, now adults with families of their own. In Newburyport, Espaillat followed up on her previous experience with the Fresh Meadows Poets by helping to launch the Powow River Poets, a collective named after a nearby landmark.

By the time Espaillat's verse first appeared in the pages of *Poetry* magazine in 1991, she had already accrued a number of achievements that the editors could use to introduce her to the publication's readership. The biographical note in the August issue identifies her as follows: "Rhina P. Espaillat formerly taught English at Jamaica High School in Queens. Since her retirement in 1980, she has served as poetry consultant to the New York Board of Education and organized the Fresh Meadows Poets program of readings and workshops. Twice a winner of the Poetry Society of America's Gustav Davidson Award, she has contributed poems to many journals, including *Poet Lore*, *Commonweal*, and *Bitterroot*" ("Contributors" 296). This issue of the magazine carried two poems by Espaillat. "Cutting Bait" meditates in blank verse on the difficulty of the bereaved to part with the dead: "How we need them / to play themselves for us . . . / Aching with absence, we tug at their deaths / to hold them" (Espaillat, "Cutting Bait" 255). The other, "Changeling," is a harrowing sonnet evoking the speaker's torturous grappling with the changes that her Alzheimer's-stricken mother has undergone. The poem, in its entirety, reads:

> I want to tell myself she is not you,
> this sullen woman wearing Mama's eyes
> all wrong, whose every gesture rings untrue
> and yet familiar. In your harsh disguise
> I sometimes need to find you, sometimes fear
> I will, if I look closely into her.
> I want to tell myself you are not here,
> trapped in this parody of what you were,
> but love was never safe: it lives on danger,
> finds what can't be found by any other
> power on Earth or over it. This stranger
> is you, is all the you there is, my mother
> whose gentler face is gone beyond recall,
> and I must love you so, or not at all. (Espaillat, "Changeling" 255)

It merits mention that an anthology published to commemorate a century of achievement by the prestigious magazine, featuring one selection each by one hundred of the poets whose work had appeared in *Poetry*'s pages since its founding in 1912 by American writer, editor, and critic Harriet Monroe (1860–1936), includes "Changeling" (Share and Wiman 178, 200). The title of the collection, *The Open Door*, pays tribute to the innovative, openminded approach that defined Monroe's commitment to the genre. The journal's objective was to welcome originality and talent irrespective of the specific aesthetic or ideological orientations to which an individual poet might subscribe. The "open door" that *Poetry* offered Espaillat in many ways matched the aesthetic inclusiveness she had found in the Poetry Society of America. In his foreword to the previously mentioned *The Golden Year*, PSA president Clarence R. Decker affirmed the organization's commitment to receptiveness, indicating that it had maintained a policy of embracing quality work irrespective of the aesthetic school adhered to or represented by a particular poet. He comments, "In the war between the old and the new, the traditional and the experimental, the PSA has been hospitable to both: It is committed to the proposition that all sides of an issue must be known and heard if the cause itself is to flourish" (Decker viii).

Espaillat nurtured her relationship with *Poetry* as a contributor over the years. The openness of the magazine proved beneficial, enabling her to enter its pages at a time when the poetry scene in the United States often found itself partitioned, with practitioners of free verse regarding those who privileged meter and rhyme as entrenched in forms that no longer spoke to the sensibility and the needs of a modern world. Likewise, formalist poets dismissed free verse practitioners as untrained artists who rejected the aspects of the craft that they lacked the patience or talent to master. Therein lies the significance, for instance, of a comment by Dorn in his letter directing Espaillat to submit work to the *Manhattan Poetry Review*: "This magazine, which is open to finely crafted work in free verse and traditional form, deserves all the support we can give it—especially at a time when many poetry editors will not even look at a poem using rhyme or meter" (Letter, 3 May 1983).

During the early 1990s, Dorn alerted Espaillat to a conference starting in West Chester, Pennsylvania, that she must, in his view, join. By then she had already met Len Krisak, a Massachusetts poet who reiterated Dorn's enthusiasm about the West Chester Poetry Conference. In 1995 Krisak invited her to go with him, and she, "a housewife at heart," worked up the courage to "take off four days to go to a poetry conference" out of state. "It was magnificent," she recalls, adding that since then she has missed very few iterations of the annual event (NK/STS). A unique poetry-only conference, the event has been held at West Chester University since 1995 with the purpose of hosting panel discussions and workshops on the craft. Despite recent fluctuations, the historical emphasis has been on formal verse, narrative poetry, and the concerns of New Formalism. Convened originally by West Chester University English professor Michael Peich and the poet Dana Gioia, the conference began modestly with an attendance of eighty-five poets and scholars, a number that would grow to several hundred by the following decade. The program every year centers on a team of teachers who lead hands-on workshops on particular aspects of the craft, and it pays tribute to one major figure who comes invited as keynote speaker. By 2000 Gioia had recruited Espaillat to conduct workshops at the conference, and by 2003, when her colleague Krisak published an essay on her life and works for a volume of the *Dictionary of Literary Biography* dedicated to the "New Formalist poets," he could report on her ascent as one of the leading voices of the movement (Krisak).

CELEBRATIONS OF CRAFT

On the whole, no aspect of Espaillat's verse has attracted as much attention from anthologists and editors as the widespread recognition of her mastery over the range of forms that make up traditional English prosody. The prestige she has enjoyed on the poetry scene nationally since she began publishing books in the 1990s has much to do with her standing alongside poets associated directly or indirectly with "formalism," whether old or new. Her circumstantial affiliation with New Formalism, a school of American poetry that by the late 1980s had become a considerable contender on the national debates among verse makers, probably helped to propel her into greater visibility than she would have acquired otherwise, given the decades she spent away from the literary scene. Chronologically speaking, however, Espaillat's adoption of traditional English prosody preceded the movement by several decades. While she has accepted the recognition extended to her by the "new" formalists, she occasionally likes to describe herself as an "old" formalist—a dash of humor given her earlier engagement with classical prosody than the overwhelming majority of her fellow practitioners (Kang 192).

Espaillat's works have appeared in numerous compilations premised upon particular fixed forms. One example is *Fashioned Pleasures* (2005), an anthology edited by William Thompson that showcases the formal dexterity of some choice contemporary poets. The editor explains the mission of the collection as bringing together word-artists "who find a technical challenge hard to resist" (Thompson 5). Thompson instructed his twenty-four contributors to compose sonnets following the *bouts-rimés* model exemplified by Shakespeare's Sonnet 20, which reads:

A woman's face with Nature's own hand painted
Hast thou the master-mistress of my passion;
A woman's gentle heart, but not acquainted
With shifting change, as is false women's fashion;
An eye more bright than theirs, less false in rolling,
Gilding the object whereupon it gazeth;
A man in hue, all hues in his controlling,
Much steals men's eyes and women's souls amazeth.
And for a woman wert thou first created;
Till Nature, as she wrought thee, fell a-doting,
And by addition me of thee defeated,
By adding one thing to my purpose nothing.
But since she pricked thee out for women's pleasure,
Mine be thy love and thy love's use their treasure.

It was imperative that contributors adhere strictly to the prescribed rhyme scheme modeled above. The results, as published in the collection, are "an eclectic variety of sonnets each fashioned around the shaping code of Shakespeare's invention" (5). *Bouts-rimés*, or "rhymed ends" in English, constitute a French verse-writing game played by various hands who followed specific rhyming patterns in a given form, usually the sonnet (Turco 137). Referencing French form specialist and scholar Clive Scott, Thompson explains that this prosodic game—rarely played today—had a reputation for trying the ingenuity of the most formidable seventeenth-century French poets (Thompson 5). Espaillat wrote two sonnets for the collection: "She Meditates among Works of Art" and "Take That Plato" (Thompson 18, 32). Both works illustrate Espaillat's virtuosity in the execution of her craft, as well as an overall good-natured resolve to participate in the work of poetry with joy as well as seriousness.

Her inclusion in edited volumes that celebrate specific poetic forms dates back to her poem "Metrics" in poet Annie Finch's *A Formal Feeling Comes* (1994). This compilation centered on contemporary American women's verse and the manifest ways it is driven by meter and rhyme (Finch, *Formal Feeling* 65). Characteristically, Espaillat's poem not only abides by established metrical and rhyming constraints but also dramatizes its own aesthetics. As the first of its three stanzas makes plain, the speaker outlines the stylistic preferences that guide her work: "I like the clattering of hoof and street / Signaling 'horse': slow course of fruit / From earth, air, water, sun, and root / Through branch to ripened flower makes it sweet" (65).

By the following decade, when the poet William Baer, founding editor of the influential poetry journal the *Formalist* (1990–2004), assembled two form-oriented anthologies, it seemed natural that Espaillat's work be included. The first volume, *Sonnets* (2005), includes her "Contingencies" and "Discovery" among the 150 texts chosen to represent the scope of American poets who have engaged the form in its latter-day resurgence (44–45). The second volume, *Rhyming Poems* (2007), gathers contemporary American verse by poets whose work subscribes to a variety of rhyming schemes. Baer includes Espaillat's sonnet "Moods," which had appeared originally in a 2000 edition of the *Formalist*. In this grammatically themed poem, the speaker guides us tersely through a thought process based on verbal options, prompting readers to reflect upon how language conveys the changing possibilities of existence:

> I am learning the subjunctive, mood of choice
> once the indicative has slipped away
> that seemed to say it all once. Active voice,
> yes, all the tenses—I need those to say
> act and remembrance, why and how we live—
> but, now, subjunctive and conditional
> ('If that should happen') and obligative
> ('Let this be said') feel truer than 'I shall,
> he did, we are,' ripening to speech
> spiced and complex and tart, past what I'm sure
> of—or was sure of—or set out to reach;
> how to acquire a taste for the impure
> provisional, that's what I need to know,
> before the last imperative says 'Go.' (Baer, *Rhyming Poems* 35)

In *Villanelles* (2012), edited by Finch and Marie-Elizabeth Mali, Espaillat's poem "Song" appears alongside work by veteran practitioners of the form dating back to Sir Edmund Gosse (1849–1928), Oscar Wilde (1854–1900), and Thomas Hardy (1840–1928). A form originating in medieval Provence, the villanelle entered English-language poetry in full force during the nineteenth century "among makers of intricate verse," and later evolved into a vehicle "for meditative speculation" (Hollander 40). Characterized by "two refrains in parallel," the form builds its meaning through a crescendo of repetitions; it is the verbal equivalent of the repetitive yet swelling rhythm of *Boléro* (1928), the one-movement orchestral piece by composer Joseph-Maurice Ravel (1875–1937), a leader of Impressionism in European classical music.

Espaillat's mastery of forms also extends to the sestina, a structure attributed to the French master-poet Arnaut Daniel (1150–1210). After gaining popularity in its native country, the form traveled to Italy, where several notable poets embraced it, including Petrarch and Dante. The sestina became widespread in English mostly during the twentieth century and especially in the United States. Consisting of six stanzas, each made up of six lines, and a final triplet that serves as the envoi, its rhyme scheme follows the six end words of the lines in the first stanza, which recur as end words in the five succeeding stanzas. Anglophone poets have typically written the sestina in iambic pentameter and, less frequently, in decasyllabic meters (Turco 251; Hollander 40). Espaillat's "People in Home Movies" is a sestina that places in relief "our visceral need for photographs to help us remember our past experience," as described by the editors of *Obsession* (2014), a poetry collection that surveys the popularity of the sestina as a formal option for poets in the twenty-first century (Whitlow and Krysl 23).

Additional compilations featuring Espaillat's work and organized around matters of form or the poetic craft broadly conceived include *Open Roads: Exercises in Writing Poetry* (2005) and *Winding Roads: Exercises in Writing Creative Nonfiction* (2008), edited by Diane Thiel; *Gondola Signore Gondola: Venice in 20th Century American Poetry* (2007), edited by Rosella Mamoli Zorzi and Gregory Dowling; *Token Entry: New York City Subway Poems* (2012), edited by Gerry LaFemina; *Able Muse Anthology* (2008), edited by Alexander Pepple; the collection *Literature: Poetry, Craft, and Voice* (2010) edited by Nicolas Delbanco and Alan Cheuse; and the third edition of Helen Vendler's *Poems, Poetry, Poets: An Introduction and Anthology* (2010), among many others. Such varied dissemination of her verse signals a widespread consensus that regardless of trendiness or other fluctuations in the what and how of modern verse, Espaillat stands among the first-rate practitioners of her art.

DIALOGUE WITH THE POETIC TRADITION

Another important premise motivating anthologists and editors to seek out Espaillat's verse for their collected volumes has been her ongoing dialogic engagement with the literary tradition writ large, which she has accomplished in diverse ways. Revisiting some of the major topoi tackled throughout Western literary history, she has returned several times to the biblical story of Adam and Eve (a topos that chapter five will consider in detail); she has also discoursed lyrically upon several myths from Greco-Roman antiquity, among other ancient traditions. For instance, Espaillat's poem "Arachne" draws upon the Greco-Roman myth of the eponymous character and the didacticism of the story. As told in book six of *The Metamorphoses* by Ovid (Publius Ovidius Naso, the Roman poet of the Augustan era), Arachne is a Lydian maiden exceptionally skilled at the loom. She committed the folly of bragging that her talents as a weaver surpassed those of Pallas Athena, a goddess widely renowned for her dexterity in the craft. The first of a series of tales of divine revenge in Ovid's text, this competition ends with the goddess exacting vengeance on the mortal by turning her into a spider. Espaillat's poem, consisting of two quatrains in iambic trimeter, evokes the state of mind of an older, subdued Arachne, making do with what scant powers still remain after the temerity of her youth caused her to challenge the uncompromising ego of the divinity:

> Aging, the mind contracts
> and learns to do with less:
> out of itself exacts
> a filament, a tress
> to trap the lightest prize,
> a joy too fine for sense,
> that passion would despise
> but for its impotence. (Kossman 156)

Another poem, "On the Walls," revisits the saga of Helen of Troy. Espaillat's Helen, speaking from inside the walls of Troy, knows she made an unwise decision when she left her home, seduced by the young Paris to come to this city, thus unleashing the current war: "The best I left behind; they're in those ships / nosing your harbor." Whatever charm she may have first found in the son of Priam proved fleeting. In the first line, she admits that "From the first look I knew he was no good," and after having undergone the fateful voyage, she confirms, "Not smart, not interesting—no, not the best / at anything, all talk and fingertips." Yet, this coveted daughter of Leda and lecherous Zeus accepts the consequences of her actions without regret, remarking, "The heart does what it does, and done is done." Nor does she seek justification by blaming higher powers: "The future finds its Troys / in every Sparta, and your fate was spun / not by old crones, but pretty girls and boys" (Kossman 219). Her equanimity may be subdued, but it is wise and poignant.

Espaillat's version of Helen is notably disconnected from the stunning, ethereal being whom we meet in the seminal texts of the Western literary tradition. Contrary to the traditional tendency to fixate on Helen's superlative beauty, Espaillat presents her to us as one who stands out, paradoxically, for her striking ordinariness. A mere mortal, after all, Helen speaks as a woman who indulged a whim with disastrous results. She has no way of undoing the adverse outcomes. Not disposed to blaming anyone else nor given to self-flagellation on account of her failings, she has simply resolved to brace herself and live with the consequences. This poem would form part of Espaillat's *Her Place in These Designs* (2008), a collection of verse encapsulating various women's perspectives on the vicissitudes of life and imperative of persevering despite adverse circumstances.

In addition to revisiting some of the favorite topoi of literary artists throughout the ages, Espaillat has engaged the tradition by staging conversations with individual poets. The work she has produced using this type of intervention has earned her spots in volumes that pay tribute to particular writers as well as those that focus on producing counternarratives to existing traditions. In other words, these are texts that "talk back"—even to the notion of tradition itself. The collection *Visiting Frost* (2005), a compilation of 101 poems attesting to the abiding influence of the former poet laureate Robert Frost, merits special mention because of Espaillat's lifelong admiration for his work. Editors Sheila Coghill and Thom Tammaro chose her poem "For Robert Frost," a piece published originally in the journal *Lyric* (2004), for inclusion. A Petrarchan sonnet, the piece ostensibly enacts the same virtues that it attributes to the craftsman it fêtes. The opening lines read, "Easy as breath, without a trace of toil, / your lines uncoil, roll off the spool you wound / so that to shift one syllable would spoil / the spin of image or the flow of sound." The closing lines display no less fluidity: "So birds / juggle their ordinary scales to say / extraordinary things. Like them, you came / to make our songs no longer quite the same" (Coghill and Tammaro 26).

Forthright admiration such as that which she bestows on Frost has not been the only tenor of Espaillat's conversations with the major poets of the Western tradition, however. She has also engaged illustrious predecessors to settle accounts with them on views that she must dispute, particularly in regard to insufficiently complex positions about topics like gender or morality. Her poem "Dialogue" spars with the idea of God advanced by George Herbert (1593–1633), and her "Answering to Rilke" quarrels with the understanding of life's options conveyed by the Bohemian-Austrian poet Rainer Maria Rilke (1875–1926). Both pieces, along with "After Frost," were included in *The Muse Strikes Back* (1997), a collection edited by Katherine McAlpine and Gail White that assembles responses by women to the work of their male predecessors in the tradition. "Answering to Rilke" would also feature in Espaillat's eighth poetry collection, *Playing at Stillness* (2005).

Espaillat's response to Rilke converses with his sonnet "Archaic Torso of Apollo." Rilke's speaker meditates on the meanings generated by the extant trunk of an ancient statue depicting the Greek god of music and poetry, Apollo. The artistic power of the sculpture—despite being but a surviving fragment—induces in the viewer a profound desire for self-scrutiny that leads to the injunction of the closing hemistich: "You must change your life" (Rilke 147). Espaillat uses the closing words of Rilke's enigmatic sonnet as point of departure for a sustained reflection, in the form of a sestina, on what changing one's life might entail. Her piece proposes an exploration of what this exhortation in Rilke's lyrical piece would translate into materially, so she ventures into hermeneutic possibilities: "I say, Good; / let's start by simplifying, by tossing out" (McAlpine and White 191). Espaillat's speaker considers the implications, existentially, of discarding in order to gain. She interrogates the worth of the now-dormant wedding gown, books that she "meant to read a good / forty years ago," her "father's coins, gathered / in lieu of travel," "Old yellowed invitations," "Early pictures of people beyond change," and even "love letters long forgotten" (191–92). The meditation proposes that the difficulty of severing ties to our former selves may lie in the recognition—conscious or not—of the promise of change contained in previous stages of our lives. The idea of life as a protean, shifting composite of experiences pervades Espaillat's sestina. Looking back, aided by the guidance of objects accumulated over time, we can ascertain the various junctures at which change has happened or could have happened. Without the engaged exploration of tangible possibilities that Espaillat's sestina provides, Rilke's overarching injunction appears a bit too abstract, emanating perhaps from a view of life as a monolithic block of experiences that one can simply break in two: the ones that came and the ones to come.

Espaillat's poem does not respond dismissively to Rilke's injunction to change one's life after engaging in an epiphanic meditation on the fragmented piece of sculpture. She disagrees by building a serious, serene, and compelling argument in favor of an alternative view. As we have seen here, Espaillat does not take lightly the judgments she might make about the work of other practitioners of the craft. Her exchange with bards from the length of the tradition generally refrains from cursory indictments. As her tête-à-tête with Herbert illustrates, she has the level-headedness to recognize the other artist's talent even while putting on the table her difference in worldview. Espaillat's response to Herbert involves a skeptical departure from his assumption that love may be equated categorically with "God." He posits that gratitude is our only reasonable attitude toward the Creator as a whole, irrespective of our particular individual experiences. The speaker in Espaillat's poem finds her "thanklessness" rebuked by the accepting disposition of the great English poet whose "pure will" enables him to remain "clean of doubt, / sweeping the world's dust out" from the "small room" of his existence (McAlpine and White 85). In the third of her poem's eight stanzas, the speaker quotes the unwavering creed of her seventeenth-century "friend" in relation to the love-God equation: "whose word is our beginning and our end. / Such thanks are what we owe; Love's debt was paid / by covenant once made / there, on the cross. / Love found, all else is loss" (85). But, wishing she could "believe him right," the speaker understands that the discourse is about more than just "wrestling with / the difference between history and myth"; to embrace his view, she would have "to go . . . past" her own limited knowledge. She thus offers a counterargument to Herbert's unmitigated paradigm of godly devotion, settling the dispute with him in the final stanza by declaring the caliber of his verse much worthier of her gratitude than the cosmic vision of the world that he wishes to impart: "For your song's sake—not what you sing to prove—I will give thanks" (86).

CULTURAL BRIDGE BUILDER AND TRANSLATOR

Significantly, the slow nature of Espaillat's entrance into the space of Hispanic literary identity occurred even while she invariably asserted herself as a native speaker of Spanish. Her immersion into the Hispanic literary scene did not happen until her family's relocation to Massachusetts. While the Hispanic presence has long been numerically greater in New York than in Massachusetts, Espaillat's life evolved in such a way that the move to New England brought her closer to her coethnics than when she resided in Manhattan and Queens. The years dedicated to raising children and teaching had kept her linked to networks of family and friends that included but a few Hispanics, chiefly relatives from both sides of her family and one or two friends of her parents. Nor were there distinct Hispanic or Dominican enclaves in her immediate surroundings. She had closer and more numerous associations with the ethnic group that she had married into via her Jewish husband. Indeed, her poems first appeared in a collection assembled on the basis of ancestry when an editor included her among a group of Jewish women poets (Wenkart). Only a few years later would her poems appear in a collection that celebrated the writings of Latinas of the United States (Fernández).

By 2000 Espaillat had come into contact with several Spanish-language poets based in Massachusetts and started collaborations with them, especially fellow Dominicans. Her compatriots in the 1990s had emerged as one of the fastest-growing ethnic communities in New York City. While Dominicans had applauded the market success of Dominican American fiction writers Julia Alvarez and Junot Díaz, they had remained largely unaware of Espaillat's work, likely due to the lesser appeal of poetry to the reading public (Torres-Saillant and Hernández, *Dominican Americans* 116). César Sánchez Beras, based in Lawrence, and Juan Matos, a resident of Clinton, were among the talented Dominicans Espaillat eventually met. She introduced both to the Powow River Poets' circle, inviting them for readings in which they performed their poetry in Spanish and she, in turn, provided English renditions of their verse.

As a result of her contact with a Hispanophone cultural scene, Espaillat increased her literary activism in her native language. For example, she contributed poems to an international anthology that brought together verse in Spanish by over two hundred poets from over one hundred cities (Alemán). The Newburyport Art Association held a bilingual reading featuring Sánchez Beras and Espaillat on November 15, 2000 ("Powow River Poets" B3). In that same year, she collaborated with the organizing committee of the Latino Arts Month Festival, held annually in November at Northern Essex Community College. In August 2003 she was the featured speaker at the Dominican Day festivities in Lawrence, Massachusetts. And as coordinator of the Powow River Poets' public readings, she organized programs that aimed to introduce her audience to the works of Pablo Neruda, Federico García Lorca, and other great poets of the Spanish language, while maintaining the practice of including poems in Spanish during readings of her own poetry.

Espaillat has also sought to expand the range of English prosody by promoting the incorporation of modes imported from the literary history of her native tongue. She recalls that when she first attended the West Chester University Poetry Conference in the mid-1990s, she realized that the occasion posed a unique opportunity to contribute something that her peers could put to good use: "I was the only Hispanic there, but I realized that these people were open to everything, that their one interest was the craft. If you could bring in something from another culture, they were open to it" (NK/STS). She has spoken emphatically, even somewhat boastfully, about her work on the Spanish styles at the West Chester University Poetry Center, where she introduced several of these while lecturing there (NK/STS). Espaillat took charge of "teaching the French forms and the forms of repetition," and always made sure to include "the Spanish and Hispanic examples of the forms."

Espaillat recalls with joy how she "introduced the *décima* [and] the *ovillejo*" at the conference to an appreciative cohort. The *décima* is a ten-line stanza in octosyllabic verse found in the works of some of the major literary figures of seventeenth-century Spain, including the poet and playwright Lope de Vega (1562–1635). But Espaillat speaks with particular zest about the *ovillejo*, a form named after the Spanish word for skein, *ovillo*, which, as the term suggests, refers to a tight-knit structure consisting of ten lines that break down into a sestet made up of rhymed couplets and a *redondilla* (a four-line stanza rhymed as *abba*) that rounds up the dramatic situation developed in the preceding sestet. Miguel de Cervantes Saavedra (1547–1616), regarded by many as the founder of the European novel with his memorable *El ingenioso hidalgo Don Quijote de la Mancha* (1605, part I; 1615, part II), figures among the authors who helped establish the form. Public interest in the form has grown significantly in the last decades much to the delight of Espaillat, who has gleefully proclaimed, "On the internet and in the stratosphere, everybody loves it" (NK/STS).

Support for Espaillat's boast may be found in the "Cheat Sheet of Repeating Forms," a short manual by Kate Benedict, editor of the online literary journal *Tilt-a-Whirl*. Benedict cites Espaillat as the source she used after finding no entry about the *ovillejo* in "major reference works." She simply refers readers to a definition provided by Espaillat, "a practitioner of the form and an enthusiastic proponent of it." Benedict quotes a relatively long passage in which Espaillat defines the form, advocates for it, and offers tips to potential users:

> This old ten-line form, whose name means 'little ball of yarn,' and, by extension, 'small, tight bundle, tricky puzzle or tangle,' was popular in my country, the Dominican Republic, until the nineteenth century. There are no specific line lengths required, but the short lines (2, 4, and 6) are usually no more than five syllables long, and the other seven lines no more than eight syllables long. The rhyme scheme gives away the secret of the form: a, A, b, B, c, C, c, d, d, A+B+C. (Benedict)

Espaillat closes her explanation with a pitch and some special instructions: "A warning for users, to be printed on the label: The writing of ovillejos is habit-forming. And a word of advice to those eager to risk it anyway: compose the tenth line first, in such a way that it divides roughly into thirds" (Benedict).

Consistent with the enthusiasm exhibited by her definition, an ovillejo by Espaillat goes meta, proselytizing about the form itself. Titled, rather transparently, "Ovillejo," it features a speaker addressing an interlocutor whom we may assume to be a hesitant fellow poet:

> Admit you're tempted by it:
> Well, try it!
> It's full of kinks and quirks.
> It works
> by stealth: you steal a kiss
> like this,
> or steal a base—they'll miss
> the ball until you've stepped
> to safety! It's a plot kept
> well: Try it; it works like this. (Benedict)

Another example, also titled "Ovillejo," covers a serious existential topic and appears in *Agua de dos ríos* (2006), Espaillat's bilingual collection of verse and prose. The poem exudes the dark, prophetic tones of a jeremiad but ultimately voices an invitation to openmindedness:

> You who attempt to bind
> The mind
> In the dark cave where guilt
> Was built,
> In rusty chains too tight
> For flight:
> If not to seek the light
> But huddle there, afraid,
> For what was reason made?
> The mind was built for flight. (*Agua* 144)

Espaillat's actively bilingual presence as a member of the West Chester poetry community helped to underscore the need for "some kind of focus on translation," an area in which her leadership again came to the fore (NK/STS). Not only has she regularly offered workshops on the subject, she has also excelled as a first-rate translator herself. A primarily Anglophone poet who never regarded the language or the culture of her ancestral homeland as something to overcome in order to achieve Americanness, she has maintained (as well as perfected) a command of her native Spanish. In that way, she came to possess the unique ability to produce fine literary translations from Spanish into English and vice versa, in addition to composing high-quality poetry in Spanish. Thus equipped, she has felt compelled to use her linguistic versatility to help expand the reach of poetry across the linguistic barriers that may hinder communication across regions, especially in the Western Hemisphere. Passionate about translation, she now regards the task as a key component of her oeuvre and broader artistic mission.

In a message dated January 28, 2013, Espaillat expressed jubilation at the news received the previous week that the manuscript of her Spanish translations of forty poems by Robert Frost had finally received a long-awaited permission from Henry Holt & Company, the American publisher holding the copyright for the late poet's work. The manuscript had languished for over four years on the desk of a patient and unfailingly committed Mexican publisher, Víctor Manuel Mendiola, the head of Ediciones El Tucán de Virginia. The joy of her words radiates out from the opening line of her message: "Please sit down, as this piece of news is so amazing that you may fall over and hurt yourself after reading it" (Espaillat, "Re: Buenas Noticias!"). In 2014, Espaillat finally enjoyed the pleasure of seeing her Spanish renditions of Frost's poetry in print as *Algo hay que no es amigo de los muros: cuarenta poemas/Something There Is That Doesn't Love a Wall: Forty Poems*.

Another translation project of similar magnitude had materialized the preceding year. The same Mexico City–based publisher had issued the volume *Oscura fruta: cuarenta y dos poemas/Dark Berries: Forty-Two Poems* (2013), a 134-page collection of Espaillat's Spanish versions of verse by Richard Wilbur, a poet she admires possibly as much as she does Frost. In her words of acknowledgment to this volume, Espaillat thanks the poet and essayist Leslie Monsour for her insightful introduction, the publisher for "his devotion to poetry, and his interest in the notion of sharing poetry across cultural and language barriers," and Wilbur himself for entrusting his poems to her (10). Monsour, for her part, celebrates the collection as "an important and unique event in the literary history of our hemisphere. Seldom have the works of a modern American poet of Richard

Wilbur's stature been introduced to the Spanish-speaking world with so little lost in translation" (26–28). Monsour characterizes Espaillat as ideally suited to undertake the task since she is "in possession of exactly the right combination of literary qualities to execute her faithful transformations with the beauty and success embodied here" (28–29).

In addition to translating works by revered senior colleagues from the American literary pantheon, Espaillat has also attended to the work of accomplished poets who are her juniors. She rendered into Spanish *The Best Gift of All: The Legend of La Vieja Belén* (2008), a whimsically illustrated children's book in narrative verse about a beloved Dominican folk heroine by Julia Alvarez. Espaillat has also published Spanish versions of poems by her Powow River comrades, especially Krisak ("Birds from Afar," "Cable TV Home Show," "Susie Trewellha") and Nicol ("Faux Pas"), which she then gathered into her own collection, the aforementioned *Agua de dos ríos* (197–201). For her own *Mundo y palabra/The World & the Word* (2001), *Agua de dos ríos* (2006), and *El olor de la memoria/The Scent of Memory* (2007)—a chapbook of poems, an anthology of verse and prose, and a volume of short fiction, respectively—she has herself translated into English texts that she wrote originally in Spanish and produced Spanish versions of pieces written originally in English.

Espaillat has also accrued a solid track record as English translator of Spanish and Latin American verse from across diverse historical periods. Nationally recognized, she is perhaps the finest living translator of poetry by the sixteenth-century Spanish mystic San Juan de la Cruz, and has also produced English versions of works by Creole Franciscan priest Miguel de Guevara (1585–1646) of New Spain, the courtly Spanish poet and playwright Gabriel Bocángel (1603–1658), and the iconic "Phoenix of Mexico," Sor Juana Inés de la Cruz (1651–1695). She has translated verse by other poets from the Iberian Peninsula, including the Seville-born Gabriel García de Tassara (1817–1875), the Portuguese Antero de Quental (1842–1891), the Basque Miguel de Unamuno (1846–1936), the Andalusian Miguel Hernández (1910–1942), and the revolutionary Catalonian Blas de Otero (1916–1979). The roster of Latin American bards whose work she has translated into English includes the Peruvian Manuel González Prada (1844–1918), the Guatemalan Rafael Arévalo Martínez (1884–1975), the Chilean Nobel laureate Gabriela Mistral (1889–1957), and Mistral's influential compatriot Vicente Huidobro (1893–1948).

Espaillat has similarly attended to the work of Dominican poets, including the little-known Quiterio Berroa y Canelo (1872–1936), the venerable Manuel del Cabral (1907–1999), and his contemporary Héctor Incháustegui Cabral (1912–

1979). Nor has she failed to translate into English some of the Spanish-language poetry by young Dominican immigrant writers in the United States, such as the aforementioned New England–based Juan Matos and César Sánchez Beras, as well as New York City–based compatriots Diógenes Abreu and Dagoberto López. The work of the dynamic Sánchez Beras has elicited particular attention and commitment from her. She has produced an English version of his *Trovas del mar/Troves of the Sea* (2002), a collection of verse that she translated in collaboration with Krisak, in addition to *Lawrence City and Other Poems* (2007), a gathering of 150 pieces highlighting landmarks of the author's adopted hometown. She produced the English text of Sánchez Beras's bilingual collection *Scar on the Wind/Cicatriz en el viento* (2013), an anthology of short poems. She has also translated several of his children's books, including *El sapito azul/The Little Blue Frog* (2010), a charming volume of verse that in 2004 won Sánchez Beras the Dominican Republic's National Book Award in children's literature.

Espaillat's English versions of Spanish poems have received wide dissemination in US literary venues. Her translations of Spanish and Latin American devotional poetry gained her a following when they appeared in the pages of *First Things*, the influential journal of religion and public life. Editor Joseph Bottum, when surveying the accomplishments of the periodical after twenty years of existence, emphasized several milestones, including the publication of "a great deal of translation," including the "extraordinary renditions of John of the Cross by Rhina P. Espaillat," which he illustrates by offering a sample:

> Where have you fled and vanished,
> Beloved, since you left me here to moan?
> Deer-like you leaped; then, banished
> and wounded by my own,
> I followed you with cries, but you had flown.
>
> Shepherds, if you discover,
> going about this knoll to tend your sheep,
> the dwelling of that lover
> whose memory I keep,
> tell him I sicken unto death and weep. (Bottum 60)

Given the caliber and detail of her work, it was not surprising that the Christmas 2012 issue of *Sewanee Theological Review* devoted the majority of its pages to her translations (Espaillat, "Spanish"). In this issue, Espaillat pays moving tribute to the memory of her father: "Homero Espaillat, who loved poetry, and in particular the works of Saint John of the Cross. The many works in Spanish that he placed in my hands as I was growing up have enriched my life beyond measure. It delights me to think that these translations may go on to please other readers, and encourage them to delve further into the works of the poets represented here" (70). The selection of the mystic's works appeared in *STR* accompanied by a prefatory essay by American poet Tim Murphy, who testifies to the personal impact that Espaillat's English versions of these poems had on him when they began appearing in *First Things* during "the bleakest days early in this century" (Murphy, "Lost" 13). In some ways, Espaillat as translator engages in and extends the spiritual work of the mystic by ensuring greater access for readers to the balm that such profoundly coded, often abstruse art can offer.

The spring 2011 issue of the *Hudson Review*, which was dedicated to translations from Spanish, also conferred a prominent place to her contributions (Espaillat, *Hudson Review* 90–94+). A good many of her renditions of Latin American and Spanish poems that first appeared in the magazine also found their way into the volume *Poets Translate Poets* (2013), a collection compiled by the journal's editor to showcase the publication's unequivocal investment in making poetry from languages other than English available and palatable to American readers (Deitz).

Having devoted considerable time and effort to bridge building between literary artists across linguistic regions, Espaillat has performed the task without privileging the literature of one language above another. She clearly believes in the universal reach of poetry, and she has approached translation as a vehicle that can galvanize the cross-cultural ties that the art, in her view, has the power to forge and strengthen. In "A Few Words from the Translator," her one-page preface to *Oscura fruta/Dark Berries*, she offers a compelling rationale for undertaking the translations contained in the volume. She speaks of Wilbur as an "author of inimitable originals that have given the world so much music, pleasure and wisdom," texts "so finished and satisfying in every sense that it feels wrong to touch them at all, even with the translator's best intentions." Yet her understanding that they "are also universal poems, clearly addressed to the human spirit everywhere," offered the necessary assurance that she must pursue the task. Translation, she contends, enables people to gain access to the literary greatness of our fellow human beings across chasms of history, culture, and language. By translating Wilbur's poems into Spanish, she fulfills what she sees as her responsibility to readers who might otherwise not have a chance to enjoy them: "Those of us who are foreign-born are compelled to claim them, and make them available through translation, for readers who speak those other languages that inhabit our thoughts" (10).

Similarly, in her prefatory remarks on her Spanish rendition of poems by Frost, she makes the classic disclaimers about the impossibility of perfect translation and the inevitability of diminishing the original. She does, however, reaffirm the value of translation as an indispensable form of mediation *and* meaning making that renders "the original at least partly accessible to foreign readers" (Espaillat, "Comments" 24). She thus advances the conviction that "diminished or not, great poems should—and do—belong to everyone, but only translation makes it possible for foreign-language readers to claim what is and ought to be theirs" (24). For her lasting service to this democratization of letters, not only has Espaillat received the Robert Frost Foundation's Tree at My Window Award for Translation, but she also had the honor of witnessing the establishment of the Rhina P. Espaillat Poetry Award at West Chester University's Poetry Center in 2010. This prize has been conferred to undergraduates for high-caliber original poems written in Spanish and excellent translations of Spanish poems into English.

As evidenced here, Espaillat has consistently aimed to link creative communities, especially those existing across barriers of language and culture. Out of this desire came the launch and development of the Pedro Mir Poetry Reading Series, an initiative named after the late poet laureate of the Dominican Republic. Founded with Espaillat's support by Matos and Sánchez Beras, the Lawrence-based project aimed to promote Hispanic letters in the region and to invite conversations and collaboration between Spanish-language and Anglophone writers. The series opened successfully with a cross-cultural reading that featured poems written in either Spanish or English performed in the original language and then in translation. There were also presentations by members of the Powow River Poets. For Espaillat especially, the success of the program, with its fluid communications across linguistic traditions in the name of art, affirmed "that poetry is for everybody and crosses boundaries" (Vartabedian B1).

Espaillat stands out for her humble and consummate dedication to the craft of poetry, its practitioners, the reading or listening public, and those wishing to expand their knowledge of its legacies and evolving presence today. After she addressed the West Chester Poetry Conference in 2010 as its keynote reader, the highest distinction conferred by that formalist hub, her commitment to teach and learn the myriad aspects of the craft did not abate. She continued to participate as a regular teacher and learner with great enthusiasm. A June 2014 email message in which she described her numerous engagements in West Chester and New England convey a sense of her undiminished excitement about the way forward: "I co-taught a workshop for high school teachers with my colleague Alfred Nicol in the Powow River Poets, participated in three panels, and took a great workshop in metrics." She described 2014 as "an eventful year altogether . . . and there's so much to do that I don't know what to tackle first, between mentoring several poets who are paying a fee to West Chester's Poetry House in order to send me poems to look over and preparing the readings coming up the rest of the year. I enjoy every bit of it, but I need to be triplets to keep up!" (Espaillat, "Re: Following Up"). The words of X. J. Kennedy describing her work with Newburyport's Powow River Poets and her overall impact on the literature and art scene of the city attest to the magnitude of her dedication to her peers: "Rhina P. Espaillat [is] . . . a teacher by vocation and by nature and, as her fellow poets will attest, a generous friend" (Kennedy xi–xii).

By the mid-2010s Espaillat had accomplished a great deal for the wider community of poets, reciprocating the gift of generosity that she had long received from Dorn and from others. In her teens she had entered their space and felt a sense of belonging as a member of their community, and although she had to stop visiting with them for many years to attend to family responsibilities, they welcomed her back with much appreciation when she was ready to return. Espaillat recalls with affection her rapport with the late Stanley Kunitz (1905–2006), whose work she had followed since her college years. She felt greatly honored to meet him in person when she attended the celebration of his eightieth birthday held at the Poetry Society of America, and her delight increased exponentially when she had the opportunity to serve on the panel that chose him as the winner of the Lawrence L. & Thomas Winship/PEN New England Award for his poetry collection *The Wild Braid: A Poet Reflects on a Century in the Garden* (2006), conferred the same year as his passing.

Though she left New York for Massachusetts in 1990, her years in Queens left a discernible imprint as well. The recognition she earned from the late painter and fellow poet Yala H. Korwin (1933–2014), author of *To Tell the Story: Poems of the Holocaust* (1987), testifies to this impression. In the acknowledgment page to her poetry collection *Crossroads* (2011), Korwin expresses gratitude to the "poet friends whose encouragement and guidance I've treasured over the years, most especially Rhina P. Espaillat and the members of the Fresh Meadows Poets." Korwin's appreciation for Espaillat has been echoed by other literary artists since the latter's arrival in New England. Among them is the singer, guitarist, songwriter, and poet Robert Moore, author of the collection *Unexpected Colors* (2009), whose acknowledgment page underlines the contribution of "the Powow River Poets who have helped me understand poetry as an art form, especially . . . Rhina Espaillat[,] who is both an excellent poet and a cheerleader for good poetry." The *Powow River Anthology* (2006), edited by award-winning poet and collaborator Alfred Nicol, gathered work by poets from the region and elsewhere who had read at the events organized by the group or attended its workshops over the preceding fifteen years. It was an affirming gesture to have the volume dedicated to Espaillat. Like Dorn, she has proven herself a gracious mentor and friend.

4 MULTICULTURAL IMPERATIVES, DIFFERENCE, AND AMERICAN PROMISE

It is not clear whether Espaillat had occasion to cheer the recognition accorded by the literary establishment to African American poet Gwendolyn Brooks (1917–2000), the recipient of the Pulitzer Prize in 1950 for her collection *Annie Allen*, which made her the first poet of her ancestry to receive this coveted award. However, around the time of Espaillat's marriage in 1952, a memorable racial incident took place in the poetry scene involving Brooks and Anglo-American poet Wallace Stevens (1879–1955). Stevens formed part of a panel of judges convened by the National Book Foundation to select the winner of the poetry prize for the next cycle. At one point of inactivity in the selection committee, Stevens and colleagues perused a wall that displayed the photographs of authors who had previously served as judges, and when his eyes spotted the picture of Brooks, he asked, "Who's the coon?" (Richardson 388–89). We might find it instructive to think of the genesis of Steven's contemptible outburst, which may very well have been the Anglo poet's genuine surprise at the photograph on a wall where he had not imagined seeing anything but male, Caucasian faces, a wall where he had expected to encounter a visual equation between great literature, whiteness, and maleness.

While Espaillat did not have to bargain with or compromise her ancestry in order for the community of poets at the Poetry Society of America to welcome her in the late 1940s and the early 1950s, the Euro-American imagination's hold over the republic of letters was still a reality in her field. We might recall that Louis Untermeyer's mammoth anthology of 1942, which proved so influential to her literary formation, included no authors from non-Caucasian groups or ethnic minority populations with the exception of the anonymous "Negro spirituals." Perhaps the very anonymity of the sorrow songs earned them inclusion in the anthology, for it afforded the compiler the opportunity to include black creativity without having to acknowledge the talent of individual black authors.

With this background in mind, this chapter examines Espaillat's trajectory in American letters by highlighting the fractious literary history that informs her biography and verse production. Her oeuvre straddles important stages of social change that prompted shifts in the cultural assumptions of American writers as they tackled the task of making worlds with words. The impact on literature of the social transformations that took place in the United States beginning in the middle of the twentieth century is reflected today in the way critics read Espaillat as compared with how they read her when she first broke into print and gained early recognition. The pages ahead will review this background, focusing on its influence on literary production, outlining the epistemological breaks in the literary history, and underscoring how ancestry and social identity are salient factors in the reading and reception of her texts. We will also gauge the impact of the Civil Rights Movement on the production, dissemination, consumption, and evaluation of literature using Espaillat's oeuvre as an example. We undertake a necessary discussion of migration, exile, transnationalism, and itinerancy as instances of human mobility worth considering as we stress the value of Espaillat's diasporic identity.

CIVIL RIGHTS AND LITERATURE

The Civil Rights Movement had a tremendous impact on US cultural production, intellectual discourse, and the arts, with creative writing standing out prominently among them. Until then, standard literary and cultural histories of the United States left little room for the narratives of people from the country's racialized minority populations to figure in the main story, so to speak. A high school or college syllabus purporting to cover American literature chronologically could easily go from the *Autobiography of Benjamin Franklin* (1791) to *The Sun Also Rises* (1926), by Ernest Hemingway, with no nonwhite writers featured and only a couple of Euro-American women authors appearing on the list. The Civil Rights Movement led to unprecedented numbers of people of color gaining access to higher education, and their presence on college campuses across the land created pressure for schools to come to terms with the bodies of knowledge and cultural heritages associated with the ancestries of these higher-education newcomers.

Out of the difficult and often contentious processes played out within and outside of the echoing halls of academia (especially through student activism in the 1960s onward) emerged ethnic studies as well as women's studies initiatives throughout the nation. Among other consequences, that development nurtured an emphasis on cultural recovery, with many scholars bringing to the fore literary and cultural production by populations whose stories had long been kept out, suppressed, or trivialized by dominant narratives of the country's heritage. The rise of multiculturalism and the critique thereof, as well as what many call the "culture wars," stem from those developments. These currents had a particular impact on what Espaillat refers to as "literary polemics," namely the uses of creative writing to advance the author's strategic social, artistic, or institutional agendas.

Though never shy about asserting her ancestry, Espaillat began her literary trajectory as an ethnically unmarked author primarily because her ancestry connected her to a family background and a foreign birthplace, not to a US minority community. Dominicans did not exist as a recognizable collective in the New York City of the 1930s and 1940s, and Latinos would only emerge as a panethnicity several decades afterward. She gained recognition during her early life as a precocious New York poet who happened to have been born elsewhere, and in that spirit, she received attention from the press and support from teachers, literary scholars, and more seasoned poets whom she had impressed with her gifts. Indeed, one likely explanation for Alfred Dorn's persistence in keeping her connected to the poetry scene during the years of her literary inactivity, in addition to his widely recognized generosity, was his bias in favor of her craft over the other attributes that defined her writing. With a greed for talent that one can regard as typical of mentors and lovers of belles lettres, he may have found it inconceivable that a person with her extraordinary gifts as a verse maker should choose to discontinue a literary career that had started so promisingly.

When Espaillat returned to poetry in full force during the 1980s, the political geography of American literature had undergone considerable change. The idea that creative writing would take a stand in social matters had become popular under the rubric of "engaged" literature in the post–World War II era thanks to the positions taken by such groups as the French Existentialists. Though the roots of the concept date back to previous literary generations, the likes of Jean-Paul Sartre (1905–1980) posited the artist's responsibility to society in a novel and telling way (Whiting 1948: 84). The Existentialist tenet that stressed the necessary commitment of writers to their fellow human beings rather than merely to their craft manifested itself with particular intensity in the United States with the rise to greater visibility of ethnically marked literary voices following the transformations spurred by the Civil Rights Movement. The urge to include the formerly excluded had become a state-ordained imperative by dint of the Voting Rights Act and Title VII of the Civil Rights Act. The law required the government to collect racial statistics for the purpose of implementing correctives to the disadvantages that nonwhite racial minorities had endured for generations. Statistical Directive No. 15, issued in 1977 by the Office of Management and Budget Statistics, formalized the classification of the US population into the five branches that became the country's federally recognized ethnic groups (Oboler). While unimpeachable in its motivation to redress the wrongs of a past wherein the US government had been complicit for centuries in the official practice of racist exclusion, the new law had consequences for literary artists that could best be described as "complex."

As curricula in many high schools, colleges, and universities throughout the country increasingly reflected their growing acceptance of the idea of the United States as a multiethnic society, the assimilationist precept having somewhat loosened its grip on the national discourse, the publication of books by nonwhite minority authors grew exponentially. However, since schoolbooks had for so long neglected the histories, cultures, arts, and overall heritages of the populations involved, the knowledge deficit about those groups was enormous. Teachers, publishers, and readers began to treat literary works by nonwhite ethnic minority writers as vehicles to learn about the communities depicted in their texts. Critical commentary tended to value their works primarily as sources of information about the groups represented, not as works of art fueled by craft and imagination. For instance, we might examine the way the novelist Daniel Stern assessed *Down These Mean Streets*, the debut autobiographical novel by New York-based Puerto Rican author Piri Thomas (1928–2011) in 1967. Reviewing the novel for the *New York Times Book Review*, Stern attributed the book's "undeniable power" to its value as "a report from the guts and the heart of a submerged population group," which "claims our attention and our emotional response because of the honesty and pain of a life led in outlaw, fringe status, where the dream is always to escape" (Stern 43).

Ethnic minority readers also hoped *their* literary artists could explicitly affirm their validity and engagement in American life. The political urgency of some ethnic community advocates, aware of an official national cultural discourse that had either omitted them from the narrative of the land or had included them in a manner that diminished their humanity, often had little patience for writers of "their own" who did not explicitly step up to the plate in defense of the "community." Less welcoming of writers invested in the supposedly selfish ideal of perfecting their craft, these detractors favored those with the clear agenda of representing their people in a way that was unequivocally positive. Those who failed to do so could be branded traitors, out of touch, self-hating, wannabes, mealy-mouthed panderers, and worse. The renowned Ralph Ellison (1914–1994), author of *The Invisible Man* (1952), had occasion to complain later in his life about the mistreatment he had received from "so called Black radicals during the late 1960s" (Rothstein). The winner of the 1953 National Book Award for Fiction for his provocative novel, Ellison would later become a member of the American Academy of Arts and Letters. Some black militant cultural activists found his work lacking an overt commitment to the "cause" of their community and overly engaged in ivory tower aesthetic demands and "obsequious bleatings of white appeasement" (Rothstein).

On the whole, a situation prevailed that caused literature written by ethnically marked Americans to be positioned as a resource to educate the overall population about the lives of formerly marginalized communities. The inclusion of these texts was supposed to attest to the resolve of the state to implement new infrastructure to rectify the history of exclusion. These writers would then have to contend with a readership that, generally speaking, seemed interested first and foremost in what their texts said about the ethnic communities to which they belonged. How they did so, through what artistic ingenuity, by means of what leaps of the imagination, and with what degree of aesthetic success were questions often subordinated to the primary imperatives of participation, bearing witness, and speaking up.

The essayist Richard Rodriguez has poignantly noted that in the Sacramento of his childhood, a time in which legal segregation still prevailed, books did not sit on segregated shelves. He recalls the configuration at the Clunie Public Library:

Frederick Douglass on the same casement with Alexis de Tocqueville, Benjamin Franklin. Today, when our habit is willfully to confuse literature with sociology, with sorting, with trading skins, we imagine the point of a 'life' is to address some sort of numerical average, common obstacle or persecution. Here is a book 'about' teenaged Chinese American girls. So it is shelved. . . . How a society orders its bookshelves is as telling as the books a society writes and reads. American bookshelves in the twenty-first century describe fractiousness, reduction, hurt. Books are isolated from one another, like gardenias or peaches, lest they bruise or become bruised, or, worse, consort, confuse. (Rodriguez 10–11)

One may fault Rodriguez for telling only one part of the story, omitting the part about the dearth of publications by blacks and other minorities prior to the emergence of "segregated" shelves. He allows himself to sound like those self-proclaimed decent, well-meaning men who long nostalgically for a time when it was easier to compliment a woman's appearance without her feeling threatened or diminished, but who omit from their plaint the part relating to the patriarchal history that had allowed men to view the objectification of women and even sexual harassment as both their entitlement and the norm. Nobody should expect for correctives to long histories of injustice and exclusion to work overnight, or to work at all without unintended consequences. But the fact remains that the segregation of bookshelves can disable literature's power to communicate across difference, especially differences relating to social identity such as race, ethnicity, religion, gender, and sexuality.

Among the challenges facing an American literature professor in our present-day university or college classrooms is that of dissuading students from ill-conceived expectations about the books they can and cannot "relate to." Typically white students will accept without much discursive intervention on the part of the teacher that *Moby Dick* (1851), the enduring novel by Herman Melville (1819–1891), may elicit in them insights about human society, including themselves as individuals. However, it may take considerable effort before they can begin to entertain the notion that the same applies to the novel *The Bluest Eye* (1970), by African American Nobel laureate Toni Morrison; *The House Made of Dawn* (1968), by Native American fiction writer N. Scott Momaday; *The Woman Warrior* (1975), by Chinese American memoirist Maxine Hong Kingston; and *The House on Mango Street* (1984), by Mexican American fiction writer Sandra Cisneros. Conversely, it will take no less effort to convince the African American, Native American, Chinese American, and Mexican American students that their communication with these works by Morrison, Momaday, Kingston, and Cisneros respectively does not precede or replace their careful reading and considered engagement with what they find on the pages of those texts. They will not take easily to the notion that their successful rapport with the texts in question will depend on the seriousness of their reading practice. That is, they need to learn the "second language" of each individual literary artist and attend to the relationship between form and métier rather than simply rely on their shared ancestry with the respective authors. Literary communication loses a major portion of its capacity to reach out in light of a prevailing ideology of reading that assumes "our" books speak to "us" whereas others' books speak to "them."

This mutually exclusionary principle of literary communication reveals an even more detrimental implication for the relationship among the ethnically differentiated segments of the national corpus that we call American literature. Since out of the five subsections of the American population that David Hollinger names "the ethnoracial pentagon," the white European-descended majority has set the terms for defining the country's culture and its sense of national community, whites have enjoyed the privilege of dispensing with named markers to their various ethnicities (Hollinger 33). Thus literary histories and anthologies have typically referred to John Updike (1932–2009) as an "American" fiction writer while identifying Langston Hughes (1902–1967) as an "African American" poet. The unnamed becomes the norm, which presumably matters to everyone in the national "we," whereas the ethnically specified suggests an appended part that matters mostly to the particular group named therein.

Perhaps the worst consequence of the segregated bookshelves that partition American literature, much to the chagrin of Rodriguez, is the unequal relations between books by white European-descended authors and their ethnically marked counterparts. Thus white readers in the library or bookstore will cross over to the shelves with specified ethnicities when wishing to learn something particularly about those groups, while staying at the ethnically unmarked shelves when seeking to learn about the general whole, the national community, humanity, and the like. In that case, the so-called *white = universal* equation lives among us still.

ON BEING RENDERED ETHNIC AND ENSUING READING PRACTICES

Because Espaillat did not experience foreigners and minorities as "abstractions drawn from debates on multiculturalism," to use Joseph Barbato's words, but rather had direct access to them in Flushing "as individuals like you and me, fumbling, reaching, struggling to survive and get ahead," she did not develop a narrowly conceived idea of ethnic solidarity (Barbato 10). Nor had she derived from her Manhattan childhood the sharply delineated sense of herself as representing Dominicans or Hispanics as social identities with political significance. She grew up, acquired an education, and established a literary reputation in New York prior to the emergence of a Dominican community with an ethnically differentiated sense of identity. This coming of age also preceded the advent of "Latino/a" as a panethnic category grouping all peoples of Hispanic descent as a subsection of the US population that could view itself as having a shared experience or common destiny. She did harbor ethnic self-respect stemming from recognition of her ancestors' human dignity along with a sound valuation of the language, culture, and art that she inherited from them. However, she asserted the worth of her heritage as an individual, never having lived in an ethnic enclave of Hispanics in general or Dominicans in particular. She wrote poems in Spanish and incorporated some of them into her first poetry collection even when she did not have reason to expect Spanish speakers among her readership. She even included Spanish-language poems in her public readings at a time when she could only assume an audience made up of Anglophones. Furthermore, she did not suppose that having an ancestral language other than English in any way reduced her Americanness.

Perhaps unexpectedly, the first time that Espaillat's work appeared in an ethnically differentiated publication was in the 1990 anthology *Sarah's Daughters Sing: A Sampler of Poems by Jewish Women* (Wenkart). Espaillat recalls the circumstances leading up to her coalition building with Jewish women poets, to the extent of becoming "a sort of honorary Jew." She had agreed to accompany a friend to a reading sponsored by a national Jewish women's group. Once at the location, she realized that the program included an "open mic" segment and signed up to read. When her turn came, she shared "Learning Bones," the poem in which the speaker enacts an argument with her late father, who insisted on calling human bones by their Latin names. The editor and scholar Henny Wenkart, in attendance at the reading, approached her and invited her to contribute the poem to an anthology she was then preparing on Jewish women poets. Flattered by the invitation, Espaillat graciously declined, explaining that she was not Jewish. Wenkart, unaware that Espaillat was married to a Jewish man, said she liked the poem so much that she was willing to overlook the detail in question, and at the editor's insistence Espaillat agreed to participate. After *Sarah's Daugh-*

ters Sing was published, Wenkart went on to include Espaillat's verse in several of the volumes in the series *The Jewish Women's Literary Annual.*

Especially after the publication of her first book, *Lapsing to Grace* (1992), critical attention to Espaillat's work has revealed, in addition to the emphasis on her superior artistry, a parallel—and at times competing—stress on her ancestry. Her verse made its first appearance in venues that showcased her specific ethnicity in 1994, with the publication of two compilations that included her work as representative of Hispanic heritage. The first was *Latino Caribbean Literature*, edited by Virginia Seeley, which intended to serve the needs of a multicultural curriculum for the high school classroom and includes her poem "You Call Me by Old Names." The other, titled *In Other Words: Literature by Latinas in the United States* and edited by Mexican American writer and scholar Roberta Fernández, includes six of Espaillat's poems. "You Call Me By Old Names" is also featured here (Fernández 79–88). We may recall this poem to be a darkly humorous reflection on the way immigration and generational shifts affect naming. It was one of the pieces selected by W. H. Auden, Marianne Moore, and Karl Shapiro for the *Riverside Poetry* anthology of 1953, when Espaillat was only twenty-one years old. Its selection by both Seeley and Fernández in 1994 demonstrates the lasting appeal of the text after four decades.

> You call me by old names: how strange
> to think of "family" and "blood,"
> walking through flakes, up to the knees
> in cold and democratic mud.
>
> And suddenly I think of people
> dead many centuries ago:
> my ancestors, who never knew
> the dubious miracle of snow. . . .
>
> Don't say my names, you seem to mock
> their charming, foolish Old World touch—
> call me "immigrant," or Social
> Security card such-and-such,
>
> or future citizen, who boasts
> two eyes, two ears, a nose, a mouth,

but no names from another life,
a long time back, a long way south. (Espaillat, *Lapsing* 16)

For *In Other Words*, Fernández also selected Espaillat's "Snapshots from an Album," six free verse stanzas, glossing the images seen on old photographs of "the elders, / looking out of / another place"; "Where Childhood Lives," evocations of the speaker's earliest years in a place "where childhood lives, / where stones and water know my name / and stroke me with diminutives"; "Translation," recollections of the speaker's work as translator for the benefit of visiting "cousins from home" who "are practicing their English"; "The Ballad of San Isidro," a narrative poem telling the sad story of two sisters wronged by the husband of one of them back in the homeland, his disappearance, and the survival of the younger sibling's child, who leaves the country to settle in El Bronx; and "Bodega," a remarkable tribute to the speaker's tropical birthplace, recreated strictly through the colors, products, and tastes offered by the neighborhood grocery store.

These same poems, minus "Bodega," reappeared in 2000 as chosen by Puerto Rican scholars Lizabeth Paravisini-Gebert and Consuelo López Springfield in a special issue dedicated to Dominican literature and culture of the journal *Callaloo* that they coedited (Paravisini-Gebert and López Springfield 1047–56). These selections in general, intended as they are to present Espaillat respectively as Hispanic Caribbean (Seeley), Latina (Fernández), and Dominican (Paravisini-Gebert and López Springfield), predictably privilege texts from her oeuvre that explicitly signal her engagement with questions of ancestry, immigrant othering, ethnic identity, land of origin, rapport between English and Spanish, and the cultural backgrounds that make up her composite heritage.

In 1999, Espaillat was also featured in the gender-specific collection *Landscapes with Women: Four American Poets*, edited by Gail White. The back cover carries a celebratory comment by Dana Gioia, a highly regarded poet of Mexican, Italian, and Portuguese descent. By the time of the endorsement for *Landscapes with Women*, Gioia had already come to admire Espaillat's work through her participation in the West Chester University Poetry Conference, a gathering in which he played a key leadership role. Clearly convinced that she deserved even greater acclaim than she had already garnered by that point, he declares, "The vastly underrated Rhina P. Espaillat demonstrates once again that she is one of America's pre-eminent Latin [*sic*] voices." A man of his time, Gioia came into American literature after the partitioning of the map of the country's letters into distinct ethnic districts, with the writings by authors from each of the officially designated minority segments of the population acquiring a differentiating hyphen while those written by members of the white majority kept their ethnicity unmarked. As a result, though the praise he bestows upon Espaillat as a poet is superlative, he inadvertently circumscribes the sphere of her achievement to a horizon delimited by the accomplishments of other American poets who share her ethnicity. Designating her as one of "America's pre-eminent Latin voices" tends to invite consideration of her merits only by comparison with other "Latin voices," discouraging us from considering where she stands in relation to American poetry overall.

As an editor and anthologist, Gioia has shown enormous regard for the quality of Espaillat's work. He includes her statement on poetry in *Twentieth-Century American Poetics* (2003), the compilation of aesthetic pronouncements by practitioners of the craft that he coedited with David Mason and Meg Schoerke. He also displays her work in *Twentieth-Century American Poetry* (2003), the anthology he coedited with Mason. More significantly still, Espaillat figures as one of the eleven living writers represented in 100 *Great Poets of the English Language* (2005), edited by Gioia and Dan Stone, an anthology spanning from the eighth-century anonymous author of *Beowulf* to the 2011 Pulitzer Prize–winning Kay Ryan. Gioia's selection of Espaillat's work for a sampling of verse meant to illustrate "the high points" of English-language poetry over the last thirteen centuries suggests that he views her words as transcending the confines of a single, ethnically differentiated segment of the American population (Gioia, 100 *Great* xxi). But given the politics of representation and the multicultural expectations under which many school curricula now operate, one can understand the compulsion of any editor to highlight the extent to which his or her choices comply with diversity imperatives. In many ways, as editor, Gioia cannot resist—one could even argue, *should not* miss—the opportunity to name Espaillat's ethnicity, since naming it will point to the virtue of dismantling the homogenizing imaginary that formerly plagued American literary history. Nor has the placement of her verse within the Hispanic compartment of the country's letters in any way displeased Espaillat, who, on the contrary, regards it as an honor to see her work gradually recognized as part of the contribution that Latino/as (and specifically Dominicans) have made to the country's literary legacy.

In the 1990s, under the title *American Identities*, Robert Pack and Jay Parini aligned a constellation of forty Native American, African American, Latino/a, and Asian American writers, along with a few Euro-Americans, to represent "contemporary American multicultural voices." The resolve of the editors to run the gamut of multicultural representations is evident in their decision to choose white males with discernible markers of regionally, ethnically, or religiously distinct identities (i.e., Southern, Italian, Jewish, and Mormon). The editors expressed their conviction that the debate over multiculturalism, having intensified in the mid-1980s, had already tapered off as a result of a general acceptance by then that "literary merit is to be found in an ever widening range of writers coming from many regions and backgrounds" (ix). Pack and Parini applaud the arrival of a new era in the study and dissemination of American literature, gesturing to multiculturalism as a movement that had migrated to "the center of American intellectual life," catalyzing "arguments over what critics call 'the canon'—the variable list of works considered valuable by editors, teachers, and critics in a position to promulgate taste and articulate a version of 'the tradition'" (ix). Whether or not they spoke too soon remains unclear. It is also debatable whether by the 1990s the country's national imaginary had so delinked from its racist socialization that "multicultural voices" would enter the pages of American literature anthologies naturally *without* anthologists committing to an intentionally inclusive agenda such as that of Pack and Parini's pioneering compilation. While recognizing the progress that has been made thus far, we cannot naïvely assume that the former barriers hindering racial minority writers from receiving proper recognition have completely disappeared.

Literary scholars might ask whether appreciation of Espaillat's oeuvre will suffer as it transfers from her previously unmarked "American" location to the ethnically specified "Latina" category. For one thing, the application of an ethnic minority label to the poet comes accompanied by a particular manner of representing her work. Notice, for instance, that for their coedited anthology *An Introduction to Poetry* (2010), Gioia and X. J. Kennedy chose Espaillat's signature poem "Bilingual/Bilingüe," a piece in which the speaker muses about the language policy in the Manhattan apartment where she grew up with an immigrant father who insisted on her retaining full command of her native Spanish, along with a statement in prose in which the poet reviews the same history with some thoughts on its implications for the craft (Gioia and Kennedy 265–66; 276–77). The editors use this complex, double-voiced text to illustrate issues pertinent to "identity poetics," ethnicity, and culture; even the study questions at the end of the poem urge readers to consider precisely those concerns (254–65). In doing so, the compilers inadvertently induce a type of reading that will not look for the formal accomplishment involved in the poet's presentation, development, and resolution of a problem in nine rhymed couplets. In light of what we know about Espaillat's open disavowal of Spanglish as an acceptable medium of expression, bringing words from Spanish into a predominantly Anglophone poem might be worth more than just passing consideration.

Purely for the sake of hypothetical illustration, one could speculate about how differently the distinguished literary career of the National Book Award–winning essayist and short fiction writer Barry Lopez would have evolved had his surname defined him as a Hispanic. Born in Port Chester, New York, the son of Alabama natives Mary and Jack Brennan, restless Anglos who journeyed west to the San Fernando Valley, Lopez grew up "white in a white man's valley." He witnessed his father walk out on the family and his mother's concomitant struggle with economic insecurity. This situation changed in 1955, when Mary wed a "third husband, a businessman from New York who offered us financial security, elevated social status and private school" (Lopez, "Scary Abundance"). Lopez received his surname from that stepfather, an immigrant from Asturias in northern Spain who hailed from a hidalgo family and who "was suspiciously alert to issues of class and race." This new parent, as the writer recollects in "A Dark Light in the West: Racism and Reconciliation," exhibited overt prejudice toward African Americans, Jews, and gay men (366–67). His stepfather also impressed upon the young Barry "the need, especially as a young man with a Spanish surname, to distinguish between people who immigrated to the United States from Spain and Spanish-speaking people who had arrived in New York from places like Puerto Rico" (367). As sensitive as Lopez is toward treating all people with respect, primarily by dint of the influence of his mother, he has no memory of interaction with minority populations as a child despite growing up in California: "I can't recall any Latino or Asian students having been in my classes . . . and I am aware now that the valley back then was home to few African Americans. The social world I inhabited at the time, as a middle-class, suburban white boy, was predominantly, if not thoroughly, white" (365). While a brilliant, award-winning essayist and storyteller, especially of meditations on landscapes, flora, fauna, and the uniqueness of the human and nonhuman inhabitants, he has arguably benefited from the whiteness that renders him an ethnically unmarked American writer and makes it natural for readers of all stripes to access his texts without having to make the "progressive" move to reach across to the "ethnic" shelves. If the surname Lopez had made him Latino, chances are that readers would seek his work mostly when in need of a Latino "take" on a subject, no matter how finely crafted, imaginatively astute, or observant his prose.

Likewise, readers who might approach a poem like Espaillat's "Agua" looking for explicit expressions of ethnic specificity on account of the Spanish word for water in the title might miss the larger, transcultural valence of that signifier. The first stanza presents the dramatic situation of the speaker's mother, severely afflicted with Alzheimer's disease:

Mother, the trees you loved are dense with water,
alive with wings darting through stippled blue
of recent and imminent rain. And that old street
you mistook for water—remember?—is flowing still,
as when we walked between its banks of pickets
down to the river, which you knew was water
and spoke to, leaning over it last summer. (Espaillat, *Where Horizons Go* 27)

In the last stanza the speaker represents the sick parent as a "balmy old Thales" with "true" piercing sight that rips through "every disguise," uncovering "the water / that links us, the current that bears us / from season to season, whose tide you greeted / in the mindless music you spoke" (27). The Spanish word *agua* marks not culture but chronology: the mother spoke Spanish before acquiring English as an adult. Those afflicted by the devastating disease tend to revert to earlier stages of knowledge while losing any consciousness of more recent cognition. The English word for water probably disappeared from her lexicon; as such, that fundamental substance, proclaimed by pre-Socratic philosopher Thales of Miletus (624–546 BC) to be the originating principle of nature, resurfaced in her mind as *agua*. Despite the sadness attached to the speaker's prodding her elder to "remember" a street that the latter had once mistaken for water, there remains an accepting disposition, one buoyed up by the thought that the mother had actually hit the mark, echoing the wisdom of the ancient Greek thinker who had, so long before, reduced everything to water.

Similarly, in a poem like "Bra," the question arises: should ethnically minded readers funnel *all* their attention to the semantic weight of the brassiere's label that "says Honduras" and the cultural implications of that reference for the speaker, who happens to be of Latin American descent? The poem invites a larger consideration of the geopolitical reality that complicates the simple act of purchasing an undergarment at a local department store. Though enamored with the garment, the speaker cannot merely overlook her awareness of the colonial history and political economy behind the transit of the coveted item from

Honduras into her hands. She senses the unequal relations between the highly developed consumer societies of the capitalist West—with the United States at the helm—and the economically dependent developing world to which the corporations export production, spurring unemployment at home while exploiting vulnerable workers abroad. Furthermore, the speaker has a moment of pause, given that she is a union member committed to US labor. Her unequivocal loyalty allows for a critical approach to the dilemma from a working-class perspective. The poem, *in toto*, reads:

> What a good fit! But the label says Honduras:
> Alas, I am Union forever, yes, both breasts
> and the heart between them committed to US labor.
>
> But such a splendid fit! And the label tells me
> the woman who made it, bronze as the breasts now in it,
> speaks the language I dream in; I count in Spanish
> the pesos she made stitching this breast-divider:
> will they go for her son's tuition, her daughter's wedding?
> The thought is a lovely fit, but oh, the label!
>
> And oh, those pesos that may be pennies, and hard-earned.
> Was it son or daughter who made this, unschooled, unwedded?
> How old? Fourteen? Ten? That fear is a tight fit.
>
> If only the heart could be worn like the breast, divided,
> nosing in two directions for news of the wide world,
> sniffing here and there for justice, for mercy.
>
> How burdened every choice is with politics, guilt,
> expensive with duty, heavy as breasts in need of
> this perfect fit whose label says Honduras. (Espaillat, *Where Horizons Go* 18)

We can even devote an entire reading exclusively to the extended metaphor of the brassiere as a site of duality and dividedness, ambivalence, weight, and the ethical difficulty of making conflict-free decisions when we remain vigilant to the impact on others of the choices we make. The article of clothing in question, called in the third stanza a "breast-divider," causes the heart to be pulled in two opposite directions, and the sense of moral partitioning is conveyed by means of a clever use of the caesura that breaks most of the lines in the poem into sonic hemistiches.

Even a poem like "Bodega," which on the surface seems to relish in the recollection of "childhood and another place / where the tang of orange sweets / golden on the vendor's tray / drifts like laughter through the streets" allows for much more than the sensorial provocation and the rhythmic tonality that the speaker associates with her tropical birthplace (*Lapsing* 18). Embedded in the visual and olfactory qualities of "saffron, anise . . . / rosemary, oregano, / clove, allspice and *bacalao* [salted, dried cod]" is the speaker's ponderings on the passage of time, the brevity of life, and the role of memory as resource to recreate the world despite our constant losses: "Fifty years have blown away: / . . . / Memory is filament / weaving, weaving what I am: / bitter coffee, musty beans, / caramel and guava jam" (18).

As the choices made by Seeley, Fernández, the *Callaloo* guest editors, and Gioia illustrate, there is a tendency among anthologists to represent ethnic minority writers in a manner that privileges autobiographical content over form, or the "what" over the "how," as Espaillat would say. Doing so reduces the range of concerns that fuel the work of literary artists. By no means do we wish to discourage the application of the labels "Latina" or "Hispanic" to the poet under consideration. We would certainly not wish to invite the kind of persuasive rebuke that a young poet earned from Langston Hughes in his famous 1926 essay "The Negro Artist and the Racial Mountain":

> One of the most promising of the young Negro poets said to me once, 'I want to be a poet—not a Negro poet,' meaning, I believe, 'I want to write like a white poet'; meaning subconsciously, 'I would like to be a white poet'; meaning behind that, 'I would like to be white.' And I was sorry the young man said that, for no great poet has ever been afraid of being himself. And I doubted then that, with his desire to run away spiritually from his race, this boy could ever be a great poet. (Hughes 175)

The question remains whether, in the context of the segregated bookshelves that Rodriguez decried at the start of this discussion, a brilliant literary artist can receive proper credit for all he or she does as a practitioner of the craft once the ethnic label has already marked the work. The question for the critic, as well as for the anthologist as canon builder, is whether we can find a way to acknowledge the contributions of literary artists from ethnic minority backgrounds that stresses their validity for readers across the board, not merely for those seeking targeted knowledge about distinct subgroups of the American population.

We may want to tackle the problem of how to speak about literature in a manner that assumes the oneness of humanity and helps to break up the monopoly of ethnically unmarked whites over the national definition of Americanness. We need to reach a point of critical development at which it becomes normal for readers to find the general yearnings, conflicts, and challenges of humanity in an ethnically marked literary work no less frequently than they would in an unmarked one. The truth of such claims as "everybody is ethnic," or "no human experience is inherently more universal than another" is not yet self-evident to most students, for instance. Yet there is arguably nothing at the level of content, form, substance, or execution that makes Whitman's "A Noiseless Patient Spider" or Frost's "The Road Not Taken" more evocative of the human condition than a poem like Espaillat's "Bra."

The commemorative anthologies that celebrated fifty years of the Poetry Society of America in 1960 and one hundred years of *Poetry* magazine in 2012 respectively featured Espaillat's work on the strength of what she had to contribute to the literary tradition rather than what she could say specifically about her own people. Dorn dwelt on her ancestral origins briefly in his 2002 review of her collection *Where Horizons Go*, but several decades prior, he had extolled the virtues of her verse without regard for specificities of heritage. He never viewed her work strictly in relation to texts by those sharing her ancestry but felt free to juxtapose it to the output of any and every bard working in the language, including Shakespeare and the Metaphysical poets. Dorn's appreciation of her accomplishment in the sonnet "Changeling" included the statement that he did not know anybody writing at the time who could match her ability to express so much so movingly within the constraints of the fourteen-line structure:

a poignant, riveting, tragic piece about your mother, [it] is one of your greatest sonnets, perhaps your greatest. I know of no contemporary poet who matches your skill, compression, and emotional power in a form restricted to 14 lines. 'Changeling' is a masterpiece. The concluding couplet, the stumbling block of so many sonnets, is one of the highlights of your poem. The couplet is not 'tacked on,' nor does it sum up what has gone before. Instead it adds something new and significant to the three quatrains. Shakespeare himself would have been pleased to see how deftly you have handled the form to which we have given his name. (Dorn, Letter, 15 Sept. 1991)

Espaillat's artistic persona is dichotomous: a notably talented practitioner of her craft who can represent the field of poetry while being a member of a racialized minority fully equipped to represent her coethnics in the republic of letters. In accounting for the duality of this presence, commentators may wish to look for (or invent) language that does not subordinate one representational capacity over the other. Whatever the precise formulation ends up being, it would ideally highlight her command of the craft while acknowledging her ancestry in a manner that turns the elements of her heritage into factors that expand rather than diminish her expressive resources. One could thereby praise her as a Latina who stands as one of the preeminent poetic voices of our times.

DIASPORIC PERSPECTIVE, CAPACIOUS CITIZENSHIP

Beyond locating Espaillat on the identity grids making up American literature, first as an unmarked and then as an ethnically marked author, we can point to a third mediating factor that influences the other two: the particularity of her Caribbean background. We might think, for instance, of her active engagement with literary initiatives spearheaded by Lawrence, Massachusetts–based Dominican immigrant poets writing in Spanish. She has similarly led a translation project at the City University of New York's Dominican Studies Institute at City College to make available in English the writings of the Dominican Republic's founding father. The effort resulted in the bilingual volume *Juan Pablo Duarte, the Humanist* (Espaillat and Aponte 2015). This third location of culture complicates the binary opposition between the "ethnic" and the presumed "nonethnic." She hails from the Dominican Republic, a country that partakes not just of the Hispanic world created by the colonial transaction under Spain in what we now call Latin America, but also of the Caribbean cosmos, a site characterized by pervasive crossings of heritages, languages, and traditions.

American writers with roots in the Caribbean—like their counterparts in Europe—have demonstrated a tendency to explore the story of humanity via the recurring scrutiny of Caribbean lives, histories, and narratives. Espaillat's poems "Bodega," "Translation," "The Ballad of San Isidro," or even "Bra" have much less to do with ethnicity per se than they do with the dialectic of "here" versus "elsewhere," a discourse intrinsically linked to diasporic identity. In Espaillat, as in most writers tied to the Caribbean diaspora, we witness the layered identity of a metropolitan poet with her civic, political, and social roots set firmly in American society but whose involvement with the memory of a history elsewhere pushes and pulls, thereby shaping her manner of belonging within the shifting parameters of Americanness. With the likes of Claude McKay, Rosa Guy, Paule Marshall, Julia Alvarez, Martín Espada, Michelle Cliff, Edwidge Danticat, Cristina García, Junot Díaz, and Rafael Campo, among numerous others, Espaillat forms part of a vigorous cadre of Caribbean diaspora writers who have contributed significantly to expanding the geography of the American literary imagination.

In recent decades, the advent of diaspora writers has had a radically transformative impact on the literary corpus of the United States. Alvarez, Danticat, Díaz, and Espaillat, for instance, have helped Hispaniola intervene into the prevailing discourses of American literature. As a result, readers can now access an imaginatively robust, geographically and culturally ample picture of Americanness that may use Haiti or the Dominican Republic as a reference point of no less importance than the US locations where these authors are based. The texts of these writers abound in moments when a character forms his or her subjectivity in the United States through the understanding gleaned from recognition of connections to another people, culture, or set of social expectations elsewhere. The awareness of a place where "stones and water know my name / and stroke me with diminutives," which we hear the speaker evoke in Espaillat's "Where Childhood Lives," refers specifically to the poet's memory of having spent her earliest years in the ancestral homeland, but for others born in the metropolis, the awareness may come as a learned recollection from stories heard or experiences interpreted from their household elders in the United States.

The community of writers that we would place within the Caribbean diaspora consists of individuals, whether born or raised in the metropolis, who owe their socialization and literary training to the land of residence where they have formed their idea of home. They do not have the Caribbean region easily at their disposal as the center of their existential or political being. The social space they inhabit in the United States—with their counterparts in England, France, the Netherlands, or Canada—is not "abroad" or "away." They reside in those spaces as their primary habitats, and they retain varied links to their ancestral homelands. These sites serve as repositories, cultural locations to which they resort when positioning themselves socially and politically as citizens of the metropolitan societies where they reside (Torres-Saillant, *Intellectual* 252). As writers, they belong recognizably in the literary communities of the metropolis rather than in those of their ancestral lands, where their works often arrive as expensive import products from the major international publishing firms and possibly even in translation, as in the case of writers of Haitian and Dominican descent who, like Danticat and Díaz respectively, received their education in English and their literary training in the United States.

At the risk of stating the obvious, we should distinguish between the "here" and "elsewhere" dialectic for writers of the Caribbean diaspora and the familiar age-old mobility of artists from one country or region to another. Literature and its practitioners have long surpassed the confines of the village, the nation, or the region to commingle with, borrow from, or pay tribute to alien or otherwise foreign forms, styles, vocabularies, and sensibilities. The anonymous composer of Genesis, the first book of the Hebrew Bible, drew much of the diction, content, and poetic logic suggested by the *Enuma Elish*, the twelfth-century BC Babylonian epic of creation. The second-century AD Roman writer Apuleius found the métier for his *Metamorphoses*, better known as *The Golden Ass*, in the search for knowledge of Egyptian traditions of magic and spirituality, particularly the sacred cults of Isis and Osiris. Shakespeare owed the substance of his play *Romeo and Juliet* to a 1554 novella by the Italian writer Matteo Bandello (1480–1562), who himself may have taken it from the fifteenth-century collection *Il Novellino* by the fiction writer Masuccio Salernitano (1410–1475). With the adoption of such poetic forms as the sonnet from Italy, the villanelle from France, and the pantoum from Malaysia, among others, Anglophone poets have long traveled across languages, geographies, and cultural heritages to find material to expand their expressive repertoires.

Additionally, writers themselves have historically defied national boundaries to secure the company of kindred spirits, to escape censorship, or to ensure an amicable reception for their works. René Descartes (1596–1650) in the seventeenth century settled in the Netherlands, and in the eighteenth century we find Voltaire passing several intellectually significant years in England. Józef Teodor Konrad Korzeniowski (1857–1924) spent the first twenty years of his life as a native Polish speaker in the ancestral homeland before settling in England, where he became a central figure in nineteenth-century British fiction under the name of Joseph Conrad. Rudyard Kipling (1865–1936), whose works encapsulated the ethos of British imperialism in the nineteenth century, was born in Bombay, India, the site of his most formative years. American fiction writers and poets hailing from the generation of Gertrude Stein (1874–1946) sought to enhance their creativity by moving to Paris. Samuel Beckett (1906–1989) left Ireland to merge comfortably into French literary life, and T. S. Eliot (1888–1973) simply decided to change his citizenship, becoming a subject of Her Majesty the

Queen and one of the artists memorialized in Westminster Abbey's Poet's Corner. Vladimir Nabokov (1899–1997) was forty before he settled with his family in the United States, a considerable literary record in Russian already under his belt. Yet, outside of the Slavic world, Nabokov may be remembered primarily for the American portion of his oeuvre, which includes such Anglophone texts as *Lolita* (1955) and *Pale Fire* (1962). Similarly, one does not think of Pablo Picasso (1881–1973) as having his locus of creativity in his hometown of Málaga or the Barcelona to which his family moved during his childhood; one thinks first and foremost of Paris, where he first visited at age nineteen.

The individual instances of cross-national mobility illustrated by the foregoing artists, however, did not fundamentally complicate the nationalist paradigms underlying the construction of histories of art, literature, and thought. This is so especially since Europe was so often characterized in the critical discourse as a site of unitary culture that could unproblematically harbor a harmonious collection of national experiences. Therefore, the literary or visual imagination could glide among and across countries without necessarily triggering a redistricting of the geographies of knowledge at stake. At present, different phenomena operate that have the effect of altering national cultures. We have entered a historical moment when the centers of the Christian West that spearheaded the colonial transaction have found themselves inhabited by the children of former slaves or colonized subjects who have come into themselves as compelling speakers with metropolitan reach. The images and stories that result from that scenario necessarily expand the territory of the imagination and invite reconsiderations of belonging, obstacles and catalysts to unity, the spatial location(s) of cultural production, and the nature of citizenship.

Explicating the concept of *diaspora* also seems prudent before expounding upon its value in the study of Espaillat's work. Diasporic citizens normally come from families that harbor different politics and cultural heritages in their midst; divergent national histories and cultural practices often undergo considerable negotiation within the sphere of the household. The experience or the memory of migration structures much of the internal dynamics between family members. But their story is hardly reducible to migration, as the act of mobility that has characterized the narrative of humanity from its beginning. Migration is too central to the human experience overall to provide clues for distinct identities. Coming out of Africa some fifty thousand to eighty thousand years ago, our forebears found it necessary to leave their original homelands to migrate across the rest of the planet (Wells 191). The work of the influential Italian geneticist Luigi

Luca Cavalli-Sforza, the author of such compendia as *The History and Geography of Human Genes* (1994), has done much to discredit the old scientific wisdom that rigidly posited the differences that presumably set each "race" of humans apart from the others based on genetically determined variation (Cavalli-Sforza, Menozzi, and Piazza). Similarly, Spencer Wells, a geneticist and anthropologist who studied under Cavalli-Sforza, has helped to popularize the now widely held view among scientists that modern humans may all trace our origins to African ancestors who left their continent and spread throughout the globe, populating all regions as they went.

Thus, the story of our itinerancy as a species began back in time immemorial, and in the twenty-first century the tendency shows little sign of abating. Espaillat has sustained the idea that migration is the perennial narrative of humankind. "Tireless travelers" is the epithet she uses to describe "all the children of Adam and Eve" (*Agua* 90). But Espaillat's own story also partakes in the large cohort of Caribbean-descended American writers whose history has a much shorter chronology, having its genesis in the sort of human mobility that colonialism triggered in the modern era. To that more recent chapter we owe the visibility of immigrant-descended (second generation or older) or even foreign-born writers who received their education and literary training in the metropolis and came of age in the great intellectual and artistic crucibles of the United States and Europe. The insights of James Clifford prove useful at this juncture to help distinguish other outcomes of migrancy from the diasporic stance that we are applying to Espaillat's oeuvre. "Diaspora," posits Clifford, "is different from travel (though it works through travel practices) in that it is not temporary. It involves dwelling, maintaining communities, having collective homes away from home (and in this it is different from exile, with its frequently individualist focus). Diaspora discourse articulates, or bends together, both roots *and* routes." What emerges are "alternate public spheres, forms of community consciousness and solidarity that maintain identification outside the national time/space in order to live inside, with a difference" (Clifford 251). While objecting to his formulation of "collective homes away from home" for the reasons we provide in these pages, we favor Clifford's view of *diaspora* as denoting something distinct, something else, not just any kind of transnational mobility.

The term *diaspora* has recurred dramatically in the social sciences and the humanities over the last two decades. Some scholars extol the virtues of the notion for its capaciousness as a theoretical paradigm. Anh Hua contends that "diaspora theorizing opens up the discursive or semiotic space for a discussion of many ideas: identification and affiliation, homing desire and homeland nostalgia, exile and displacement, the reinvention of cultural tradition in the New World Order, and the construction of hybrid identities, as well as cultural and linguistic practices, the building of communities and communal boundaries, cultural memory and trauma, the politics of return, and the possibility of imagining geographical and cultural belonging beyond and within the nation-state formation" (Hua 191). Evidently, this scholar posits diaspora as an all-encompassing theoretical paradigm with the versatility to cover an enormous social field. In another vein, Roza Tsagarousianou recommends that "diaspora should be seen not as given communities, a logical, albeit deterritorialized, extension of an ethnic or national group, but as imagined communities, continuously reconstructed and reinvented." She likewise asserts that "diaspora can refer to constellations of economic, technological, cultural, and ideological and communication flows and networks" (Tsagarousianou 52, 61).

Khachig Tölölyan, founding editor of the journal *Diaspora*, offered early on the clearest mapping of the advent of émigré or expatriate communities that one could call diasporic in the latter half of the twentieth century, arguing for the value of the term beyond its earlier application to the dispersion of the Jews in antiquity, Africans in the wake of the transatlantic slave trade, and Armenians, among others, in more recent times (Tölölyan). William Safran made an early attempt to provide a typology of constituent elements that may justify our applying the term to describe differentiated populations, including such indicators as a dispersion from an original center to peripheral or foreign regions, a collective memory or myth of a lost homeland, an experience of marginality in a host society, a yearning to return to the lost homeland, and a continued engagement with the land of origin (Safran, "Diasporas"). At this early stage in the cultural history of the term, Gabriel Sheffer points to the roles occupied in international politics by expatriate or émigré communities, such as that of Cuban exiles shaping US foreign policy against Cuba, or people of Jewish descent in the United States and elsewhere sustaining the State of Israel in the Middle East (Sheffer). Similarly, Clifford's well-received essay suggests that we might derive more benefit from locating the concept of diaspora in relation to "what it defines itself against" rather than in a set of central features (Clifford 307).

The concept of diaspora has become ubiquitous in the nomenclature of contemporary criticism to the point of making it difficult to understand what scholars mean by it or, even worse, to ascertain its full range of explanatory powers. Ironically, the pioneering voices who gave currency to the use of the notion concur in advising some caution. Tölölyan has coedited a collection whose introduction establishes that the concept of diaspora, like transnationalism, "still awaits a conclusive definition" (Kokot, Tölölyan, and Alfonso 3). Safran, on the other hand, has gone so far as to decry the proliferation of uses of the concept, which he alleges "has become an academic growth industry—not only in political science, but also in anthropology, sociology, psychology, religion studies, history, and even literature." This proliferation, in his view, has stripped the concept of historical meaning, reducing it to a "useless metaphor" (Safran, "Deconstructing" 9–10).

Recognizing its status as "an all-purpose word used to describe a growing number of populations," a spread that he ascribes to the recent influence of such notions as postmodernism, globalization, and transnationalism, scholar Stéphane Dufoix devoted an entire book ostensibly to clarify the place and utility of the term (Dufoix 30). Contending that the word often stands in for immigration and emigration, he proposes a typology of his own that classifies diasporas according to mode: enclaved, atopic, and antagonistic (60). Ultimately, however, his inquiry continues to revolve around a view of the populations in question as being "far from one's native land and feeling nostalgic for it" (80). He, like other thinkers, leaves the question of diaspora unresolved, settling for its multiform reality and ubiquity by deeming it "a global word that fits the global world" (108). Perhaps more notable in this regard is Sudesh Mishra, who conducts a significant *compte rendu* of the intellectual history of the concept from the 1980s onward. The author defines the body of writings that has amassed as "diaspoetic," a term coined to refer to diaspora criticism as a field in and of itself (Mishra 14). This body of knowledge is "at its best when taking stock of the variety of historical continuity and rupture that exist (1) within and across the different diasporas, (2) within and across their cultural and aesthetic practices, and (3) between a single diaspora and its cultural and aesthetic conditions" (175).

It is not unreasonable to doubt that a critical term could be made to serve so many disparate functions and still do so well. However, the fertile development of diaspora as concept has made it difficult to harness in a way that could render it optimally useful for literary criticism. We thus find it necessary to establish our approach with some precision so as to enhance the notion's applicability to a reading of Espaillat's oeuvre. For the purposes of this study, we limit the application of the term *diaspora* to the migratory flows that, for long, have left the Caribbean to find their destination in the large cities of Europe and North America. We refer here especially to instances when the mobility of populations results in the establishment of immigrant settlements that build communities with characteristics that differentiate them within the receiving society. Generally, starting with the second generation, we can therein attest to the emergence of a collective formation with ancestral links to the Caribbean, displaying the distinguishing marks of a palpably diasporic identity.

The distinctive profile of that identity allows for the hypothesis that diaspora differs substantially from exile even though the close link between both forms of itinerancy may often make the latter a sort of anteroom to the former. The exile is characterized by his or her separation from a native land temporarily or permanently. Mentally, the exile lives in a maternal, autochthonous abode that he or she hopes one day to recover. An evocative poem by Bertolt Brecht titled "Thoughts on the Duration of Exile" represents these individuals as hesitant to unpack their luggage and disdainful of any gesture of permanence in the receiving society, such as studying the local language or planting a tree (Brecht 301–302). One gathers from such reticence a mental state imbued with the fear of betraying the ancestral origin, suggesting that perhaps the indifference towards the present surroundings nurtures the possibility of returning to the native land.

The diasporic citizen, on the other hand, exists in a state of mediation—be it political or existential—between the country of residence, upbringing, as well as civic loyalty and an ancestral homeland that prompts long-distance identification. Unlike exiles, diasporic citizens do not live abroad. Nor do they lack *a home*. In the United States, for instance, Espaillat is as much at home as she could possibly be, irrespective of her continued rapport with the Dominican Republic. She and the Caribbean-descended diasporic citizens under consideration here live at home in the spaces they inhabit even when they may recognize a certain precariousness to their dwelling place. They have pitched their tent in the place where it has been their lot to grow up and live despite the insufficient firmness of the ground beneath their feet. To a large extent, one must look for the identitarian basis of diasporic citizenship in precisely that duality: the awareness of the precariousness of belonging in the land of civic location and the absence of an original homeland to which one might "return" in search of the solace of belonging without undue conflict.

Migration precedes diasporic identity, but it need not lead there. Dominican writer Alan Cambeira, for example, lived in the United States for nearly five decades, until in 2005, not having successfully crossed the identity border from immigrant or exile to diasporic citizen, he made the decision to return *home* to

Samaná (Torres-Saillant, "Dominican-American" 433). In a sense, immigrants and exiles can go home again no matter how long they remain abroad. Diasporic citizens are home, and their ancestral homeland does not constitute a site of probable return, although it remains viable as a source of identification often needed in societies like the United States for ethnic self-fashioning.

As we stress its utility for the study of literature in general and its relevance for our reading of Espaillat's oeuvre in particular, it should be clear that diaspora is neither good nor bad; it serves a primarily descriptive rather than interventionist function here. Its relevance lies in its power to interpret rather than prescribe collective behaviors or social developments. As such, a human group does not seek to become diasporic; the diasporic experience merely happens to people. Diaspora does not describe people on the move; it does not name migratory flows. It most productively refers to the identity location of some communities that have come into the fold of particular societies as a result of their earlier need to part with an ancestral homeland. We contend, therefore, that the term *diasporic* will do a better job than *ethnic* or *immigrant* when accounting for the layered identity of a major American writer of Caribbean descent like Espaillat.

Literary critic Jahan Ramazani has appealed to critics and scholars to delve more deeply into "globe-traversing influences, energies, and resistances" that have characterized writing in English "from the modernist era to the present" (Ramazani 334). Ramazani illustrates his claim by referring, inter alia, to the mobile locations of Eliot, Stein, Auden, Langston Hughes, William Butler Yeats, Amy Lowell, Mina Loy, D. H. Lawrence, Ezra Pound, H.D., Claude McKay, Robert Graves, Laura Riding, C. Day Lewis, and William Empson, all British and American literary figures whom he views as "migrants" (334). While acknowledging the significance of the contacts with others that he describes, we propose that the phenomenon that Ramazani terms "a transnational poetics" differs emphatically from the diasporically informed literary imagination that we see operating in Espaillat's oeuvre. We are placing her work and the overall Caribbean diasporic corpus of which it is a part in a historically and geopolitically differentiated locus that activates the engagement with an "elsewhere" whether or not individual authors have the ability or desire to transcend the national space of their civic belonging.

In a book titled *Global Diasporas*, Robin Cohen builds on Safran's typology by classifying dispersed groups into victim, labor, trade, imperial, and cultural diasporas (Cohen, *Global* 26–29; Little and Broome 221–26). Prior to that, Cohen had authored an article theorizing the "special and qualified sense" in which the term *diaspora* may apply to the Caribbean ("Diaspora" 168). Hispanic Antillean countries like Cuba, the Dominican Republic, and Puerto Rico, no less than the rest of the Caribbean, form part of an Atlantic region that harbors numerous religions, tongues, cultures, and discrete national histories. Populations from all over the world ended up voluntarily and coercively in the Caribbean from 1492 onward, and people of multiple ancestries have left the Caribbean for other destinations, again both voluntarily and coercively. Cities throughout the United States have received immigrant populations from across the linguistic map of the Caribbean region: speakers of English, Spanish, French, Dutch, and the numerous creoles that evolved there over the last five centuries. Generations after the arrival and settlement of their ancestors, the children of immigrants remain imaginatively engaged with their ancestral homelands even when they have not worked to preserve the ancestral language. The Caribbean experience, put differently, has been the site of an inherently cross-national and global experience given the planetary implications of the events unleashed by the conquest and colonization that unfolded there as of 1492.

Clearly, the case Ramazani makes in favor of recognizing transnational dynamics in literary history warrants attention. His analysis succeeds at identifying the tendency of artistic writing to escape the confines of the immediate site of creation and its attraction to alternative resources elsewhere. But we find it especially necessary to place Espaillat outside the field of inquiry that the term "transnational poetics" shores up. Ramazani's nomenclature invites a semantic association with the baggage that "transnationalism" acquired when the notion gained ascendancy in the social sciences during the early 1990s. The transnational perspective boasted the explanatory power to make sense of entirely new dynamics in the history of human mobility from native geographies to sites of destination. Transnationalism presumed radically novel geopolitical conditions that, becoming most pronounced in the 1980s, fueled new patterns of mobility across the globe. It purported to reveal that, unlike the conventional studies of migration that drew the line of mobility from a point of origin to a point of destination, the new migrants pitched their tents on mobile ground, moving back and forth between alternating homes in the land of origin and the site of destination.

The itinerancy of Caribbean peoples, however, does not correspond to the chronology of a phenomenon datable "from the modernist era to the present." Transnationalism and globalization do not explain the particular plight of the populations connected to the Antillean world. Nor does the history of mobility of intellects across languages and regions shed useful light on the diasporic identity of Caribbean-descended writers in the United States or the other metropolises of the Christian West. We would not describe the rapport between the here and elsewhere in Espaillat's verse as partaking of that kind of "transnational" mobility. It becomes too apparent that, whatever virtues the "transnational" paradigm could boast to shed light on other realities, it simply could not contribute much understanding to historical dynamics in the Caribbean, a region whose people, from the start of the colonial transaction to the present day, have seldom enjoyed the luxury of having their future and their daily lives determined solely by national or internal forces (Torres-Saillant, *Diasporic* 31; Torres-Saillant and Hernández, "Dominicans" 230–33).

As applied to Caribbean-descended Americans, then, the term *diaspora* does not refer "specifically to the movement—forced or voluntary—of people from one or more nation-state to another," as the editors of *Theorizing Diaspora* suggest in their attempt to "differentiate diaspora from transnationalism" (Braziel and Mannur 8). Understood as a process of people on the move, a meaning that *migrancy* or *itinerancy* could most perfectly subsume, the notion of *diaspora* fails to convey a differentiated meaning. We can far more profitably use the term to refer to a condition, a manner of belonging, a state of mind that shapes social interaction with dominant populations in the nation; in other words, it is a locus of identity. On the basis of the discernible centrifugal force that has typified the human experience in the region, we may regard the Caribbean as a primary source of diasporic displacement irrespective of the previous dispersion that may have brought diverse peoples from across the globe to form part of the Caribbean population.

Writers ancestrally connected to the Caribbean tend to link "the old country" seamlessly or else problematically with the metropolitan world of their civic belonging and socialization, ushering in a sociohistorical phenomenon that has made it necessary for scholars to imagine new ways of fashioning our understanding of cultural history. These literary artists differ radically from their non-Caribbean predecessors, especially those whose families checked their histories and many of the trappings of their difference at Ellis Island. Now, their ancestral past forms part of their present. As such, the literary imagination of the Caribbean diaspora has brought something new to American letters, an existential crucible whereby a character may feel incomplete until coming to terms with a chapter that took place elsewhere in a former time. For instance, Espaillat's aforementioned "Bodega," "The Ballad of San Isidro," "Where Childhood Lives," and "Bilingual/Bilingüe" attest to a component of the poet's consciousness that hinges on the memories, stories, or experiences of elsewhere.

The poem "Coca Cola and Coco Frío" by Martín Espada, a poet much admired by Espaillat, tells the story of a Nuyorican boy who travels to the ancestral homeland and comes back transformed as a result of direct contact with everyday practices that are less driven by consumer consciousness: "On his first visit to Puerto Rico, / island of family folklore, / the fat boy wandered / from table to table / with his open mouth" (Espada, "Coca-Cola" 44). The elders there had offered him Coca Cola, a drink preferred in the US mainland where he comes from, and, therefore, for colonial reasons, on the island too. However, "at a roadside stand off the beach," he then chanced upon "coco frío, a coconut / chilled, then scalped by a machete" that he could drink by simply inserting a straw (44). The boy returns to Brooklyn marveling at the contradiction of an island with so many coconuts that hung "swollen / and unsuckled" from the trees because "the people drank Coca Cola / and sang jingles from World War II / in a language they did not speak" (45).

Likewise, the novel *The Dew Breaker* (2004), by Danticat, presents us with the challenges endured by the main character Ka when she learns that her father, whom she always viewed as a decent man in Brooklyn, has a dark past dating back to life in Haiti at the service of the Duvalier dictatorship. Not only did he excel as a torturer and executioner for the blood-drenched regime, but the maternal uncle Ka never met figured among those her father killed. Here we have an instance of past events in the ancestral homeland thrusting themselves into the present existence of a young woman in Brooklyn who now must contend, like Oedipus, with horrifying knowledge about her own flesh and blood. On the other hand, the young Selina, the Brooklyn-born child of Barbadian parents in the novel *Brown Girl, Brownstones* (1959) by Paule Marshall, establishes a clear sense of herself as an American by finding a middle ground between her father's obdurate desire to return to his homeland and her mother's perhaps uncritical acceptance of the host society's ideology of advancement and success.

GENESIS OF A DIASPORIC POETIC VOICE

Espaillat's birthplace sits squarely at the center of the Caribbean cosmos. Like most Caribbean societies, from the start of the twentieth century the Dominican Republic has sent sizable portions of its population to host countries overseas. The portions that, over many decades, have settled in the United States have become the most distinct for their production of generations of offspring with a strong sense of their rootedness in American society and a concomitant aware-ness of the difference that Dominican ancestry makes. The writings of Espaillat and her coethnics in addition to Alvarez and Díaz—namely Annecy Báez, Jose-fina Báez, Angie Cruz, Ana-Maurine Lara, Loida Maritza Pérez, and Nelly Rosa-rio, among others—quite discernibly evince the diasporic worldview that cre-ates an interlaced field of consciousness straddling the American here and the Caribbean elsewhere without necessarily living psychologically "between two worlds."

Poet Leslie Monsour covers key biographical details of Espaillat's life in *Rhina Espaillat: A Critical Introduction*. Discussing Espaillat's bilingualism, Monsour offers the compelling suggestion that although English "is technically [Espail-lat's] second language," it could conceivably stand as "her 'mother' tongue," for after the family settled in New York, [Espaillat's mother] Dulce María took to English with a passion, letting the young Rhina speak to her in that language. This openness was "a luxury undreamed of" when addressing her father (13). In view of the strained political circumstances that caused Espaillat's family to set-tle in the United States, Monsour reasons that "Espaillat would almost certainly not have become the award-winning US poet and translator she is today" had her homeland not suffered the scourge of the Trujillo dictatorship (17).

Monsour draws causal links between the events surrounding the family's break with the oppressive government and the girl's childhood experiences. She reviews Espaillat's beginnings in the United States as a toddler whose parents had settled in Washington, DC, following her father's appointment in 1934 to the Dominican Legation there, at the time headed by her father's uncle Rafael Brache Ramírez, or "Nino Fello," the godfather who would buy her Untermeyer's pricey anthology of verse that her parents could not afford back when she started dis-playing her zeal for poetry. Appointed by the country's dictator Rafael Leónidas Trujillo, Nino Fello indicted the October 1937 massacre of tens of thousands of Haitian immigrants and their Haitian-Dominican offspring in the towns along the Dominican border by command of the nefarious ruler. As a consequence, the family fell from grace with their country's government and sought to stay in the United States as political exiles. There began an abrupt new chapter in the life of Rhina and her parents, who left the nation's capital for New York City "to look for work and a place to live." Probably "as a result of stress and insecurity," her mother miscarried what would have been Espaillat's "American-born kid brother" (Monsour, *Rhina Espaillat* 21). The loss left her mother "depressed and in very frail health," to the point that some feared for her life (22). The grieving woman then resolved to travel back to La Vega and Jarabacoa, the Dominican cities where her extended family lived, with the five-year-old Rhina in tow, "to say goodbye to her siblings and her mother, whom she feared she would never see again" (23). She left the child in these good hands as she foresaw difficult times ahead for the family in New York. Espaillat recalls that her mother made it out of the Dominican Republic shortly thereafter to join her husband in Manhattan, bringing little more than her sewing machine. It was a tool that ensured her ability to work and rebuild. Espaillat reflects, "I'm convinced that she thought she would not live to return from there, but she was much more resilient than she herself thought" (NK/STS).

Dulce María recovered from her illness, and the parents braced themselves for economic hardship as foreigners new to an immense metropolis "still in the grip of the Great Depression" (Monsour, *Rhina Espaillat* 23). It took the couple until 1939 "to secure steady jobs and an apartment and save up enough money to send for their daughter" (23). Monsour stresses the formative influence of the two years Espaillat spent with her father's family in La Vega, all the while making frequent visits to Jarabacoa to see her maternal grandmother. Espaillat herself encourages this emphasis, as she unfailingly points to that period as a sort of genesis of her poetic awareness, a time prior to any formal literacy. Under the roof of her maternal grandmother, she first heard and was enraptured by the sound of poetry, giving her the sort of aural education in Spanish that predisposed her to identifying with the sonority of verse in English.

Monsour hypothesizes that Espaillat's distinct form of utterance—that which makes her idiom, sound, and vision compelling—draws substantially from the productively absorbed elements of her life. The poet had a beginning that marked her in the US, with political events of traumatic significance to her parents, which then caused her to spend part of her early childhood living with extended family. As such, she had her ears educated, as it were, by the sounds of poetry in the ancestral homeland. Perhaps the fractious early chapters of her life account for the texture of the poetic voice that by the 1950s earned her considerable praise. The adult literary artist who would return to the poetry scene in the 1980s to reclaim her old spot simply had to build on what was there already. She would enhance her early assets by means of training, experience, keen observation, emotional depth, and psychological maturity, as well as productive rapport with fellow artists and thinkers.

On September 3, 2013, Espaillat journeyed to the Dominican embassy in Washington, DC, to be fêted alongside several individuals of Dominican ancestry who had achieved great distinction. Among them was the then US Secretary of Labor Thomas E. Perez, the poet's cousin. She left that diplomatic site appreciative of the recognition that the government of her birthplace had extended to her. The occasion must have triggered thoughts of her life in the United States, which began precisely at the Dominican embassy in Washington when she first came as a toddler in the early 1930s. Being celebrated by the Dominican ambassador in the nation's capital seventy-six years after her father had severed ties with that diplomatic site must have represented a kind of internal peace accord with the authorities of her native land. Being honored alongside her politician cousin must have been particularly evocative given his own consanguine relation to Nino Fello, his maternal grandfather, who served as Dominican ambassador to the United States in the 1930s until he spoke out against his home country's regime, which rendered the ambassador persona non grata ("Secretary of Labor Thomas E. Perez").

The peace accord was short-lived. Espaillat felt compelled to interact with the Dominican embassy again in October 2013 via a letter to the ambassador in which she invited him to join the people of goodwill—Dominican and non-Dominican alike—in repudiating the ruling of the Constitutional Court that had disempowered such a great number of his compatriots, reducing them to destitution for what she argued was the "irrelevant fact of having been born of Haitian parents." On September 23, 2013, a newly created Constitutional Court in the ancestral homeland had issued a cataclysmic ruling that denationalized hundreds of thousands of Dominican-born citizens of Haitian ancestry. Previously, the country had adhered to the principle of jus soli, whereby the land of birth confers citizenship automatically. Now, not only was the ruling deemed "unappealable," it was also applied retroactively all the way back to 1929. When Espaillat became aware of this law, the best-known precedents of which are those that denationalized Germans of Jewish ancestry under the Third Reich during the 1930s and Ugandans of South Asian ancestry under Idi Amin during the 1970s, she joined the voices of protest against an action of the Dominican State that reduced a large portion of the national population to abject vulnerability and statelessness overnight. An article by Fausto Rosario Adames published in the Santo Domingo–based online newspaper Acento covers Espaillat's correspondence with the embassy. Her letter condemns the "manipulation of the country's laws" by judges with the most "impure motives" and urges the ambassador to do whatever he can to save the country "from being morally stained with this ruling that is incompatible with justice" (Rosario Adames).

As exemplified by Espaillat's involvement in Dominican affairs, whether in the ancestral homeland or in the diaspora, we can now account for a brand of US citizen with ancestral links to the Caribbean that seems unlikely to relinquish all ties to the land of origin. As an outcome of the colonial transaction, we face a situation that makes the human experience of formerly subject people very difficult to relegate to an elsewhere overseas. A meaningful number of the children of formerly subject peoples now speak as citizens of the metropolitan center; they can usher in a more humanized image of formerly captive populations. No longer do they reside in a realm of insurmountable alterity. Julia Alvarez and Junot Díaz, the coethnics of Espaillat's who have garnered the widest acclaim in the realm of contemporary American letters, went public in 2015 as signatories of a letter that urged then US Secretary of State John Kerry to demand of the Dominican government immediate correctives for the civil and human rights of Dominicans of Haitian ancestry. Here we see operating an instance of diasporic citizens seeking to use their political rootedness in the country of civic loyalty to exert influence on the rulers of the land of origin.

The Caribbean remains a place of beginnings, the previous bodies of knowledge and historical experience of its inhabitants having been rendered native. With its histories of voluntary and coerced mobility, the Caribbean informs Espaillat's tolerance for panoptic remembering, namely her ability to make room for all the human experiences that fused into her present self. Her sonnet "The Old Ones," in which the speaker ponders the history of colonization that made her the child of both master and slave, asks us to meditate upon the inescapably tragic condition of ancestral legacies in the hemisphere. The careful phrasing of each iambic pentameter line, the seemingly effortless music made by the three quartets and the closing couplet, and the overall sedate tone of this Shakespearean sonnet combine to make the meter and rhyme hardly noticeable. Overall, the astute handling of form and the quiet gravity of the thoughts conveyed lexically induce a calm understanding of the weight of our shared historical drama:

> If they could rise out of their graves in me—
> that slaver and his captives, each cool knave
> who bought or sold or shackled them at sea,
> the nameless few who vanished between wave
> and auction-block, that clever Spaniard who
> left me his old name with his new land,
> those drifters from all ports who, passing through,

settled in every cell of brain and hand—
what should they do? List grievances, forgive
themselves, each other? Justify each crime
that built my body's house? Send me to live
clear of their quarrels, in some blessed time
less brutal than Earth time, some clearer place
where everything that lives lies down in grace? ("Poems by Rhina P. Espaillat"
   127)

"The Old Ones" limns the heritage of pain inflicted by colonial domination, the inevitable family ties that such a history has forged, and the seeming pointlessness of holding a rancorous vision of historical injuries into the present day.

National histories in the Americas trace their roots to tales of woe—the violence of one ethnos overpowering the resistance of another—which the nationalist imagination turns into glorious epics that sing to the virtues of the "winners" and diminish the humanity of the "losers." Triumphalist in outlook, the nationalist imagination regards the outcome that *was* as the one that necessarily *had to be*, allowing hubris to squash any semblance of the humility that a cautious winner ought to observe, wisely mindful that the wheel of fortune could easily have turned the other way. A supplement to the expansiveness of Espaillat's diasporic perspective, then, is that she does not hail from the side of the winner. A child of mixed-race, cross-cultural Caribbean parents, she came into the world as the product of the tragic events whereby adventurers from Christian Europe encroached upon indigenous societies in that region. Diasporic uprooting occurs mostly as a result of dispossession. The offspring of the dispossessed, when endowed with the prescience to learn about uncertainty from the history that has tossed them about from geographic space to geographic space, ought to think twice before gloating over the dispossession of others.

The poem "Cartography," from Espaillat's *The Shadow I Dress In* (2004), communicates a macro-level understanding of the cruel and multilayered history that eventually propelled her to Newburyport, Massachusetts, where she envisions her progeny leaving their own mark on posterity. The speaker is a loving elder guiding her grandchildren through the map of the region they inhabit, pointing out the surrounding cities, towns, and waterways. Scanning the landscape of the country's verse, the reader may find it difficult to name a more expansive vision of American promise and possibility than that which "Cartography" conveys. This is a result, we could argue, of Espaillat's understanding of the manifold lessons bestowed by her diasporic experience. The speaker in the text embraces the country that she calls home even with the baggage that it carries: the unfortunate pillage, erasure, and domination that essentially brought it into being. Acknowledging the tragic beginnings as microcosm, she comes to terms with this freight as historical contingency of the sort that led to the creation of all the other nations and peoples birthed by the colonial transaction in the hemisphere.

5 QUIET REVOLUTION
DOMESTICITY AND CREATION STORIES

When Espaillat and other former winners of the T. S. Eliot Poetry Prize visited Truman State University's campus in 2012 to promote poetry among the students, Espaillat granted an interview in which she defined an aesthetic principle that serves as a template for understanding many aspects of her literary vocation and life. "Dancing in a box" describes how she was able to retain her artistic fervor in the years monopolized by domestic duties and public school teaching:

> It's impossible to "think outside the box" unless you first have a box to get outside of! The pleasure of poetry is that you first get to make the box (by learning how to build it, with language) and then willingly climb into it, then tempt the reader into it with you, and then manage to get out of it without destroying it, all while dancing. It's one of the oldest arts, after all, and art is the only activity I know of that can take a profound sorrow and turn it into an artifact that inexplicably provides comfort without changing anything. (Sharp 2013)

Poet Alfred Nicol refers to Espaillat's path as that of a "woman's life fully experienced," arguing that her awareness of constant constraints has been deftly woven into the warp and weft of her creative works (Nicol, "Rhina P. Espaillat" 97). The preceding chapters have established how Espaillat innovates within the realm of received forms and traditional English prosody. Her artistic trajectory, with its long absence from publishing between her early years as a teen poet and her postretirement "boom," also illustrates the paradoxical duality of freedom within constraint. Such a pattern has dictated her decisions as a woman coming of age in the 1940s and 1950s, all the way to the present moment in the early twenty-first century.

When situating Espaillat's oeuvre within the ethnic cartography of American literature, we might consider to what extent she may have dealt with the biases held by scholars, literary communities, and the reading public against writing and other forms of artistic self-expression by women of color. One such bias involves the historical marginality endured by women poets from minority groups, including Latinas, given the country's insufficiently integrated and often blatantly racist literary scene that did not consider women of color's voices as worthy of publication, let alone inclusion in any broader canon of US letters. In Espaillat's case, these problems may have been further exacerbated by her publishing her first book at the advanced age of sixty. By this age, many of her contemporaries might already be planning commemorative publications of their life's work.

In popular media and literary representations, women of mature or advanced age tend to be sequestered into roles associated with mothering and the home. Age often confers respect in the world of traditional families, with women elders standing as repositories of wisdom for younger generations, a model evidenced, for instance, by La Grande, the heroine in Chicano writer Rudolfo Anaya's seminal novel *Bless Me, Ultima* (1972). Within Latin American folklore and other traditional stories, they need not be benevolent in the sense of the *curandera* (healer) or devout *abuelita* (granny); less-savory character types include the community gossip, the meddler, the unyielding matriarch, and the bitter crone (sometimes a *bruja*, or witch/sorceress) whose aim is to complicate the lives of others because her own is devoid of ambition or joy. Rarely do these women have sexual power, unless it is for some comedic purpose, such as being paired with a young man as a ruse or aesthetic experiment, or for some point of instruction, as when warning young people about the perils of love. Older women's agency is hardly a priority in many of these narratives. This stereotyping is not unique to Latinas; however, Dominican American novelist Loida Maritza Pérez has observed that Latinas are further "ascribed traits such as nurturing, caring, [and] submissiveness" and face pushback after displaying "other traits that are not considered womanly, for example, independence, defiance, and for that matter, sexual aggression and hostility" (Chancy 13). In light of the negative freight generated by gender, ethnicity, and age-based biases, this chapter grapples with the ways Espaillat's poetry about women's experiences—not just Latinas, but not to the exclusion of them—offers a paradoxically empowering perspective of home life within her composite feminist worldview.

Among other locations of power, Espaillat views the home as an artistic workshop and a sanctuary. In literary critic Maureen Corrigan's review of businesswoman Sheryl Sandberg's best-selling memoir *Lean In: Women, Work, and the Will to Lead* (2013) for National Public Radio, she comments, "Sandberg is following the first axiom of political organizing: Start where you live" (Corrigan). Since home is where Espaillat lives and writes, especially given her status as former housewife and retired schoolteacher, it would follow that the home must also be a place with revolutionary potential. As a CEO, Sandberg does not work from home; her perspective, while touted as a kind of new feminist exemplar, is inherently individualistic, failing to address the social problems facing poor women and especially women of color who have encountered great barriers when seeking to enter professional spaces typically reserved for elite whites (hooks, "Dig Deep"). Sandberg's perspectives on leadership resonate with the details of a controversy that exploded shortly before the release of her book. Yahoo CEO Marissa Mayer, whom the *LA Times* has called "corporate America's most famous working mother," built a nursery for her child at her workplace. She banned telecommuting for her employees, resulting in protests from those working mothers in her company who used "home days" as a way of spending time with their children while remaining committed to their occupations (Guynn). Sandberg's and Mayer's cases, while extremely different from Espaillat's in terms of professional field and circumstances, do bring up an essential issue for feminists and for working women broadly. In the quest to provide increasingly diverse options for women outside of the home, in places where, as Sandberg urges, they should cultivate leadership, what has happened to the home itself as a site of leadership and power?

FORMULATIONS OF HOME

Espaillat dedicated *Her Place in These Designs* (2008) to her two grandmothers, thanking them for conferring "clear and complementary notions of [her] place." Here, "place" does not convey the sense of containment associated with the injunction that one "know one's place"; rather, it is an invitation to inhabit—a kind of ontological open house—when the position has been passed down to a relative who needs to decide how and whether she wants to live in it. The complementariness Espaillat refers to here is layered, even deceptive. The poet recalls in an interview that her maternal grandmother, Mama Julia, and her paternal grandmother, Mama Polincita, held contrastive places despite both being working-class women in the early twentieth century. Mama Polincita, outside the home, was educated to a degree that was professionally gratifying, and she was able to express herself artistically and communally. Espaillat explains that this older woman "entertained thoughts; she played the guitar; she sang; she played the piano; she's the one who had the visitors to the house who told stories and recited poems" (NK/STS). In contrast, Mama Julia was "very submissive, very, very religious . . . very, very traditional, and 'good' in the old-fashioned sense. She would go out and take care of sick people, even if they were strangers. She would feed anyone who came to the house—and they were very poor" (Kang 189). This illiterate widow, a seamstress with numerous children, was totally immersed in "her poverty and her submissiveness and her silence." Espaillat recalls poignantly, "She never argued" (189).

The poem "Find Work" recreates Mama Julia's heart as "anaesthetized and mute / with labor" to the extent that her floors were "scrubbed white as bone" and her dishes shone "painfully" (*Her Place* 17). The language here evokes thoughts of the Old Norse and Anglo-Saxon poetic use of kennings, or metaphorical circumlocutions such as "whale road" for the sea and "bone house" to refer to the human body. In "Find Work" the contents of the house both contribute to and reflect Mama Julia's psychological and physical pain. She is a "bone house" in a house that is working her to the bone. Even her dishes (perhaps of bone china) are extensions of her body given the deep fragility residing in their flat, seemingly strong exterior. Espaillat's characterization of her grandmother in the poem offers clues to Mama Julia's psychopathology, in particular her inability to enunciate verbally, let alone through art or other form of expressive release, her frustration as an economically unstable single mother without the educational resources or array of opportunities to better her life. Work had become her sole premise for living; finding it and doing it assuaged her lack of fulfillment in other areas of her life, and yet she had few, if any, alternatives: "So her kind was taught to do— / *Find work*, she would reply to every grief" (17). The poet uses the phrase "her kind" to specify that this is not just an individual problem but a generational, gendered, and collective one.

Though unhappy, Mama Julia fulfills the image of the ideal woman according to the Latin American gender ideology of *marianismo*, an allusion to the Virgin Mary. To quote legal scholar Berta Esperanza Hernández-Truyol, this is a trans-cultural construct "that demands a Latina must be *la buena mujer* ('the good woman') and requires of women self-sacrifice, self-effacement, and self-subor-dination" (Hernández-Truyol 536). Jenny Rivera, a judge and legal scholar of civil and women's rights, elaborates upon these expectations: "A Latina must serve as a daughter, a wife, and a parent, and must place the needs of family members above her own. The influence of Catholicism throughout Latin America solid-ifies this image within the community, where Latinas are expected to follow dogma and to be religious, conservative, and traditional in their beliefs" (Rivera 502). Even though the husbands of the twice-widowed Mama Julia are long gone, the obligation-driven structure of *marianismo* obtains, buttressing an existence "spent in the lifelong practice of despair" (*Her Place* 17).

Aware of the contrasting models offered by her two grandmothers, and con-scious of her own experience, Espaillat had choices far different from those of Mama Julia. She did not repudiate the elder's legacy completely, having herself assumed domestic responsibilities when she left her parents for marital life in the New York of the 1950s, a period associated with steep conservatism in US society. Immersed in expectations about good housewives and self-sacrificing mothers, Espaillat straddled domestic and nondomestic spaces in a way that piv-oted on choice and agency even amid constraint.

Feminists of different stripes have construed domesticity as restrictive and mentally stultifying for women whose professional goals lie outside of the home. Euro-American feminist writer Charlotte Perkins Gilman (1860–1935) exposed the existing model of gender relations allegorically in her 1891 story "An Extinct Angel," whose main character, a member of a lost breed of earthbound angels entirely devoted to their masters, dutifully takes on all the dirty work while remaining spotless. Denied the benefit of a formal education, these angels had to understand how "to assuage, to soothe, to comfort, to delight" on their own (Gilman 48). White feminist readings of home recall the nineteenth-century ideology of separate spheres that placed assertive and enterprising men outside the home while women remained inside it as "angels of the house." That women across identity categories and locations do not experience the domestic arena in the same way, however, may be gleaned from the dilemma faced by middle-

and upper-class African American women who hesitate to hire domestic help because of the history of black women's relegation to (and mistreatment in) such positions. This history involves being underpaid, physically and verbally abused, even sexually assaulted from the postslavery era through WWI especially (Bates, "History"). Indeed, the habit of construing the domestic arena as inherently oppressive correlates with a typical Betty Friedanesque reading that concentrates on the travails of white middle-class women.

As legal scholar Elizabeth Iglesias maintains, white middle-class feminists may favor increasing women's opportunities outside of the domestic sphere, an orientation that has resulted in a conservative backlash against these supposedly negligent mothers and selfish wives. Their critics conveniently overlook the greater roles that men can play in homemaking for the sake of a fairer distribution of labor within heterosexual couples. Iglesias contends that a "lack of individual freedom (even from gendered obligations) is not the same as lack of power, autonomy, or agency" (Iglesias 510). When a woman states her desire to become a homemaker or at least devote a significant portion of time to home-related matters, some may look askance at her, suggesting her decision to be "a waste of talent," a capitulation to patriarchal expectations of the past, and a source of future regret. These kinds of judgments, when lacking nuance, would suggest a dearth of understanding of women's differences and a homogenization of the so-called feminist agenda to empty homes of women for their own good. When British writer Virginia Woolf (1882–1941) famously voiced the need for women to have spaces in which to write and think—hence the title of her seminal essay *A Room of One's Own* (1929)—she clearly did not mean to suggest that a woman would clean the home and then proceed to sit down in the selfsame space to write about the very endeavor of cleaning. The recursivity involved in such an exercise would seem a bit too postmodern for a poet invested in the value of tradition, but it does appear to correspond to an important thematic facet of Espaillat's *Where Horizons Go* (1998) and *Her Place in These Designs*, the latter standing out as the most explicitly gender-centric of her poetry collections. Espaillat's work questions the extent to which it is possible or desirable for a woman to choose the home as imaginative incubator, not because she has to, but out of sheer will and volition.

Preference for work outside of the home does not categorically bar women from staying at home. Not every woman, let alone every Latina, wants to leave the home, especially if it is a space where she is comfortable and productive. This is the difference between being "at home" and being "in the house." Among other locations of power, Espaillat views the home as an artistic workshop and a sanctuary. Lessons drawn from writings by feminists of color on the notion of home enable us to identify elements in Espaillat's verse—much of which is autobiographical—that align with what we might call a *complementary domesticity*. This term encompasses a paradigm of empowerment that describes the location of the (Latina) subject who can remain domestically minded without subscribing to the ideologies that deprive her of alternatives in the public sphere. In that respect, her social location differs from the positions evoked by such terms as *marianismo*, understood as cultural values that encode the woman's dutiful subservience to the patriarchal regime.

In her essay "Homeplace: A Site of Resistance," black feminist writer bell hooks insists that the home need not be synonymous with a jail. For women of color especially, home may serve as a "site of resistance and liberation struggle" that, while still privy to personal constraints and gender politics, should be a place where white bourgeois norms do not necessarily predominate (hooks, *Yearning* 47). hooks theorizes that "home is no longer just one place. It is locations. Home is that place which enables and promotes varied and ever-changing perspectives, a place where one discovers new ways of seeing reality, frontiers for difference" (148). On the other hand, the aforementioned Loida Maritza Pérez, author of the semiautobiographical novel *Geographies of Home* (1999), defines the concept as an internal phenomenon forged from "bits and pieces of all the people that I love, all the places that I love." Her understanding is intensely subjective: "anyplace can become home if I have home within myself" (Chancy 17–18). Alison Blunt and Robyn Dowling observe that feminist geographies of home are able to differentiate and accommodate this fluidity, understanding the variations between the material space, the metaphorical connections, and the effects lived experiences have on "support[ing] and shut[ting] down identities" of women from various walks of life (Blunt and Dowling 20–21).

Our concept of complementary domesticity in the case of Espaillat reiterates the need for women's self-definitions of the homespace and affirms the Latina's right to determine how, when, and where she will enter or exit the doors and borders that constitute it. What hooks terms "the primacy of domesticity as a site for subversion" emerges in Espaillat's endorsement of Mama Polincita's professional satisfaction and *joie de vivre* without completely excluding Mama Julia's staunch (if also desperate) work ethic and personal call of duty (hooks, *Yearning* 48). The key question here seems to be whether a woman can embrace the domestic space while remaining able to discern, achieve, and pursue other options as well.

Espaillat's literary trajectory epitomizes the title of Jewish American writer Grace Paley's 1974 short story collection *Enormous Changes at the Last Minute*. Espaillat is very aware of how powerfully time constraints, coupled with awareness of her own mortality and aging body, make for an accelerated appeal to the Muse. As discussed earlier in this book, the bulk of Espaillat's adult life was spent being a teacher, wife, mother to three children, and homemaker. A commitment to domesticity, combined with teaching, prompted her to subordinate her own literary interests in a major way. This much is clear given the veritable rush of publications that followed her first full-length collection in 1992: five collections of poetry, three chapbooks, two bilingual multigeneric texts, multiple individual poems in various venues, and extensive translation work. What is quietly revolutionary about her personal timeline is that she chose her own pace; likewise, her homespace was of her own making. The question arises whether she traded her literary birthright, so to speak, for a mess of domestic pottage that was meant primarily to feed others. Espaillat denies that was the case, citing the premier importance of family in her life. While she acknowledges that some women—including Mama Julia—are oppressed in the home, she does not identify herself as one of them. Even though a consensus is difficult to reach in terms of which roles and guises are *most* empowering to Latinas, "a genuinely inclusive feminism will seriously consider these differences in the struggle over the production of alternative images of motherhood and sexuality" (Iglesias 509).

Ironically, while Espaillat's path may be deemed "traditional" given that she privileged domestic duties above her art for a good portion of her adult life, the self-certainty and volition behind her choices as a working mother strike a note of politically advanced awareness. Fellow poet Nicol has surmised that her success "resists the commonly held belief that domestic responsibilities have an oppressive and entirely negative effect on the creative spirit" (Nicol, "Rhina P. Espaillat" 105). Furthermore, the elevation of passivity and submissiveness as core aspects of *marianismo* remains inherently problematic given that it is virtually impossible to run a household without attending to manifold tasks in active, assertive ways, among them childrearing, eldercare, cleaning, cooking, and financial management, as well as other time-consuming and labor-intensive activities.

hooks stresses a multipronged approach to making the homespace more intelligible and welcoming to women: the need for domestically centered women to build meaningful communities with one another; the need for societies to understand that work at home is not the same as leisure (an equation often discernible in sexist discourses); the need to acknowledge that working at or in the home has integrity while inviting multimodal skill development from those who do; and the need for work to be flexibly connected with the nondomestic world through knowledge-sharing and network-building activities. After all, as hooks would argue, the homespace may also serve as a site for spiritual uplift and self-actualization that far surpasses the intellectual and practical resources offered by an outside workplace.

On this note, Espaillat's poetry envisions the home—and those presiding over it—as paradigmatically linked to the work of the universal mother, Earth. In line with her conservationist beliefs, many of her poems convey this sense through their numerous references to gardens and animals that exist outdoors but within the radius of the poet's residence. Espaillat captures this conceptual and experiential nexus in the very title of her first bilingual collection, *Mundo y Palabra: The World and the Word* (2001). Writer Gloria Anzaldúa casts the woman's body as a home *within* the home "by virtue of creating entities of flesh and blood in her stomach . . . in tune with nature's cycles" (27). She also explains that housework, while sometimes tedious, is also a kind of meditative practice. For Espaillat, the mundane realities of everyday life—serving as mother, wife, grandmother, senior citizen, mentor, friend, neighbor—also constitute a worthwhile topic for poetry. In the poem "For Evan, Who Says I Am Too Tidy," the speaker chides her young grandson for suggesting her fastidiousness "smacks of age and tameness, of desire / banked by gray prudence" (*Where Horizons Go* 29). She reminds him that the aged emissary of "tidy" creates the circumstances of enjoyment for others and hence should be celebrated rather than impugned. In her own defense, she reasons, "But tidy sets the table, mends the toys, / lays out clean bedding and such minor joys / as underpin contentment and at least / nourish with daily bread, if not with feast" (29). In that sense, this Dominican American *abuela* from the East Coast verily echoes the Chicana *lesbiana* Anzaldúa from the Southwest, who states, "In my head I sometimes will say a prayer—an affirmation and a voicing of intent. Then I run water, wash the dishes or my underthings, take a bath, or mop the kitchen floor" (Anzaldúa 67). Even though Espaillat avows that "tidy seldom goes where genius goes," she laughs that few ascend to glory anyhow, especially in the domain of letters, and that honest work itself merits a hearty reward: "And heaven knows / there's work for us who watch the time, the purse, / the washing of small hands" (*Where Horizons Go* 29). She hints that other forms of genius also exist beyond intellectual skills; for instance, in its older denotation, *genius* meant the spirit of generosity that propels one person to provide for another (*Oxford English Dictionary*).

Amid these instances of rhetorical self-defense, Espaillat's speaker builds up an argument that persuades even as she refuses to take herself too seriously. In "Through the Window," a poem included in *Playing at Stillness* (2005), the speaker humorously passes judgment on a pond that she deems "undisciplined." Of course, upbraiding a body of water seems fastidious if not ludicrous, but the speaker admits her folly, casting herself as someone for whom "work is waiting / and must be taken up again: this real / soberly threaded needle, socks for mating, vegetables to peel" (*Playing* 6). As these musings suggest, in Espaillat's poetry, the word engages with the world holistically without presupposing that the homespace is the site of *either* repose *or* drudgery, and that the real work of living only occurs outside of it.

WORK/LIFE, HOME/WORK: THE POLITICS OF RECOGNITION

The domestic arena's impact on literary productivity and subsequent recognition occupies American poet June Jordan (1936–2002) as well. In her essay "Where Is the Love?" Jordan decries the relative obscurity of poet Georgia Douglas Johnson as compared with the celebrity of many of her male peers during the Harlem Renaissance or more broadly, with that of many canonical Euro-American writers of the same era. She grieves the fact that work by talented women of color has failed to elicit the same critical attention as that of their white counterparts of *both* sexes: "How is it the case that whether we have written novels or poetry or whether we have raised our children or cleaned and cooked and washed and ironed, it is all dismissed as 'women's work'; it is all, finally, despised as nothing important, and there is no grace, no echo of our days upon the earth?" (Jordan 1198). Jordan's critique echoes that of hooks, not merely in that they are both contemporary black feminist writers with a stake in literary production's connection to social justice but also because they express similar frustration about endemic biases that fail to take seriously a woman of color's possible affinities for the home, dismissively construing them as a natural or expected place for her. Thus misunderstood, a woman supposedly inhabits the home without effort, thought, or appreciation, making it unnecessary for her to receive any recognition for her life or work there—unless, of course, it is for other people.

Jordan goes on to imply that artistic production is hardly distant from the domestic universe given that "homemade" creations have a long and often forgotten history; we need only think back to cottage industries to understand how painstaking and labor-intensive such work can be. Home work is also inextricably tied to gender-inflected self-expression. Jordan's argument pinpoints the often thankless nature of domestic work, paid or unpaid, and the way its lesser significance translates into a curtailed sense of relevance and self-worth, especially for women of color. The assault on self-worth worsens when we consider the ephemeral nature of the worker's achievement in domestic labor, which, unlike more high-profile types of endeavor (for instance, scientific breakthroughs or corporate empire building), appears to leave but a meager mark on the slate of posterity ("no echo of our days upon the earth"). When a woman fails in the domestic arena, she is more likely to be given public attention, such as being cast as a slovenly, careless, rebellious, unfeminine, and generally "bad" role model.

Espaillat's repositioning of domestic work as a legitimate topic for writing and, indeed, as legitimate substitute *for* it partially addresses Jordan's concerns. The homespace may even function as a training ground for creative endeavors. Espaillat's oft-cited poem "Workshop" constitutes a reasoned response to a friend's query about what she has been doing for the past few decades in lieu of writing:

> Well, I've been coring apples, layering them
> in raisins and brown sugar; I've been finding
> what's always lost, mending and brushing,
> pruning houseplants, remembering birthdays.
> ...
> Spoon-fed to me each evening, history
> puts on my children's faces, because they
> are the one alphabet all of me reads.
> I've been setting the table for the dead. (*Rehearsing* 34)

Visual artists, including Espaillat's late sculptor husband, typically have a studio or other specialized space in which to concentrate on creative work. It is differentiated (even literally separated) from the living environment based on the assumption that the daily motions of "coring apples," "mending and brushing," and "pruning houseplants" do not relate to the creative spirit and may be distractions—if not downright impediments—to the artistic process. This kind of thinking is corroborated by the distinct class statuses assigned to such activities.

Cooking and cleaning typically do not command massive salaries and may be viewed as menial labor. Studios and practice rooms, let alone extra space in general, are scarce in economically depressed households. Of course, the view of art as requiring isolation risks representing the creative act as a narrowly conceived, even elitist feat, akin to passing straws of hay through the spindle of a rarified consciousness in order to yield gold. The friend's query about Espaillat's "lost" years presupposes her internalization of this paradigm. But instead of construing the question as a reproach that elicits regret, shame, or embarrassment, the speaker finds herself propelled into a kind of self-reflexive metapositionality: a poet meditating in verse on the relationship between her poetry and other facets of her life. These are facets that actually fuel her creative fire rather than dampen it. "Workshop" acknowledges that daily life can be central to art just as art can be central to daily life. Critic and poet Leslie Monsour makes the case succinctly: "The poem is also, in part, a vindication of the ordinary and domestic as legitimate themes for art of every kind, including poetry" (Monsour, *Rhina Espaillat* 82).

Espaillat elevates the quotidian, task-oriented, concrete world of the home by attributing to it the consolidated capacities of workshop, classroom, office, and even tangentially, place of worship. All of these sites function as locations where the self comes face to face with its limits, including—and especially—of knowledge, the body, consciousness, and time. In "Workshop," the speaker reads her children's faces like letters of an alphabet, and because these youngsters are products of her body, she is essentially learning self-literacy as well. The eerie image of history donning the children's faces like a macabre body snatcher offers a sobering reminder that we all become "history" through death, which also claims those individuals closest to us as the years pass. Death sits and eats at any table, the poet reminds us, and the work of artists is to mediate the shock of mortality by setting a place for it in our stead.

In other words, the busy-ness of ordinary life becomes the business of artists such as Espaillat. Through the oddly reductive trope of being "spoon-fed" history, she urges readers to recognize that each of us must continue to learn what appears simple and fundamental, like eating or memorizing an alphabet. Sometimes the choice is not even ours, as the poet suggests by including the acts of being fed as an adult and (re)learning one's ABCs. These are two instances that bring old age and childhood full circle as states of dependency and newness by turns. Setting the table for the dead is mildly frightening in the way a Día de los Muertos mask (*calaca*) is when it acts to commemorate the passed/past. A smiling death's head garlanded with brilliant but fast-fading flowers, it laments the departed while celebrating the living's memories of them. In this spirit of recognition, Espaillat's speaker views the time she could have spent writing as reconfigured, not lost.

Evocative of the 1966 short story "Where Are You Going, Where Have You Been?" by prolific American fiction writer Joyce Carol Oates, Espaillat's "Workshop" begins with very similar queries: "'Where have you been . . .' / 'and what have you been doing?'" (*Rehearsing* 34). In Oates's much-anthologized text, a teenager named Connie undergoes a kind of accelerated aging because of a misogynistic, consumerist environment that "cons" her into believing her looks are "everything" (Oates 293). There is only one question mark in the title because the first query, which is future-oriented, requires the second's historical sense to approximate any fullness of response. However short and superficial it may be, Connie's life deserves at least that much depth of inquiry. Ironically, the questions about the teen's whereabouts might be posed with equal legitimacy to an elderly person with Alzheimer's, like the poet's own mother.

This intergenerational parallel invites further comparisons between Oates's story and Espaillat's chilling poem "January '41." The unnamed child in the piece resembles Connie in that both texts feature a male sexual predator targeting a female minor. The encroaching adult in the poem calls the child "Little girl," an affectionate epithet used by Oates's ironically named villain, Arnold Friend. Both young females also experience a bifurcation between the acting body and the witnessing mind. Just as in Espaillat's poem, the victim feels "numb and cold / as in a dream through which my body went / unmoving" (*Her Place* 7), the corresponding passage in Oates's story features Connie stepping as if drugged into the arms of her would-be rapist and possible murderer: "She watched herself push the door slowly open as if she were safe back somewhere in the other doorway, watching this body and this head of long hair moving out into the sunlight where Arnold Friend waited" (Oates 308). Each scenario attests to the precariousness of life for young women in environments where a perverse lust for their bodies subsumes any consideration for their minds and right to safe existence.

FRESH FRUIT: "EVANISMO" AS ALTERNATIVE TO *MARIANISMO*

During an interview, Espaillat expressed horror at the December 2012 gang rape and eventual death of a young female student named Jyoti Singh on a bus in New

Delhi. This disturbing incident led to worldwide outrage, renewed attention to the pervasive role of patriarchy in this simultaneously modern and ancient society, and a call by Indian citizens for their government to implement harsher penalties for sex-related crimes (Kang 186). Conversations also emerged about the greater need for protection of women in public spaces, particularly mass transportation. This is not an odd idea considering the force of tradition that persistently questions why women need to be outside the home. Preferring them to stay clear of working in professional environments alongside men, patriarchal tradition construes them as "inviting" trouble by being active in public spaces during evening hours. One brand of harassment experienced there, as NPR reporter Julie McCarthy elucidates, is "Eve-teasing," or the "everyday sexist abuse of India's everywoman, or 'Eve' as the Biblical name denotes" (McCarthy). This is powerfully allusive naming in a country that is not majority Judeo-Christian. The connotations of Eve here are less sacred or laudatory than ironic and mocking. When they are summoned to atone for their disobedience against God, Adam blames his wife, while Eve points to the snake as the instigator of the entire debacle (Gray, Meyers, and Wolpe, "Commentaries"). Everywoman Eve comes across as a naïve dupe, an undiscerning victim of a wily man/snake who stands as a living platform for the continual ritual enactment of masculine mastery in the most quotidian of spaces: streets, public transit, theaters, shops, parks, and offices.

Similarly, Eve-teasing at once highlights the sexuality of the victimized women in order to embarrass, belittle, and threaten them, thereby progressively eroding any form of sexual confidence they might have. They are thus made aware—even hyperconscious—of masculinity as possessive and dominative rather than complementary, nurturing, or collaborative. This inheritance of punishing women for sexuality yet encouraging a culture of straight male spectatorship of women's bodies has been amply supported by the femme fatale archetype and its variants: the fallen woman/whore, the Jezebel, the precocious nymphet, the mysterious harem dancer, the coy geisha, and so on. Of course, other forces like the intersectional concerns of race, class, and generation are at play here as well, but even the mythic Medusa, with her fatally serpentine hair, conveys how the threateningly powerful female must be cut down to size for fear of male paralysis or female domination. While the popular tale of Perseus uses the decapitated gorgon to amplify his male heroics, Ovid's version of the story in *The Metamorphoses* relates how Medusa started off as a ravishing woman who found herself victimized through sexual violence—and by a god, no less. It is ironic that she remains so emblematic of dangerous women (literally arresting men with her gaze) and the body part so brutally excised from the monstress's body should serve as a reminder to *men* about their need to protect themselves from fatal violence. It is also emblematic of a legacy of sexist bullying and outright misogyny that prompts women to think twice before seeking out sexual knowledge on their own terms. Espaillat believes that "all these snake stories are really warnings to women: be careful. It's like the awful operations that take place in many parts of the world that keep women from being fully sexual" (Kang 188).

A further irony is that women, in Eve's blundering shadow, may often be interpreted in art and popular culture as temptresses of men, with emphasis placed on their physical attributes rather than their intellectual gifts. In Genesis 3:5-6, the snake promises that the fruit will "make [her] wise" and her "eyes shall be open, and [she] shall be as gods, knowing good and evil" (*Bible* 4). Thus it could be argued that, if anything, instead of keeping her arcane, forbidden knowledge to herself, she opts to share it with her partner, making her a democratically minded disseminator and ostensibly more of a *teacher* than a seductress. To her credit, had it not been for Eve's actions and presence, neither love, sex, warfare, nor shame would have existed. As Rabbi David Wolpe points out, Eve offered a welcome respite from humanity's first emotion, which was a negative one: loneliness. And while less misogynistic perspectives can be—and have been— taken of the *felix culpa* (fortunate fall) to construe Eve's actions as necessary to humanity's eventual salvation through divine forgiveness, the stigma against her remains for posterity. She represents the source of our first disobedience, with Adam willing to eat the fruit she offers instead of following divine edict himself, thereby letting terrestrial love supersede metaphysical duty.

Espaillat supplemented her concerns about Singh's victimization with a nod to concurrent activism in 2012 by American writer Julia Alvarez. The author of *In the Time of the Butterflies* (1994), a historical novel about the Mirabal sisters who fought against the Trujillo dictatorship, Alvarez was campaigning on behalf of women in the Dominican Republic over proposed changes that would have increased female vulnerability had these amendments become part of the penal code. Among other prospects, emotional harassment would have been excluded from definition as a form of abuse, and abortion would have been deemed illegal under any circumstances (Alvarez, "La ñapa"). Gender-based violence creates a shameful continuity between this Caribbean nation and the aforementioned South Asian nation.

Espaillat, embracing a global ideal of gender parity, reflects in particular on how metanarratives like sinning Eve and sinned-against Adam create a false dichotomy and Manichean sense of gender difference. As with *marianismo*, the expectations and biases are skewed against the female. One way for Espaillat to fight back as an artist has been through her Creation poems, particularly notable examples of which may be found in *Where Horizons Go* and *Her Place in These Designs*. Espaillat's Creation poems attempt to depolarize the heavily bifurcated gender roles in the story. She identifies a fundamental coexistence of attributes in all people, an intriguing point given that in human genetics, all embryos begin in utero as female: "'In the men there is something female, and in the women there is something male.' Because, you know, we're a continuum; no one is strictly one or the other. We all have each other's traits" (Kang 187). This is a decidedly contemporary, even queer reading of gender dimorphism in the First Couple. Because Eve was derived from Adam's rib, some may argue that this model works, but along the lines of her being an exegete to his original. Espaillat is not so far off the mark with her continuum: if Eve really did emerge from such asexual reproduction, then maleness—as well as divinity—must be sources of the female, and as such, the two sexes cannot be so radically different.

Espaillat's evocation of a hybridized gender continuum may remind some readers of queer theorist Jack Halberstam's paradigm of "female masculinities," which posits a range of gender identities that supersede the typical binary configuration. This range includes types of "genderqueerness" and ways of negotiating gender roles in conjunction with other fluctuating, historically contextualized forms of identity, thereby accounting for the intersectionality of race, gender, and class (Halberstam 48). Though the product of critical thought generated in LGBT studies, a field that gained currency long after Espaillat completed her formal education, genderqueernesss does correspond to the coexistence that the poet describes in her model. Genderqueerness encompasses all that challenges, disrupts, and transcends the male/female binary; it need not correlate with what is denoted by the word *transgender* (Nestle, Howell, and Wilchins).

Espaillat goes on to grapple with the snake motif, typically understood as phallic and masculine in Western cultures. The poet reconstructs a decidedly modern view of the Adam and Eve story from Genesis, speaking in the sonnet "If You Ask Me" from the snake's perspective. The easiest avenue of feminist response would have been to feature Eve articulating her own concerns about being blamed for "the fall of man," but Espaillat eschews the glib predictability of such a scenario. The subversive assumption informing the poem is that typical Christians would tend not to inquire after the "me" for its opinion, inasmuch as the snake has traditionally represented Satan in disguise. The titular phrase is also reminiscent of gossips who offer unsolicited observations and advice, butting their heads into conversations that really do not concern them. As such, this serpentine representation of uninvited participation is perhaps more human than many would wish to acknowledge. While not creating a heroine out of Eve, the poem adds complexity to her character; it is precisely the lack of unity between the couple that leaves her a willing listener to Satan's forked tongue. Thus, the imperfect domestic circumstances of the couple—not Eve's actions alone—are inextricable from her victimization. In the first line, the snake confides to the reader that the pair appears "doomed" because they are so subservient and meek, taking orders from God without any dialogic interaction with their Maker. The reptile scoffs, "They started naked, not a thing to need, / a thing to wonder at / since orders boomed over the speaker" (*Where Horizons Go* 1). The poem then rhymes "blind" and "mind," which suggests that the innocence of these new beings seems constraining as well as liberating. Just as they could be led forward obliviously as if blind, their lack of awareness of precedents frees them from comparisons and leaves all options open in terms of imagination. The snake characterizes Eve as an intelligent woman "bored out of her mind," someone who plays stupidly with her hair while her husband "gawk[s] at birds and flap[s] in vain" (1). Adam's antics, situated somewhere between clownish and childish, convey the need for something more stimulating in his life as well. Perhaps his imitative zeal is meant to communicate his malleability and a concomitant willingness to try something new, thereby foreshadowing his taste for the forbidden fruit.

This incomplete happiness is a very different picture from the one associated, for instance, with the Edenic bliss depicted in John Milton's *Paradise Lost* (1667) or even in Espaillat's own poem "Blest among Women Was Eve." The latter is a short meditation on how Eve enjoys being in love because of the sheer novelty of the feeling, as she knows of nothing else. In contrast, contemporary women may come to marriage "with strange sorrow, / as if Eden were lost" because of the burden of mythological strife and the premonition that passionate love cannot last forever (*Shadow* 5). Unlike Eve, their minds are not blank slates but rather palimpsests, with memories piled on top of past experiences, some of which will never be effaced completely.

In "If You Ask Me," the snake deploys a fruit metaphor, stating that the humble gardener Eve is "ripe to risk herself" by moving beyond the confines of the life she knows (*Where Horizons Go* 1). Instead of blaming her for being tempted, the poem praises the woman for being inquisitive enough to venture beyond the "estate, so green, so plain" (1). The text also acknowledges that perhaps she did so not because of an innate flaw but rather through curiosity and loneliness. While the notion of the fortunate fall is hardly new, Espaillat specifically underscores the salutary effect of Original Sin on Adam: "they need to die; / unbanished, he's an ornament, a brute" (1).

Most surprising is the poet's choice to make the Satanic agent both pleasant and observant, even cleverly ironic. In the very last line, the trickster figure grinningly declares an intention to "go visiting, with fruit," since that is what "neighbors" might verily do (1). Instead of muttering oaths, criticizing God, or leering at Eve's body, this genteel snake emerges as a kind of understated hero, a suave manipulator and con artist. It not only targets these human "marks" in an ambitious way, it also facilitates the salvation of the couple for all posterity. Satan, after all, was an angel once. Although we know the outcome of this "neighborliness," Espaillat does not go so far as to rewrite the Creation story; she does, however, add depth and a resistant reading to Eve's construction as a foolish woman guilty of humanity's first sin. Instead of focusing on the sinner, Espaillat inquires, what were the circumstances of the sin? She follows in the contestatory footsteps of other woman of color feminists who have critiqued the skewed, misogynistic portrayal.

Another Creation poem by Espaillat, a sestina titled "As She Tells It," constantly repeats the word *clearing* (*Her Place* 40–41). This word denotes a meadow, a space of freedom, and a desire for absolution or cleansing, among other possible meanings. Another example of repeated diction is *recalcitrant*, a more nuanced choice than the frequently used synonym *stubborn*. The echo between the titles of this and the aforementioned poem is undeniable as they both concentrate on different versions of the same story. Eve is no radical feminist separatist; she expresses love for her partner and acknowledges that he, in a sense, gave birth to her through a kind of divine midwifery: "the wound in his side that closed / after God drew me out of him." The very metaphors of birth and midwifery are typically identified as women's work, so they contribute to Espaillat's implicit endorsement of Eve as integral to the functioning of the newly created world. She also acknowledges Adam's sexuality as comforting: "the sweet recalcitrant / pull of him afterwards that always / felt like a return." Eve is obedient in the sense of participating in the labors of the garden clearing. One supposes the garden clearing was home, so both she and Adam were domestically inclined. But, the woman admits, "I could not always / run to God's call, as he did," adding later that she lingered "with questions, brooding doubts, recalcitrant / to law and season even as they bound me, closed." In this atmosphere of endemic constraint, she confesses, "thought was my clearing."

The central irony underlying this open/closed dichotomy is that Eve is actually open—critically open—while Adam is not. He epitomizes something akin to the happy servant at best and contented slave at worst. The poem explains: "He went willing and joyful to the clearing, / worked it to order" (40). Adelaida R. del Castillo considers this broad duality in the context of gender stereotypes in Mexico, a relevant perspective because Adam's obedience may be compared to humble indigenous peasant Juan Diego's attitude toward la Virgen de Guadalupe. In the traditional Mexican household, the obedience expectations in terms of gender tend to be that females defer to the males. Del Castillo explores how in prevailing Mexican gender ideologies, the meanings of open and closed are also quite different: the woman is open, vulnerable, needy, and sexually penetrable; the man is closed, protective, self-sufficient, and sexually penetrating (del Castillo 500).

Another ideology that feminist scholars regard as important among the sources of indoctrination for Latina domesticity is *familismo*, or the "family-first" mentality. This belief system can be circumscriptive because, like *marianismo*, it "keep[s] Latinas right here within our own *fronteras* (borders), hiding behind the proverbial priva[te] closet door of family" (Hernández-Truyol 536). Borders and doors are tropes that signify securing something in while keeping something else out. Borders tend to be grand-scale and associated with geopolitical discourses, while doors usually refer to entry and exit points for buildings or rooms. When circumscriptive, these two encompass the economic, cultural, and physical constraints endured by women. They render the home a private space, but that privacy does not guarantee the comfort, affirmation, or stability typically connoted by the term *home*. Rather, Hernández-Truyol's phrase "closet door of family" implies a kind of commingled secrecy and shame *held in* that is not too distant from the motif that queer theorist and literary critic Eve Kosofsky Sedgwick examined in her book *The Epistemology of the Closet* (1990). Instead of referring to nonnormative sexualities and the schism between self-knowledge and public knowledge, however, the metaphorical architecture that Hernández-Truyol evokes is one in which victims of domestic abuse at home—as well as perpetrators and witnesses, to some degree—hide because of the perceived need to keep private matters private. Loyalty to family and the fear of public ostracism serve as the hinges of the closet door, and women are caught in the uncomfortable liminality of the threshold because they can lose out whichever way they step. Beyond threats of violence, there are such access-related issues as precarious citizenship status or language difficulties that discourage vocal resistance and perpetuate the challenges US Latinas face in gaining mainstream social support away from family.

Del Castillo quotes the passage in *Labyrinth of Solitude*, the influential 1950 essay by Nobel Prize–winning Mexican poet and writer Octavio Paz (1914–1998), that states, "The female . . . is pure passivity, defenseless against the exterior world" (Paz 29–30). As such, women must be protected and contained, a state of vulnerability captured by Espaillat in such lines as "we played like children, learned, recalcitrant / as buried stones, those rules we kept" (*Her Place* 40). For Espaillat, the private becomes public through a swinging door of language, namely the vocabulary and freedom of personal disclosure. What differentiates silent sufferers and speaking resistors is the capacity to pass through borders *and* doors. Espaillat's vision for women's empowerment involves traversing these arenas via the language of social critique.

It is possible to argue that Espaillat's poem rewrites the biblical creation story as an allegory of domestic containment, making both humans gendered female and hence living behind closed, guarded gates to God's *ür*-male. They are the inside, He is the outside; they are human Eves to His divine Adam. It is the woman, thus, who initiates their (re)gendering through her rule-breaking and risky "mistake." She genders herself male by her experimentation and knowledge-seeking behavior. The closing of the gates of Paradise leads to the "mind clearing itself free," culminating in a physical banishment from Eden (*Her Place* 41). Eve recounts a harrowing scenario resonant with any number of carceral scenes from recent history. The difference, of course, is that the humans are locked *out* rather than in:

> The gates were closed
> the woods outside them dark, searchlights always
> combing the sky, the borders of our clearing
> towered and sentried. The end of it—the *clearing*
> *of his good name*, as Adam called the sword
> of his confession and betrayal. (*Her Place* 41)

A contrast to the sword-wielding angel who protects the garden, Eve sets about using language as a weapon ("recalcitrant / words learning to be a sword") to arm herself against her husband's patronizing attitude ("unforgiveable forgiveness"), the disapprobation of her Heavenly Father, and the disturbing implications of equating the desire for knowledge with disobedience and subversion (41).

As much as Eve's choices become generalized as women's weakness, Adam's pride and arrogance also complicate his gender identity, but these leave no lasting legacy for which men have had to atone. Espaillat's Adam is flawed but not flat: he feels keen disappointment in himself for failing to be an obedient child of God. He also senses his own privilege because like God, he helped to create Eve and should thus be above her, commanding her submission to his microcosm of patriarchal power. He feels ambivalence toward his partner because love for her fueled his indiscretion, making him look poorly to their mutual Father. Eve, on the other hand, admits *with pride* that she "did the thing that closed / that brief first chapter" of their lives (41). Nowhere in the speaker's account is the character vying to appropriate or outperform her husband in terms of his *raison d'être*, which is to be an excellent worker. Her approach is less competitive than corrective of Adam's primary deficiency, one which is intellectual rather than physical. Eve criticizes him for naming without "find[ing] things behind [the] names" (40). She declares that "thought was [her] clearing" once she lost interest in gardening (40). Adam might be contented in his pursuit of routine work and profound faith, but her mind wanders—less sheep than shepherd—into a new clearing. Her choices—social engagement and risk-taking—did not pay off in the short run, but in the long run, closing the door to compulsory obedience opened the door to critical thinking. Of what use are deeds without thoughts, she asks. Her intrepid act opened the gates to self-awareness and called attention to the need for personal accountability. This achievement might be termed *evanismo*, derived from the Spanish word for Eve, a counter to *marianismo* and a means of reconfiguring women's supposed weakness into a source of long-held, underacknowledged, and indubitable strength.

Perhaps the most important injunction from the Creation story broadly is to open doors to the forgiveness of others, a fundamental Christian value not readily demonstrated in these poems by the banishing Patriarch, whom the poet has colloquially termed "Big Daddy" (NK/STS). The epithet is freighted with both deference and distaste, while the chastisement received by the couple pushes readers to reassess the nature of this Old Testament God, whom Nicol describes as being "too distant and hardly trustworthy" enough for Espaillat's taste (Nicol, "Rhina P. Espaillat" 109). Nicol also evokes Jan Schreiber's take on the poet's resistant attitude toward God: Espaillat "attempts to invoke the feeling of a remembered religious heritage while retaining the skepticism and ironic detachment that shape her primary perception" (Schreiber 41). This sort of critical consciousness deviates from the attitude that might be expected of a woman married for more than six decades to the same man starting in 1952. If an impulse to partake in some "Adam-teasing" does exist, it is likely in the spirit of furthering discussion about the ways in which men and women need to cultivate complementarity as well as conjugal autonomy rather than insisting on neatly contrastive notions of place and selfhood as being "what God intended."

RETURNING TO OUR MOTHERS' GARDENS

In "Current," a poem that immediately—and perhaps deliberately—follows "If You Ask Me" in *Where Horizons Go*, an unnamed contemporary speaker talks about the cord of a coffeemaker and how it is "coiled to spring" at her as she peers at it in the darkness (2). This serpentine imagery arises from a rather unspectacular domestic setting, but Espaillat likens the kitchen to the Garden of Eden. She parallels the painful literal shock that comes from ignorant childhood inquisitiveness with the figurative shock that accompanies the acquisition of new knowledge. The older female "I" recalls her childhood experience of sticking a metal hairpin in an electrical socket. Thus "probing the wall's secrets," she finds herself chastised by "an angry god" (2). More mature but no less excitable, she shivers with the repressed memory that returns in the form of an oddly predatory electrical cord, a kind of ghostly umbilicus to a more naïve past and distant ancestress, Eve. The parent-child analogy suggests that the god-human relationship is one of guardianship and punishing authority, but the personification or even deification of electricity (literally, power) is both enlightening and disturbing because we are not quite sure who the "angry god" is. The poet adds sexual nuance to the divine power, conflating the "angry god" as Christian Father with Satan the devilish tempter.

More specifically, the speaker recalls how, as a child being electrocuted, she received "a licking all over / by fire, a rod of ice in the marrow" (2). The "rod" here evokes the old-fashioned hickory stick yielded by an authority figure (usually a teacher, principal, or parent), but is doubly suggestive of the phallic rod of the metaphorical molester/monster from which the child hides "night after night" to avoid this "licking" (2). While "lick" denotes a beating in more antiquated phrasing, the invasive act becomes even more complex and morally loaded in conjunction with the snake image, as such creatures use their tongues as sensory wands, simultaneously testing, tasting, and smelling the air for prey. The result is being literally and figuratively burned by knowledge that has a distinctly sexual flavor: "in dreams, flicking your quick tongue / lewdly from the safety of familiar things; / you crouch in my walls; you ripple your braid of / muscle among dark leaves in the mind's garden" (2).

The flicking tongue "lewdly" induces discomfort in the speaker, not merely because it was frightening to be electrocuted, but also because the encounter remains perversely memorable as an initiation rite into a world of cautious (sexual) knowing. Because Adam cannot monopolize her mental space, the Eve-like speaker is able to linger erotically on the rippling muscle that insinuates itself among the "dark leaves" of her mental garden. Perhaps herein lies some liberation, however fleeting. The power morphs into a "braid of muscle" that moves stealthily through the narrator's mental garden, the coiling now less phallic than cerebral like pulsing, intricately twisted brain matter. Made of three interwoven strands, the braid offers a symbolic parallel between the triangulation of Adam, Eve, and God with the speaker, her past fears, and her current awareness, all captured ambiguously in the title "Current."

Undergirding the power struggle between the First Couple and their heavenly Master is the reality that both individuals are sexual beings. This premise is something that shuts God out as a participant, even though He may be a witness. For conservative Christians, sex is one form of knowledge that is forbidden outside of the bonds of marriage, but as the speaker in "Current" bristles at being stalked and harassed (electrically Eve-teased), this sense of victimization oscillates between annoyance and curious pleasure. The literal shock of experience renders her more vigilant to her surroundings and appreciative of the vulnerability—and value—of her life and body. She learns that knowledge is not neutral insofar as the electricity could have dealt her a final, fatal lesson. At the same time, knowledge also surrounds her spatially; it can be everywhere and nowhere, much like divine power. She considers how ubiquitous the force of electricity is, as if Lucifer himself, whose name is derived from "light" (and also, one manifestation of electrical power), ambushes her wherever she goes.

Beyond expulsion from Eden, another facet of their punishment is the need to cover their nakedness and intimacy, a self-consciousness that links moral mistakes with sexual transgression. Their postlapsarian intimacy bears the stamp of sin and the results of their union, children, emerge only through Eve's labor pains, an unpleasant and unequal punishment visited only upon the woman's body. This scenario is a thoroughly *unerotic* evolution of what used to be a natural, unfettered enjoyment of each other's bodies. Eve's perpetual sin is perhaps why "fallen woman" is a contemporary epithet signifying sexual immorality even when the woman may not have been the instigator and no such comparable epithet as "fallen man" targets expressions of male sexuality as irreparable misconduct. Furthermore, contemporary society views sexual precocity in children—especially girls—with unequal disapproval and employs such phrases as "getting herself in trouble" for teen pregnancy, enacting the same Edenic model of wayward children needing the moral guidance of a larger, overarching male authority in order to return to the fold of the acceptable and the good.

The memory of this first supposed human transgression, Eve's foolhardiness, dies hard; it is a legacy meant to rein in the subject, making her cautious and passive rather than assertive and daring. That is why the sense of being surrounded by a hotly wired house is fundamentally carceral—constraining like a cell, compound, or enclosure—while the "garden of the mind" offers release, being more permeable, personal, and equivalent to a sanctuary, refuge, and homespace. "Current" returns to the idea that Espaillat enunciated earlier when discussing rape and female genital mutilation in a global context: there are constant warnings to women about sex as forbidden knowledge. The so-called sins of voluntarily partaking in or enjoying sex are akin to tasting "forbidden fruit"; as such, dire punishments are more than likely, usually from an angry father/God, especially for women.

The fruit/knowledge/sexuality connection participates in an exhausting discourse of normative patriarchal privilege, as women have often been compared to fruit themselves, going through such processes as budding, blooming, ripening, plucking, being deflowered, and then "eaten." In turn, they may "bear fruit" in the form of children, or alternatively "wilt on the vine" if unwanted, at least by men. Some remain "barren" like nonarable, deserted land and are thus devalued as failed women. Not all of this imagery is surprising given that in botanical terms, fruit actually is a ripened ovary. Eve's act of accepting and passing on the fruit to her partner is sexually suggestive, even gynocentric and symbolically self-serving. It is not surprising that Adam, the first man, was a gardener, thus charged with tending and harvesting fruit.

The Adam and Eve story is hermeneutically dense, whether understood as an early instance of externally mediated conjugal strife or part of a model for justifying patriarchal gender norms as divine ordinance. Espaillat's poetry tends to resist religious dogma, so the biblical creation story as she revises it is sketched in fine pencil lines rather than broad brushstrokes. Even the snake itself may be nothing more than a backyard animal struggling to live. In *Lapsing to Grace*, the poem "Treaty" has the speaker spy one such unfortunate reptile trapped in her garden-side pool. Comparing herself to the prophet Aaron, whose staff miraculously turned into a snake to prove his divine power, she humbly offers a stick of salvation to the moribund beast. After liberating the animal, the speaker muses,

> I watch him steal
> like rain into my flowerbed.
> He will not bruise my heel,
> nor I his head.
> Not every story so begun
> subverts itself to make amends,
> nor enemies have done
> to part as friends. (*Lapsing* 41)

The allusion to the fall of humanity through the Edenic encounter emerges in the lines "He will not bruise my heel, / nor I his head," which correlates with Genesis 3:15. Here, the Lord curses the snake and prophesies the ongoing metaphysical confrontation between those believing in Him and those following Satan: "And I will put enmity between you and the woman, and between your seed and her seed; it shall bruise your head, and you shall bruise his heel" (*Bible* 5). The biblical lines are notoriously cryptic, with "the woman" possibly prefiguring the Virgin Mary as antitype of Eve, whose "seed," conceivably Christ and his followers, will compete against the spawn of the Beast. Some artistic depictions of the holy mother have placed her foot on top of the snake. The forward-looking title of Espaillat's poem ("Treaty") and the gesture of goodwill on the gardener's part forecast the possible reconciliation between historical enemies, but always in an environment without certainty, hence the final stanza's qualifying, "Not every story. . . . " By casting the female gardener as savior to the snake and hence subverting the gender and ontological dynamics of the Creation story, Espaillat reminds us that it is the individual who has moral choices to make, whether to be "saved" or to save others, regardless of—or precisely because of—the cultural burdens or blessings carried by each role we play.

Finally, the poem "In the Garden" from Espaillat's *The Shadow I Dress In* refers not to the biblical story directly but to the search for what appears to be a snake in the speaker's garden. The voice speaks in the same first-person, conversational style as in "Treaty" and includes this oblique reference to a possible reptilian interloper: "his satin loop forked in a bend / of apple tree or shrugging toward the rim / of that small pool." The speaker's insistent search for the snake, "as if indeed / we had been friends," provokes the reader to recollect the encounter from the earlier collection, thereby expanding the biblical rapport of the first couple that was so iconically mediated by their ophidian enemy—or friend (*Shadow* 22).

Espaillat's versions of Creation depict a woman who, along with her husband, is essentially forced out of her home. Speaking in contemporary terms, she is not just a deportee but a refugee, a migrant, and a castaway. With a bite of fruit moving her across centuries from enclosed work in Eden to work in the terrestrial homes of any number of gardens, fields, farms, and indeed, fruit orchards, Eve is one foundational figure in a long, dissident, narrative tradition of "troublesome" women. As Anzaldúa describes them, they form part of *los atravesados/las atravesadas*: "those who cross over, pass over, or go through the confines of the 'normal'" (Anzaldúa 3). One of Eve's dilemmas is that she lacked precedents, the combined blessing and burden of being "first" in a particular tradition. Women in many societies today do not necessarily lack precedents as much as awareness of and access to them. What remains as feminist legacy should be the capacity to draw and redraw the notion of Eve's "clearing" (that is, the homespace) and the clearing of her record as perpetrator of original sin. If anything, better access to previously forbidden knowledge, especially education that remains restricted on the basis of gender, needs to be tackled with as much zeal as has been used to shame and punish women who are "in the know." Fear of being branded a *mala mujer* (bad woman) is no viable freedom for modern descendants of Eve. Perhaps a term like *evanismo*, in honor of Eve, best conveys the recuperation of Eden with a focus on women's manifold paths to self-knowledge and collective cultivation.

6 | THE SPIRIT IN THE WOUND
DECAYING BODIES AND POETIC THANATOPSIS

'The man is father to the child.'
'The child is father to the man!'
How can he be? The words are wild.
GERARD MANLEY HOPKINS, "THE CHILD IS FATHER TO THE MAN"

In our January 2013 interview at her Newburyport home, Espaillat recalled an episode when her elderly mother began to accuse a trusted maintenance worker of stealing brassieres from her dresser. Doubtful of this possibility, the daughter went to verify the claim and found the garments bedded neatly in their respective drawers, untouched from having been laundered the previous week. This was just one of the decentering moments when the poet began to experience a set of powerful paradigm shifts that would usher in a new dynamics of filiality. Chief among them was a realization of Dulce María's diminishing mental capacities, changes prompted by Alzheimer's disease. As a mother of three herself, Espaillat was forced to face the concomitant realities of parental mortality and, indirectly, personal mortality, each abstraction and impending experience shedding stark, uncomfortable light on the other.

The paradoxical title of Gerard Manley Hopkins's 1918 poem "The Child Is Father to the Man" comes to mind at this sobering juncture. In Espaillat's case, the poet "child" now realizes she is mother to the woman. Of course, she is an adult who inhabits two typically polarized familial roles: child and parent. The poignant last line of Hopkins's poem ("The words are wild") captures the psychological turmoil—indeed, ineffability—associated with losing a parent to such an unrelenting, personality-effacing disease as Alzheimer's. But whereas in Hopkins's work the ascent to parental role is triumphant, in Espaillat's it is tragic. In a similar vein, "My heart leaps up when I behold" (1802), William Wordsworth's poem that serves as intertext to Hopkins's agonic meditation, weighs the relationship between innocence and experience in a way that privileges the former but does not discount the latter. Wordsworth's speaker asserts that "the Child is father of the Man" while pointing to the speaker's own inevitable aging and death: "So be it when I shall grow old, / Or let me die!" (Wordsworth, *William* 122). Here, the processes of gaining knowledge and adding years are wedded to natural wonders rather than to any abstract mysticism. The beauty of the environment provides consolation for mortality because it reflects the ubiquity and constancy of God's love, even as our corporeal selves fade and ultimately return to the earth.

While Hopkins's speaker perhaps imagines the Christ child's "wild" incursion into the realm of humanity as salvific, like being surprised by joy, Espaillat's poetry of illness, aging, and death instantiates the "wildness" in a different way; that is, it stresses the desperation, disorientation, and emotional flux of the witnessing psyche who knows this precarious slippage between health and illness is one that she will encounter herself someday, sometime. Whether the confrontation with death will be gradual or sudden is another space of "wild" prognostication and anxiety. Wildness is a signal metaphor for the shocking precariousness of human life and the collision of the healthy body with its shadow selves: the aging, sick, debilitated, dying, and the dead.

The speaker in Espaillat's Alzheimer's-themed poems typically faces the challenge of accepting her mother's mental decay and accelerated aging by articulating the unpredictable, savage course of the illness. Finding the right words serves as a balm for the grief and guilt of the living witness. As established in preceding chapters, Espaillat started publishing her book-length manuscripts when she was nearly a senior citizen, an anomalous delay that equipped her with a worldview straddling concerns of a chronologically advanced generation as well as those of a more recent, technologically entrenched younger generation. Her overall preoccupations, then, at the social, individual, and artistic levels partake of a cross-generational engagement with the word and the world. Even from the titles of such collections as *Rehearsing Absence* (2001), *The Shadow I Dress In* (2004), and *Playing at Stillness* (2005), we gather an awareness of senescence and death both unequivocal and nuanced that encompasses the approaching end as well as the concomitant possibility of new beginnings.

Aging is everywhere, but it does not proceed in accordance with a set formula or reliable timetable. Other artists and wordsmiths, especially those interdisciplinary physician-authors who write for popular audiences as well as for colleagues, have tackled the issue from different existential angles. Finding novel ways of coming to terms with aging and death is a task that artists as well as healthcare workers and family members are drawn to, as if responding to a call to conscious action—and active consciousness—that unites the arts and sciences. Atul Gawande, a surgeon and bestselling writer, succinctly expresses the prevailing attitudes toward senescence: "People naturally prefer to avoid the subject of their decrepitude. There have been dozens of best-selling books on aging, but they tend to have titles like *Younger Next Year, The Fountain of Age, Ageless, The Sexy Years*. Still, there are costs to averting our eyes from the realities. For one thing, we put off changes that we need to make as a society. For another, we deprive ourselves of opportunities to change the individual experience of aging for the better" (Gawande, "Way").

In English-speaking North America, much talk circulates in the popular media about the plight of aging Baby Boomers, the projected stress their declining years will have on healthcare infrastructure, and the unique psychological needs of the caregiving adult cohort. The media often coin epithets like "the sandwich generation" to refer to those who are raising children while also supporting elderly parents. The stress of such dual caregiving may not immediately evoke thoughts of poetry, nor might the specificities of care associated with a given illness, let alone a fatal one like Alzheimer's. Espaillat evokes the losses associated with aging in terms of both her mother's increasingly chaotic mental state and her own body as a latent reflection of that entropic possibility. She does so by tackling assumptions about what it means to die facing medical "facts" and "truths," seeking reprieves from these threatening pronouncements through creative commentary and imaginative resistance. Poetry, after all, is one space where control can be wrested back by the individual amid the onslaught of changes brought by outside agents, human or otherwise.

Espaillat's death- and aging-themed verses form a composite poetic *thanatopsis*—a meditation on death—that transcends the didactic injunction offered by the poem "Thanatopsis" by American poet William Cullen Bryant (1794–1878). The crux of the argument in Bryant's piece lies in its assurance that, unsightly as the idea of death might be, we will not face our mortality alone. He is referring to the countless streaming masses we will join in the grave and the innumerable others who will accompany us after we have departed. Building on the age-old representation of death as the great equalizer, assuring us that everybody else, irrespective of wealth, power, prestige, talent, learning, or beauty, will meet the same fate, the poem imagines the accepting state of mind with which we should ideally approach the end of our days:

> So live, that when thy summons comes to join
> The innumerable caravan, that moves
> To the pale realms of shade, where each shall take
> His chamber in the silent halls of death,
> Thou go not, like the quarry-slave at night,
> Scourged to his dungeon, but sustain'd and sooth'd
> By an unfaltering trust, approach thy grave,
> Like one who wraps the drapery of his couch
> About him, and lies down to pleasant dreams. (Bryant 675)

Espaillat's composite thanatopsis turns mortality into a site of inquiry about our lives as projects of possibility. Her discourse seeks to move beyond the fatalistic circularity of assuming that because of death's inevitability, we must accept it willingly and, by our meager actions, bring to coldly comforting fruition that which has always been foretold.

DANSE MACABRE

The pain of Alzheimer's disease for the witness is centered on the patient's loss of abstract and higher-level intellectual capacities, including memory, and uncharacteristic changes in behavior. The effacement of personality deals a particularly painful blow. Surgeon-writer Sherwin B. Nuland (1930–2014) observed in his bestselling *How We Die: Reflections on Life's Final Chapter* (1994) that the progression of the illness is relentless and affects more than just the sufferer: "Each family needs help to understand the viciousness of the attack not only on the patient himself but on those who stand with him. Not that help of any sort should be expected to provide release from the torment—it can only make the suffering understandable and offer some respite from the ordeal" (107). With a rapidly aging population, the knowledge that others are enduring similar struggles remains key to a sense of mutual comfort and perseverance for family, friends, and caregivers. The prevalence is expected to increase "nearly four-fold to between 4.2 and 15.4 million whereas annual incidence is expected to rise from 360,000 new cases in 1997 to 1.14 million in 2047" (Bloom, Pouvourville, and Straus 158). Nuland goes on to suggest that diagnosis—"the pronouncement of the words that give the alarming symptoms a name"—is the first step to bringing those witnesses back to a conversation with "the millions of others who walk alongside them" (107). Here, the doctor is the hero, offering one discursive avenue whereby the patient's loved ones gain access to answers. The effect is almost Adamic, naming that which marks the end of ignorance and descent into sometimes bitter knowing.

Diagnosis also attempts to offer a measure of certainty for something whose course may be mysterious and unpredictable, eschewing easy answers. This space of uncertainty is the bailiwick of the creative writer, a contrast to the self-assuredness, perhaps even hubris, conveyed eloquently when physician Ken Murray differentiates the final leave taking of doctors from that of the layperson: "For all the time they spend fending off the deaths of others, they tend to be fairly serene when faced with death themselves. They know exactly what is going to happen, they know the choices, and they generally have access to any sort of medical care they could want. But they go gently" (Murray). This heroic characterization of doctors, like the wounded warrior who makes the choice to perish valiantly in battle, may be self-serving, but it also illustrates the sense of helplessness that terminal illness sufferers and their supporters face whatever their occupation or current state of knowledge.

The schism between the desire for certainty and the tolerance, even appreciation, for uncertainty is the differentiating factor between Nuland's "medical certainty" approach to witnessing and narrating death and the nonmedical, "poetic uncertainty" approach characteristic of Espaillat's thanatoptic verse. What differentiates her take from those of many of the popular physician-writers is her attitude toward uncertainty: she invites, encourages, and even celebrates it. While this force is perhaps a liability or source of great anxiety in medicine, where the physician is perpetually relied upon to be correct, the poet finds the acts of questioning the certainties of aging, illness, and death to be a comforting source of subversion. The stubborn persistence of the imagination gives her speakers leave to push back against the seemingly inevitable and the arrogantly self-certain.

In "Review," one of the longest poems in *Where Horizons Go*, Espaillat's speaker finds herself disturbed by Nuland's *How We Die* because the latter articulates mortality in a way that chafes against her emotional and ethical sensibilities. She starts out mildly annoyed by the *New York Times* reviewer's "liberal quotes" from the book, offering a tongue-in-cheek assessment instead: "'Heart failure, lung collapse,' more, in clear prose / with nothing softened and no truth left out" (*Where Horizons Go* 32). The chapters of Nuland's work narrate the devastating course of such illnesses as cancer, heart failure, Alzheimer's, HIV/AIDS, and sudden death (by homicide or suicide). The writing style is notable for its assertive and precise "doctor-prose," which the speaker of the poem likens to "good sutures" (32). The surgeon's impressive Ivy League credentials help to buttress the bestseller's expository power and assumed authority.

With gentle sarcasm, the poem praises the "good title" of Nuland's work because it offers "stress on the process, necessary prose, / the work of bodies not our own, but time's" (32). The repeated references to the prose, apart from signaling awareness of formal elements in another piece of writing, prompt us to notice the deliberate generic juxtaposition of a poem dissecting a nonfiction text. The phrase "work of bodies not our own" critiques the sense of depersonalization associated with these medical case studies, fitted with fabricated names but otherwise having "no truth left out." Espaillat refers to Scripture to rationalize the reality of "inherent limits" to life, and describes physicians obliquely as "zealous pros / armed with contraptions work[ing] to overcome / disease" (32). What proves particularly jarring to the poet's persona is the realization that death is neither easy nor romantic: "Those final moments that we dreamed would come / smooth as remembered poems . . . are rough prose" (32). Instead of nonfiction prose having the last word on poetry, here we see poetry giving prose a taste of its own medicine, as it were, through a poetic review.

Nuland's unequivocal message is that no one really dies with dignity. This argument offends the speaker in "Review" because she understands death differently. Eschewing statistics and expected outcomes, she aligns herself with surprises, miracles, and the seemingly impossible: "But facts (says Proust) never obey us, come / as we least looked for: people, places, times / defeat prediction" (32–33). Clearly, she is suspicious of the certainty with which Nuland characterizes the final exit. Perhaps it is the seeming arrogance of the book's title or the crushing nature of the message that is summarily off-putting. Nuland and his colleagues in surgery, among other specialties, have the composite burden and privilege of close contact with the seriously ill and dying; these professionals' experiential authority comes from bearing constant witness to mortality. Perhaps jadedness—even numbness—is an inevitable, even necessary defense mechanism against the trauma of such proximity. Yet Espaillat's speaker implies that nondoctors may have suitable credentials to partake in this discourse as well.

The greatest irony, of course, is that the speaker has not read the book, judging it only secondhand from the assessment in the *New York Times*. This mildly humorous revelation is a reminder that death is not merely a public reality, a kind of template that is met and reproduced ad infinitum, but rather an experience that changes once we confront it in person (thus we "re-view" it with our own eyes). The speaker enacts her ambivalence by moiling over whether to buy the book, offering a performance of the very uncertainty she craves. She ends without resolution, but stands content with a tentative pledge to honor both the practical *and* the speculative. What assuages her fears is the ability to use her imagination as a buffer against the harshness of an obligatory fate:

> Maybe I'll buy this book, then throw it out
> unread; or send this poem to the *Times*;
> or ignore death till it decides to come;
> or read the damn book; dye my hair; work out;
> consult the pros, the tarot; pretend time's
> not after me; just do, till Kingdom Come. (*Where Horizons Go* 33)

The speaker oscillates between commitment and denial, between becoming informed and playing dumb. She contrasts the *Times* with Time broadly, a doctor's visit with a psychic's divination, an invocation of God's plan with a cosmetic attempt to turn back the clock.

Nuland obviously does not represent all doctors, let alone other medical writers in any broad sense. Espaillat wishes to complicate the assertion that death is "rough prose," a function of facts and lived experience only. There must also be that consolation offered by poetry or other arts, that "smoothness" that acts to lessen the pain of loss. Granted, there *is* spirituality in doctoring. The pioneering surgeon-writer Richard Selzer (1928–2016) declared that although he was an atheist, he consistently found spiritual sustenance from the power and presence of the flesh. His ministrations represented a form of soul searching for him and soul seeking in the patient. He posits the innate spirituality residing in our vulnerable beings, rendered even more revelatory when sick:

> Being a surgeon, confronted with death on a daily basis, it becomes an old adversary—one you recognize and deal with. . . . For me, the body is a sacred space. Now, you will be amused to hear words like piety, sacred and blessed from a person who claims not to believe in God. I am a highly spiritual person, so evidence of the spirit is present in many things—in people and in the body especially. I am always touched by the revelation of the human spirit when I look at the body, a wound or a lesion. I can see the spirit of the person—the aura of the spirit—in the wound. (K.)

Like Selzer, Espaillat's approach to her mother's condition shies away from the elegiac or sentimental. It is not a heroic salute to the passing of a vibrant life or a self-congratulatory reflection on how honorable a child she has been, a stereotypical immigrant topos. Some of her poems reflect upon—and dispute—current approaches by physician-writers like Nuland and Selzer on coping with mortality. Espaillat's thanatoptic verse, particularly the way the poems dealing with the subject negotiate the necessary acts of witnessing, reconciles the mind to mortality's claim on the body but does so with unrepentant resistance.

PSYCHIC, PHYSICAL, AND PHILOSOPHICAL LANDSCAPES

In the essay "The Psychic Landscape," poet Alexander Long discusses a metaphorical terrain that exists as "a place where severe losses can be observed, dissected, razed, and raised." This paradoxical pairing of "razed"/"raised" speaks eloquently to the process of witnessing a loved one who has raised the witness from birth being razed by illness. By applying the tools of imagination, figurative language, and memory to the devastating existential truth that we are all in a staggered process of dying, poets like Espaillat construct psychic landscapes as philosophical fora to help us keep going. Doing so is a function of personal as well as artistic necessity. As Long would have it, "There is only one bearable corollary for loss: the imagination realized, controlled, expressed, and offered. Loss is a catalyst for, not a detriment to, the psychic landscape. Only the poet who understands and accepts this paradox will enter—and repopulate—his or her psychic landscape" (Long).

Pressures on artists to tackle and reconcile their grief privately are compelling, though sometimes at cross-purposes with the intensely public pressure to help other people—the world even—cope with losses. In the proverbially optimistic post–WWII United States, many creative writers went against a "national predilection for the upbeat and cheery," thereby risking the possibility of appearing melodramatic or embarrassingly self-centered (Sadoff, "Flat" 188). The corollary theme of aesthetic incommensurability between loss and the personal representation of loss also surfaces. Poet Ira Sadoff recalls Roland Barthes's struggle with maternal mourning in *Camera Lucida* (1980). The French theorist's discussion and deployment of photography underscore the irony that "the work of art cannot sufficiently express or bring back 'the thing itself': that death can never truly be assimilated or transcended" (Sadoff, "Flat" 189). While this pronouncement challenges Long's model, for Espaillat, the psychic landscape coincides with physical and chronological landscapes as premises for art. All of these make up the aging body, a memento mori in the flesh. If the changes that the body undergoes cannot be defined, described, and conveyed with poetic language—much like the effect of diagnosis on a hitherto undefined disease—we find ourselves tragically reminded that one more part of us has slipped away from our already provisional control.

This awareness permeates Espaillat's poem "September." The title connotes autumn harvesting and a slow migration toward winter, an expected pattern of life in the eastern United States, a region the artist has called home for three-quarters of a century. The speaker muses, "Time for the body / to come back home, to reacquaint the body / with its slow unbecoming" (*Her Place* 28). The tone is grave and unadorned, filled with vowel sounds, reflective of the changing landscapes of the outside world and the body itself as microcosm. The fluid imagery and repetitions, especially of the word "body," emulate a steady rhythm, like the flow of blood through veins or the creep of a wave on a shore before receding. Almost incantatory, these effects convey the process of coming to terms with physical erosion through philosophical resolve and the complementary canvas of nature:

> Afterward comes a harder, harsher breaking,
> a wave more final that assails the body
> like recognition reached over and over:
> what was lost once is lost, still and again,

the knowledge persevering, one reflection
inside the next, unchanged, moving away. (28–29)

"The body," ironically, is a synonymous term for corpse, or that which signifies what is "lost, still and again." Yet "lost" contrasts with "unchanged," meaning stable, and "still" with "moving away." The overall impression conveyed by these lines is one of progressive diminishment ("harder, harsher breaking") that threatens to break the spirit of the aging subject. However, there is a rhetorical turn near the end of the poem, one that marries multiple meanings of "breaker" and offers a change of perspective, a "moving away" from loss. The speaker concludes, "Better to let the body / ease into breaking, seem to stir again, / avoid reflection, forget how much is over" (29).

One denotation of *breaker* is a large wave that disperses into foam once it contacts the shore; another is a reef against which the wave crashes, an ironic doubling of meanings that reflects—much like mirror images on water—the mind/body duality. The human equivalent of a breaker is someone who deviates (breaks away) from a pattern or convention. This meaning characterizes the speaker, who wishes to "avoid reflection." Since the body is, in essence, an electrical system wired through by neural currents, thanatopsis acts as a kind of intellectual circuit breaker that protects the system from overload, namely the awful shock of realizing that one's ultimate mortality is fast approaching. When the realities of death and loss become too much, the mind resets itself to disperse the anxiety, much like ocean foam dissipating on the sand. The waves will undoubtedly return, but the poem advocates "forget[ting] how much is over." While a blunt individual might call this denial, and a physician term it false hope, Espaillat suggests it is a legitimate, indeed healthy, alternative to facing the inexorable sea that will break against and disperse us all. If time were a stream of electrically received moments of perception, the speaker asks for a moment to pause and push reset. The thoughts are willing, even if the body is not.

To Espaillat, aging is not an illness. Decrying changes that come with age does not necessarily mean a desire to reverse time or an idealization of youth. In "Sioux Falls at Thirty-Seven," the speaker valorizes the experience that age confers: "Who would be young again? Not I; / the skin's too thin at seventeen. / It takes this long to count as joy / the mercy of the years between!" (*Her Place* 42). The aging body reminds us of our heightened proximity to death, but it also attests to our having survived thus far, and hence our undeniable strength and resilience. That said, the vulnerability generated by old age often prompts a kind of hyperawareness of the body, manifested in the sometimes joking observation that the older we become, the more we complain about what does not work anymore. Bodies change with or without our awareness and explicit permission, hence the intensity of the fear associated with growing older. In Selzer's view, "the engine that drives modern culture is the denial of death. Look at all the plastic surgery and cosmetics people use to make themselves look young. It's an unrealistic way to live" (K.).

The anxiety over aging worsens with a condition as uncompromising as Dulce María's terminal disease. The decline of the mother and the decline of the self are parallel discourses for Espaillat, not only because of the family connection but also because of their concomitant timing. While recuperation may not be possible in cases of incurable ailments like Alzheimer's, the disordered body of the patient serves as an impetus to explore what the witnessing mind must do to take stock of the situation and—as Wordsworth's "Ode: Intimations of Immortality from Recollections of Early Childhood" (1807) exhorts—"find / Strength in what remains behind / . . . In the faith that looks through death, / In years that bring the philosophic mind" (Wordsworth, *William* 145). Espaillat's "philosophic mind" is mindfully grounded in the here and now. The altered, weathered, refracted self that sees herself in the sick mother is central to her poetic thanatopsis, which aims to diminish the fear of death through the consolation of gratitude for the life experienced thus far.

COMPATIBILITY OF PHYSICIAN AND POET

Thanks in part to Shakespeare's ubiquitous declaration, "All the world's a stage," uttered by Jaques in act 2, scene 7 of *As You Like It*, it is a familiar conceit to imagine humans as actors in the grand production of life. Espaillat likewise uses theatrical metaphors poignantly in *Where Horizons Go* when referring to the stages, roles, and performances (including entrances and exits) of life. "In Absentia" features the poet asking her stillborn brother whether he has "found room on some congenial stage / less brutal than live flesh," since he "stayed pure" during his "one brief scene" but ended up missing his cue to appear altogether (5). In the same collection, the sonnet "Interlude" conjures up a middle-aged woman counting her blessings and considering "memory's curtains as they close / on this good Second Act." With a mixture of anxiety and regret, she stays vigilant "for exit lines as yet unheard / although foreshadowed, as the deed undone / cries out in retrospect" (44). Here, as in "Review," Espaillat reiterates the power of uncertainty in the lines that follow the "good Second Act": "There's more ahead, / but what—and how it ends—nobody knows" (44). Instead of being a premise for worry, this lack of certainty can be liberating, even a source of hope.

It goes without saying that a poet will not—indeed, *cannot*—approach terminal illness in the same way as a physician, with an eye on testing, diagnosis, and treatment. American filmmaker Alexander Payne's differentiation between actors and directors offers a provocative analogy for comparing a poet's approach to illness and death with that of a typical acute-care physician who deals with the phenomenon daily. Acknowledging that "film is technical as well as emotional," Payne suggests that directors envy a strong actor's "ready access to emotion and how beautiful that is," while actors, in turn, envy a talented director's capacity to deal "more clinically with emotions, ordering them about dispassionately" (Payne). Here, the poet is to the actor as the physician is to the director. Obviously, some overlap exists between the roles: actors may serve as directors (and vice versa), and the cinematic product requires both groups to invest conscientiously for the sake of the overall product. Poets do not participate in the same sphere of care as do physicians, and their roles are passive rather than interventionist. Further, as mentioned above, some doctors double as creative writers, or at least write for a popular audience about their craft. Both poets and physicians ponder what physician-writer Oliver Sacks (1933–2015) sums up as "the deepest, darkest, and most fearful parts of ourselves, the parts we all strive to deny or not-see" (Sacks xix). Payne observes that any surfeit of emotions can lead to personal problems for actors who fail to disentangle their onscreen personae from their lives beyond the set. A neurologist, Sacks argues in the preface to his bestselling book *Awakenings* (1973) that contemporary medicine requires a "metaphysical theme," or the capacity to supersede the idea that disease exists in "purely mechanical or chemical terms." With only technical emphases, practitioners are prone to "intellectual regression," which accompanies "a lack of proper attention to the full needs and feelings of patients" (Sacks xviii). The intellectually "regressive" worldview, like the one that Payne outlines, is myopic and ultimately untenable because humans far exceed the mere status of wonderful machines.

Internist Joan Teno points out that US families tend to avoid the difficult conversations relating to end-of-life care, largely because it is easier to follow a practical course of action. She comments, "We pay for another day in I.C.U., . . . But we don't pay for people to understand what their goals and values are. We don't pay doctors to help patients think about their goals and values and then develop a plan" (qtd. in Gorenstein). This lack of attention to the "emotional side of dying," when not dealt with by patients, doctors, and loved ones alike, often results in "a high price for difficult and unscripted deaths, psychologically and economically" (Gorenstein). The Hippocratic understanding of medicine is that it is an art comprising three factors: the doctor, the disease, and the patient (Nuland, "Up from Hippocrates" 33). From this triangular schema alone, reductive as it seems, the patient does not appear to have any precedence over the physician or the cause of the illness. Family, friends, and emotional attachments are also not explicitly present, although they may fall under the aegis of the "patient." Espaillat's thanatoptic poems shed necessary light on the perspectives of this latter group.

The rational, depersonalized, and resolution-oriented mindset, one that, like Superintendent Gradgrind in Charles Dickens's *Hard Times* (1854), privileges facts above all else, tends to be a dominant stereotype associated with the medical professions. Similarly, emotion and subjective experience, the jurisdiction of much contemporary poetry about illness, may appear secondary or even inappropriate in some contexts, especially when confidentiality issues arise. Gawande begins his bestselling *Being Mortal: Medicine and What Matters in the End* (2014) with the following confession: "I learned a lot of things in medical school, but mortality wasn't one of them. Although I was given a dry, leathery corpse to dissect in my first term, that was solely a way to learn about human anatomy. Our textbooks had almost nothing on aging or frailty or dying" (1). The one occasion on which he *was* able to engage these subjects presented itself during a discussion of a novella by Tolstoy during a seminar meant to cultivate "more rounded and humane physicians" (1). The first observation complements what he has elsewhere posited, that his peers in medicine may find themselves told to "turn off" their emotions. In the introduction to his book *Better: A Surgeon's Notes on Performance* (2007), Gawande avers, "As a doctor, you go into this work thinking it is all a matter of canny diagnosis, technical prowess, and some ability to empathize with people" (8). Yet the practice of medicine in the United States is "a colossal and impossibly complex machine" that functions according to its "own arbitrary rhythm." In this controlled chaos, the physician reveals, "the effort to do better for people" in areas beyond the hospital or examining room may slip to the wayside or even be construed as "hopelessly naïve" (10).

In a similar fashion, physician-writer Pauline W. Chen comments in her autobiographical piece "Resurrectionist" that during training, "even medical students chosen for their humanitarian qualities and selected from a huge pool of applicants may have their generous impulse profoundly suppressed by their medical education" (33). What may result from the wholesale diminishment or effacement of the dead's humanity is a severely skewed understanding of death-as-process and its corollaries—witnessing, suffering, surviving, healing—as experienced by that person's loved ones. One attempt to combat this interruption of sensitivity during training, recalls Chen, involves death-and-dying modules that incorporate such rituals as memorial services for the dissected cadavers. Gawande's anecdote from the seminar discussing Tolstoy captures the work of one such class. Students perform music, present essays, and share poems composed especially for these anonymous donors (Chen, "Resurrectionist" 33). By doing so, the future physicians supplement the technical expertise gained through the painstaking anatomy lessons and tune in to their first "patients" as once-living subjects rather than now-dead specimens. Imaginative language and the arts, broadly conceived, remain key catalysts in the rehumanization process of the dead and, in turn, their student caretakers. The cadaver no longer represents all bodies but becomes individualized, the physical trace of a larger repository of lived experiences now inaccessible save through imaginative reconstruction. As Chen's title reads, they undergo resurrection through the skillful use of words and creativity, a kind of extended, posthumous care offered by the living to the once-living.

Such connections emerge via greater openness to interdisciplinarity, among other bridging methodologies. Twenty-first-century physicians have been made increasingly aware of the need for an empathic imagination while treating their patients. Citing the endorsement of medical school instructors at Harvard and Yale, among others, Chen explains that "as the medical profession places more and more weight on approaches that emphasize the patient and wellness, doctors are once again turning to poetry for inspiration. And education" (Chen, "Doctor"). Audrey Shafer, an anesthesiologist and professor at Stanford University School of Medicine, is also a poet who directs "Medicine and the Muse," an integrated training program for future doctors that is meant to elicit productive conversations between healthcare fields and various art forms, including poetry (Rizzo). Beyond the instances described above, other means of nurturing compassion and awareness include shared reading programs, discussion groups, reflective writing exercises, and fine-arts-based activities that work both as emotional outlets and platforms for critical consciousness-building during medical training (Chen, "Resurrectionist" 34). What Nuland observes—albeit a bit idealistically—about the medical memoir rings true for poetry as well: "What better way to come to the realization that the more one reveals his most intimate experiences and thoughts, the more he is expressing universal themes, understood by every reader?" ("Uncertain" 131).

Apart from a shared interest in rhythm, such as cardiac beats for doctors and metrical beats for poets, Cuban American physician-poet Rafael Campo—winner of a Guggenheim Fellowship, among other national awards—reasons in an April 2017 interview that because poetry is arguably the "most embodied and visceral form in literature," each clinical encounter between doctor and patient may be seen to resemble a poem. He elaborates: "In order for me to understand the way my patients describe their symptoms, I have to be attentive to issues of language, such as metaphor. Listening to their hearts and breathing through my stethoscope is much like hearing the rhythms expressed in poetry." Well-wrought poems also fuse the acts of healing and curing: "The disease is cured, and the patient feels healed, as do I. I think the same can be said of a good poem, except that poems more rarely cure diseases but more frequently can heal us" (qtd. in Dockser-Marcus).

Attributing such salutary powers to poetry enlarges its scope as a democratic medium, applicable to everyone. In his review of Espaillat's *Rehearsing Absence*, the poet and scholar Robert B. Shaw describes her verse as "less egotistical, more meditative" than diary-like poetry of the self. It is thus able to speak "not from some cramped corner but from somewhere close to the center of life" (Shaw 351–52). Although Nuland quotes a former mentor's declaration that "doctors are the only real philosophers" because only *they* can assess a full range of healthy and unhealthy human behaviors, poets would seem no less qualified ("Uncertain" 132). That a psychological schism exists between the arts and sciences is profoundly ironic given that poetry and medicine are not incompatible disciplines. The Greek god Apollo presided over both, and such canonical poets as John Keats and William Carlos Williams, both trained physicians, demonstrated their fruitful coexistence. More currently, Campo and other doctor-poets stress the complementary potential of these two broad arenas. In the field of popular medical writing, the late Selzer remains among the most revered of the surgeon-writers, with over ten volumes to his name and a nomination for a PEN/Faulkner Award for fiction. Fellow physician Luis Toledo-Pereyra claims that Selzer "extract[s] humanism" through the skilled choreography of his tools, and that "knife and pen [are] intertwined to reach higher heights for the good of the healing patients. The surgeon-writer cures effectively with knife and pen by offering patients the best solutions to their daunting problems" (Toledo-Pereyra 320, 322).

Of course, hierarchies still exist between the knife and pen even though both may be wielded effectively as weapons against humanity's "daunting problems."

Nuland senses that although each act is infused with emotion and excitement, surgery "grounds" while writing "lifts" ("Uncertain" 129). Terms and phrases he associates with the former include "precision," "tour de force," "supremacy of planning and forethought," and "structure and substantiality." In contrast, writing offers "freedom" and a "sublime detachment from the here and now," as if one is "being borne along on a Ouija board" (129–30). Ouija boards tend not to have any standing among those in the scientific community, let alone the public, who may laugh them off as occult playthings. Perhaps the analogy is a bit too hasty, given the fact that writing, like any deliberate act, is governed by rules and expectations, especially in fields meant to avoid as much ambiguity as possible. On the other hand, the trope is also startlingly appropriate if applied to creative writing. Espaillat's thanatoptic poems imply that death—like inspiration or genius—is still largely a mystery, something that supersedes the empirical world of medicine much like the machinations of the Ouija board. Language and conjecture remain fundamental. She does not discount either approach to understanding illness and death; she simply insists on their coexistence.

Just as the word *psychic* in adjectival form refers broadly to the workings of the unconscious or conscious mind, its nominal form refers to a seer, someone with access to a world of knowledge beyond the layperson's ken. Medicine, too, can be highly specialized and exacting in its quantitative demands, but it also involves seeing into the future or past and making complex ethical decisions about divulging or withholding information from the seeker/querent. Sociologist Nicholas A. Christakis, author of *Death Foretold: Prophecy and Prognosis in Medical Care*, points out that prognoses are difficult to offer and tend to be accurate only 20 percent of the time (qtd. by Gorenstein). In some ways, the psychic, poet, and the doctor are navigating futures in the same precarious waters: each seeks meaning out of uncertainty and offers insights without a guarantee. Recalling the epigraph to this chapter, the words really *are* wild. Espaillat's references to the speculative realm, namely religion and the occult, underscore the imperative of acknowledging the limits of both the arts and sciences when it comes to confronting the omnipresent specter of death in our lives.

AGING BODIES

Our discussion thus far has touched on three discursive arenas that define Espaillat's thanatopsis: a response to aging, acknowledging the presence or power of illness, and reconciling oneself to mortality in a variety of ways, usually some combination of gratitude, despair, hope, and rebellion. We shall now take on the aspect that most directly engages the gender dimensions of her thanatopsis. In her feminist classic *The Second Sex* (1949), Simone de Beauvoir (1908–1986) describes an endemic prejudice in Western cultures against the aging and older woman: "Before all things, then, she will be called upon for youth and health" (de Beauvoir 157). When these desirable traits steadily fade, the woman's value supposedly depreciates and she tries to recuperate them by any means possible—including drastic surgical interventions. Informed by a reading of Foucault, Sandra Lee Bartky explains that in view of these long-held sexist biases, women discipline their bodies as "part of the process by which the ideal body of femininity—and hence the feminine body-subject—is constructed; in doing this, they produce a 'practiced and subjected' body, that is, a body on which an inferior status has been inscribed" (Bartky 283). While men are not immune to body prejudice themselves, feminist activist Jeanne Kilbourne contends in her documentary *Killing Us Softly 4* (2010) that such pressure is greater for women because projected social value and self-esteem depend so much on physical appearance. The popular media constantly enforces the false relationships between looking good, being good, and deserving love, respect, opportunities, and even safety.

The powerlessness ascribed to women tends to be ageist and deceptive as well as misogynistic. Of course, there are abstract manifestations that do not denigrate the mother—Mother Earth, Mother Ship, and Mother Nature, among other popular examples—but the matron, old maid, widow, divorcée, witch, and crone are frightening archetypes to those who do not trust or like women in the first place. De Beauvoir forwarded a hypothesis about this targeted disdain: "The old woman, the homely woman, are not merely objects without allure—they arouse hatred mingled with fear" (160). Part of this aversion stems from the archetype of the monstrous mother, someone who is "disquieting" because of her power to create as well as destroy. In contemporary society, she represents the threat of social loss or even regression in men, as well as possible "theft" of guaranteed leadership privileges, since a select group of older women may hold high social standing, having reached such heights by equaling (if not besting) men. She also stands as a sobering reminder of what will remain once "the charms of the Wife" have disappeared, especially for heterosexual men (160). She symbolizes the past when adults were dependent children as well as the future when wives will no longer be sexually attractive—at least according to ageist assumptions that mature women cannot be as appealing as their more youthful counterparts.

Espaillat does not shy away from examining the psychological toll exacted by age-related physical and lifestyle changes. Her poems on the subject tend to be evenhanded, even wryly humorous, with a philosophical tone that avoids any *ur*-message such as supernal uplift or overweening despair. "Pruning," for instance, features a woman gardener contemplating her husband as he works alongside her in a kind of flashback of Edenic labor. She salvages while he prunes, a symbiosis of "making one motion with two minds" (*Shadow* 12). Without ardent feeling, she notices, "He has forgotten wedding, bride, / in favor of my aging face: / the future is his chosen place. / And still we garden side by side" (12). The past and future merge through their lifetime connection, a legal and experiential bond; the language of the witnessing present makes their marriage a kind of Möbius strip of mature companionship, the twist being the difference between memories of a more carefree youth and the fragility of old age and an uncertain future together—at least on earth where gardening can be a quietly joyful pastime.

Staying close to the semiotic field of the aging body, "Weighing In" is a composition that toys with the titular expression for giving one's opinion and the dreaded task of measuring one's body mass. Cleverly, the poet envisions a deep connection between the earth and the physical self, with the pull of gravity a measure of "how much the earth / has missed you, body, how it wants you back" (*Where Horizons Go* 43). Instead of shaming the body for its heaviness, literal or otherwise, she creates an affectionate scenario of a recuperated bond between the human and nonhuman world. Superficial injuries like bruised knees and bloody shins are, to her, reminders of a lost intimacy with the ground and by extension, a nature that will reclaim us all in death. Eventually, as advanced age arrives, the body becomes a "soft old shoe / that love wears when it's stirring." In turn, teased and caressed by the shoe, the earth "wants what you weigh, needs what you know" (43). By these descriptions, death proves to be a return to the earth, an unfrightening consummation of a lifetime's worth of abiding love, suggested by the crescendo of romantic verbs (stir, want, need). By this positive logic, the aging process is not a perversion of freedom or cumulative loss of power but rather a homecoming to an original place (a natal land, literally) where one has been much awaited. We will find ourselves welcomed, the cold abjection of death layered over by a comforting earthen embrace.

Referring to the typical milestone for retirement and senior citizenship, "Sixty-Five" has the tone of a jesting yet intimate conversation between friends.

A humorous allusion to Dylan Thomas's "Do Not Go Gentle into That Good Night" (1952) accompanies a witty apostrophe to W. B. Yeats, author of "Sailing to Byzantium" (1928), which is referenced directly as well. The speaker claims a space for "old women" alongside their male counterparts, aware that both groups feel undermined by their age: "you said this is no country for old men— / or women either—and you got that right" (*Where Horizons Go* 48). Sassy exaggerations ("You want the truth? Disaster") accompany the refrain ("It's not a year I'd care to do again") at the end of each octave (48). The poem is a catalogue of physical breakdowns, at times even a parody of the blazon technique so recognizable in Shakespearean love sonnets as a way of assessing the physical attributes of the beloved. Rather than enumerating admirable traits in another, the poet dissects her own body, deriding her uncooperative bladder, a heavier frame than in youth, and the looser landscape of her face:

> My body hates me. And it's mutual too.
> We never speak these days except to fight.
> There's less and less I like it still can do.
> My bladder yells at me; my clothes are tight.
> I loathe these dewlaps and these jowls that blight
> The profile boys would notice, way back when.
> I'm sagging gentle into that good night.
> It's not a year I'd care to do again. (48)

Although self-deprecating, a subtle self-love seeps through; the speaker obviously knows she will not be "doing" sixty-five again, and this "disaster" of a body is the only one she has. The strong verb "hate" is used with flippancy rather than vehemence. The intertextual tribute to Thomas's poem also keeps the tone light; if these are tragedies for the body, they are relatively small. Furthermore, the flaws remain viable premises for immortalization in verse, another Shakespearean topos. Sixty-five, while certainly a pivotal year, is also just one of many and hopefully a precursor to more. If twenty-one is the typical marker for coming of age in the United States, sixty-five is the one at which we have fully arrived; some, after all, do not have the privilege of doing so, let alone with humor intact.

Selzer proposes that the ill body harbors greater spiritual potential than does the fit, healthy, and able one. This is because we usually construe sickness as an aberration and interruption of normative good health. Ruptures of the norm arouse pity and fear as well as empathy. He opines, "The body is the only thing that, the more wounded it is, the more beautiful or holy it becomes" (K.). This description may be too romantic for some, but in its idealism and representational breadth, it more closely approximates Espaillat's attitude than Nuland's in *How We Die*. The latter author construes the body as a means to an end; each story generated by a patient illuminates a greater reality for all. The patient him- or herself is instrumental rather than the *telos*, the end itself. Nuland reasons, "Writing is not an exercise in discretion; it is an exercise in seeking the clues to our lives. . . . In short, what I do is change the names [of patients] and never consider the consequences that may result from my efforts to achieve the essential truth" ("Uncertain" 132). To what extent does "essential truth" exist when it comes to unpredictable, fallible human bodies? Poetry and nonfiction prose are different genres, of course, but it is perhaps hubristic to assume truth can be accessed and transmitted exclusively through any professional pen or voice, let alone a single expert (or set of experts) in a lone discipline.

An analogy based on Greek poet Archilochus's contrast between the hedgehog and the fox, discussed by Isaiah Berlin, offers a comparative platform for Nuland's and Espaillat's respective quests for thanatoptic truth. If the fox "knows many things" and the hedgehog "one big thing," then Nuland's objectives accord with the methods of the spiny, digging animal: "a single central vision . . . a single, universal, organizing principle." Espaillat's view, on the other hand, correlates with the inquisitive forest canine that stands for "those who pursue many ends, often unrelated and even contradictory, connected, if at all, only in some de facto way, for some psychological or physiological cause" (Berlin 1–2). Nuland adjusts Archilochus's duality to be one of scope: the hedgehog is "master of several of its smallest settings" while the fox is "master of the panorama" ("Up from Hippocrates" 32). It would serve us well to be able to move between the vertical, single-minded, diligent, and painstaking perspective of the hedgehog and the lateral, adaptive, roving, and broad-minded world of the fox.

THE ADVENT OF ILLNESS

When facing sickness of any kind, some degree of anxiety is expected, even inevitable. This process emerges in Espaillat's "Lately," whose speaker issues a series of eerie complaints that detail escalating ripples of disempowerment throughout her daily life. Anticipated letters arrive but are sent back without having been seen by the recipient; the speaker's own body makes no impact on the outside environment. She mutters, "the light of stars / sifts through my body / Where I walk, the grass / is unbruised" (*Shadow* 8). Even an affirming reflection in the mirror has been erased by unknown assailants. These thoughts sometimes appear to be those of a ghostly apparition, but what proves most disturbing to the persona (whether human or spirit) is the sense that all of these thefts happen in spite of her unequivocal desire to intervene and stop them. She witnesses her own terrifying effacement from the hybrid perspective of a loved one narrating the decline of the sufferer and the sufferer herself watching her lucidity flicker, her mobility falter, and her grasp on reality slacken.

Espaillat again captures the surreal horror of these disconcerting possibilities in a piece titled "Happening." This word may be a verbal form (as in, "it's happening") or a noun ("an odd happening"); whatever the case, it underscores the acute fear of disorientation. In what appears to be an autobiographical "dream," Espaillat reconstructs what her mother may have felt once the elder's memory began to disintegrate. The text opens with a child (or what seems to be a child) lost "far uptown" in Manhattan after watching cartoons at a local theater. She calls home but has difficulty discerning the dial on the rotary phone, describing it as "only five holes / cramped by a strange alphabet" (*Shadow* 48). The child's mother, who answers, is rather "too composed" at the girl's desperation, and fails to mention that the father being sought for a ride has been dead for nearly two decades (48). This revelation signals the collapse of known time as the speaker admits that she is currently the age of her distant, confused mother and lives "in [her] own map now" (49). The poem offers a shrink-wrapping of past time—once familiar, now foreign—and depicts how the divestiture of family comforts resembles a Rip Van Winklesque awakening. No mother soothes with warm words, no father hurries to retrieve the frightened daughter, and even language dissolves into a "strange alphabet." It is a rendition of mental confusion that recreates the turmoil Dulce María may have experienced in the early moments of her mental decline. Sharing this pain, Espaillat's speaker blurs the lines between mother and daughter, cared-for and caring-for, both under the disfiguring shadow of the uncompromising disease.

Similarly, "How It Begins" uses techniques reminiscent of horror genres to depict the breakdown of the living body. Menacing vagueness, escalating suspense, allusions to grievous impending injury, and an indeterminate ending allegorize the body's confrontation with terminal illness—or aging itself. Following its ominous title ("it" could be anything, after all), the voice in the poem addresses readers directly from the second-person point of view. Through deceptively neat rhyming couplets, the tension mounts through the actions of a vague aggressor named "somebody" who is "picking body's lock, / tapping the glass, hefting a rock" (*Where Horizons Go* 45). As with the poem "September," familiar tropes like the blood as tides, the heart as a bird, and the nerves as electrical wires recur to construct the body as a hitherto secured home. The unnamed intruder repeatedly attempts to violate the integrity of this cozy domestic sphere. Either way, the self is under attack from without; as with the long-dead father in "Happening," there is no savior in sight. The sufferer/victim must attempt to ward off the threats by her- or himself. The terror proves to be harrowing, embodied, and visceral:

> Somebody's blade fingers your chest,
> out for the bird in its warm nest
> rocked in those tides that come and go.
> Somebody's thumb is on the flow
> memory rides through secret places
> to find the doors, to name the faces. (45)

Memory is one of the frantic inhabitants within, wildly attempting to recall the geography of escape ("secret places") and brainstorm possible sources of aid ("name the faces"). There is no explicit indication that the poem refers to Dulce María's Alzheimer's battle, but if it does, the encroaching failure of memory heightens the subject's sense of helplessness and doom.

The poem "You Who Sleep Soundly through Our Bleakest Hour" resurrects these images but with more specific allusions to health gone awry: "You stand by while madness picks the lock, / stroke cuts the wires, tumor rigs the mine" (*Shadow* 71). As we shall see in chapter seven, Alfred Nicol offers a compelling reading of this poem that considers primarily Espaillat's philosophical quarrel with God. Here we might concentrate on the irony and ingenuity of featuring the "somebody" as an inherently ambiguous figure with or without divine powers. This individual also does not have to be the malevolent agent of the earlier poems; the blade that surveys the chest could very well be that of a surgeon, the thumb checking the flow of the body's "tides" a nurse or loved one ascertaining a steady pulse. But the tone darkens as the wires/nerves that connect "motion to desire" are progressively severed. We envision a person unable to move, frozen from fear and physical incapacitation. The horror plot escalates as a foot extends onto the threshold of the residence/body. By asking "What if this once nobody's there?" the poet suggests that while it is horrific to be attacked consciously, it may perhaps be more so if one is throttled from within by silent disease. Like the earlier poem "Happening" with its literally absent father and emotionally absent mother, this text uses the trope of a missing guardian to underscore the patient's dilemma as fundamentally lonely. Such a scenario is most suggestive of Dulce María's debilitating condition but speaks to a larger frustration about the inability to protect the body in any foolproof way. Precautions such as the immune system and conscientious attention to self-care and prevention do exist, but once struck by the "thief" who deactivates our comfortable, usually healthy status quo, the hemorrhaging losses are difficult to stanch and recuperate.

Espaillat's tone is less frightening and more comforting in "Body's Weight." Here, the speaker stresses the need to offset "the soul's hard perfections" with "what the body knows" (*Her Place* 56). She exhorts readers to avoid overprivileging abstract spirituality above the body's mundane but still pleasurable rituals. The flesh is the site of professional ministrations as well as private caresses. She scoffs, "Spare me soul's hard perfections; let the hands / of surgeons—lovers, too—learn to revere / and memorize what soul cannot hold dear / but body understands" (56). She goes on to juxtapose simple comforts that can be found in daily life with more complex technologies like anaesthesia, and with the judgments of heavenly observers. All of these examples stress an awareness of death but act to blunt its force with a combination of worldly and otherworldly examples, explored in the here and now, mindfully and with gratitude. The speaker uses the jussive mood to send readers off, content for now on their respective paths: "Let there be anaesthesia and fresh bread, / warm clothes in winter, and in summer, shade, / and let the saints forgive us what we weighed / as we forgive our dead" (56).

In both of the stanzas quoted above, medical images recur to acknowledge the role of science in the phases of aging. They are meant to counteract and balance the spiritual emphasis that does not have much standing in the empirical world. Anaesthesia and fresh bread obviously come from different places: the former acts to deaden the senses during surgery, mimicking death in order to prolong life; the latter prompts an awakening of senses through a staple food prepared newly and well. That it is *fresh* rather than stale bread underscores how eating is pleasurable even though doing so fulfills a basic need for fuel. Its novel simplicity encourages a connection between awakening from a time of trial and beginning anew. The symbolic crux between feeding the body and feeding the soul also resides in the evocation of bread; it may allude to the daily bread of gratitude found in the Lord's Prayer or the loaves that Jesus miraculously offered alongside the fishes when feeding the multitudes. Alternatively, it may refer to cooked dough resting on a table, whose heat heightens the taste and joy of the experience. "Fresh bread" is an ironic image evoking home comforts and communion (hence, "breaking bread" with others) that contrast with its rhyming phrase "our dead," which carries connotations of quiet reckoning, cool stillness, and irrevocable repose. In turn, winter clothing preserves the body's warmth and is shed in the summer when shade offers relief from atmospheric heat. Both acts—putting on and taking off—are for the same purpose, to ensure a fine balance (homeostasis) within the body. While the soul may demand perfection, the body has its own assertive demands, making them both a "shared encumbrance" (56) that all of us must work to maintain, individually or as an enlightened collective. Democratically, the poem proposes that physicians and home cooks occupy comparable footing in the sustenance, as the title implies, of body's weight.

THANATOPTIC FULFILLMENT AND THE LIMITS OF THE LIVING

As an artist and elder who has intimate awareness of sickness's effects on herself and loved ones, Espaillat remains committed to acknowledging mortality's pervasive hold over our lives. She harbors much sensitivity to the medical profession's Charon-like role of ushering the unsalvageable out of this world. In her own practice, she eschews obsessive morbidity in the same way she avoids overt sentimentality. Her thanatoptic poems continually ask readers to defer to unpredictability and wonder, but the abstractions they offer are rarely without concrete, grounding, identifiable examples. Only a few poems, such as "Alzheimer's" and "Tooth Poem," for instance, deal directly with her mother's condition; even then, these works do not explicitly delineate autobiographical resonance. She is not aiming for documentary realism any more than she strives to offer elegies, eulogies, or epitaphs for the dead. There is also a marked ambivalence that informs her perception of those meant to be the primary vanquishers of death, the healthcare industry's soldiers fighting tirelessly to keep the Reaper at bay.

In "Intensive Care," Espaillat guides readers into one of the units of a hospital most frequented by death. She constructs it as a space of order, both "discreet and earnest" (*Shadow* 13). She then upends that calm with images of war: fruit and flowers stand at "stiff attention," machines resemble sentries, and nurses are "camouflaged in cool pastels" (13). Shuffling by, relatives, friends, and other "near survivors" seem to dissolve away "penitent / in their bored, guilty grief" (13). Yet in such a place of rigorous surveillance, the feared enemy still "slip[s] / through vinyl artery and needle tip, / past blood and spleen and inundated lung," coiling in the center of a patient's eye as a metonymy for the larger mortal coil that encircles us all (14). Conspicuously absent is the figure of the physician as warrior-conqueror; this omission is not a reproach or jibe at doctors acting *in loco dei*, in place of God. By delaying their arrival or keeping them out of the drama altogether, she is making a statement about acknowledging human limits. The snake imagery recalls the ancient symbol of the Rod of Asclepius, often confused with Hermes's caduceus in symbolizing the medical profession; it also begs comparison with the Edenic tempter who slips into sacred spaces to instigate the acquisition of necessary but painful knowledge. Espaillat reminds us that our wars for health (with harmful microbes, fear, lack of access, ignorance, and with human and institutional errors, among others) demand more than just a scientifically gifted battalion.

Taking a less allusive approach than "Intensive Care," the poem "Cutting Bait" is a blank-verse poem whose title alone seems to demystify the final exit with an oddly recreational metaphor. The colloquial phrase "fish or cut bait" is used to prompt an individual to make a quick decision, since both acts are imperative for the process of catching (or salvaging) anything, let alone fish. The choice is typically a difficult one, with life-changing consequences. "Cutting bait" also means letting go of attachments in the grander, Buddhist sense, whether of an idea or ideology, a person, a memory, or a treasured object. This is more likely the denotation that Espaillat espouses when she critiques the living's dependency on the dead. The poet revealed during our 2013 interview that Dulce María had become a Buddhist in her later years, thereby foregoing the idea of a ready heaven that awaited her as a reward for good Christian living (NK/STS).

Letting go of attachments for freedom is a complex demand on the acquisition-oriented Western psyche, but the spirit of the concept is not arcane. According to the speaker in the poem, we require the deceased "to play themselves for us" in order to provide comfort and a semblance of ontological order. They thus become something we depend on with or without direct witnessing, like the transit of the sun or the change of seasons. This expectation blunts the disruptive effects of grief and loss on everyday life (*Shadow* 46). It is the witness and survivor who "ach[es] with absence" while the dead do not—

indeed, cannot—respond, at least in any verifiable scientific sense (46). As such, the bait that we cut is the idea of ongoing reciprocity, fallacious since the dead "untangle themselves from our hunger, / our lame grief" and do not ask to be either commemorated *or* forgotten. The poem speculates that speaking of children as a legacy and even producing poetry, among other memorializing tributes, are forms of self-serving exchange between the living and the living, *not* the living and the dead. These acts and items do not bring the dead back "into / their gestures, the flesh we remember," but alongside the other rituals and commemorations, do help us to come to terms with ourselves (47). *Cutting bait* encompasses our paradoxical desire to cling to painful grief from soul-stirring memories while requiring the release of them to continue living.

A poem like "What It Is" proves more abstract than the paradigm of unrequited loss, turning the spotlight on the failings of the moribund body. It is a rhetorical experiment that functions through preterition, defining such acts as falling, aging, and dying oppositionally. The meaning of each, thus, emerges through a strategy of contrast, denial, and negation: for instance, discussing *x* by emphasizing that one will *not* be discussing *xy*; or, constructing *xy* by denying its similarity to *z*, and so on. This circumlocution emphasizes the idea that conventional tropes, expressions, and our extant vocabulary for such concepts are not always adequate. The anaphoric "Not falling . . . / Not aging . . . / Not dying" are contrasted with evocative descriptions of what these acts actually do entail, with aging being "the backward yearning / over the shoulder / for lives gone flying / away" (*Shadow* 9). The section on dying, however, stops abruptly at two lines instead of fulfilling the expected five-line stanza. This choice by the poet enacts the interruption represented by the end of life. It also invites us to see death as a space to be filled in, an invitation and demand different for each reader. She repeatedly evokes the trope of the shadow (except when defining death, probably to avoid the cliché) to suggest that we are often trained to understand metaphysical concepts by descriptions of concrete realities that we actually do recognize. While the reliance is comforting, it always lays bare our truly limited store of expressive resources.

Less abstract, and yet able to maintain an emphasis on the body as mysterious territory, the sonnet "Exploratory" features a speaker undergoing a mammogram to test whether a suspicious nodule is cancerous. Espaillat casts the potentially ill body not only as foreign but as one that also comprises its own solar system. A red planet symbolizes a mass of anomalous cells:

The first x-ray
shows the troublesome nodule that she needs
to train the lens on like some inner Mars;
now pain—a silent siren—while she reads
my body's horoscope in its own stars. (*Her Place* 67)

As much as it is a scientific reality, not much of the solar system is visible to the naked eye. Similarly, the inner terrains of our bodies far exceed the layperson's field of view. Just as our planetary consciousness comes from a mixture of empirical knowledge and educated assumptions about their existence, we accept that our bodies work; this acceptance is an act of faith—in science. The presence of a cancerous nodule or other internal ailment must be ascertained through exploration by an expert. That, too, is an act of faith, but in human knowledge rather than in any celestial being. Trusting our caregivers can thus be a profoundly liberating and humbling experience.

From the stanza above, we see that the speaker's body is no longer even human or tethered to the ground; it hovers in cosmic darkness where pain emerges mechanically as a "silent siren." The sound reference touches earth but remains aloft and unheard. What could sound be on unpeopled Mars? Since technicians, radiologists, oncologists, and other specialists can see into these abstruse inner workings of the body, we assume that what they say is real and true, a point taken up by Nuland's aforementioned philosophy of disclosure—that is, telling "the essential truth" in his medically themed narratives. Because most people lack access to the scientific literacy of these practitioners, and because the latter are not necessarily correct in all cases, we still must have faith, and sometimes that takes esoteric forms ("my body's horoscope in its own stars"). Espaillat uses the space metaphor to illustrate the epistemological gap between not-knowing and knowing, and how the descent into illness can be as alienating as leaving the planet we inhabit, destined for a new and frightening frontier.

What is subversive about Espaillat's figurative language is that she simultaneously casts the healthcare worker as an astronomer (able to "train the lens . . . [on] some inner Mars") and as an astrologer. She thus equates a member of the complex healthcare apparatus evoked by Gawande (that is, the conglomerate of workers, equipment, technology, facilities, services, firms, research and business personnel, and overall infrastructure required for caring for the ill) with a highly individualized occult practice like horoscope charting. She makes the act of diagnosing a potentially fatal disease proximate to the business—some might say charlatanry—of predicting future events based on factors like birthdate, birthplace, and planetary cycles. The former profession tends to command public respect, even reverence; the latter often struggles to maintain credibility and is often lampooned as a means of fleecing the desperate and the gullible. Either way, each person—technician and diviner—offers fateful news.

At the text's conclusion, Espaillat's speaker breathes, "But no, a false alarm, a gift, a grace— ," returning to both the sound imagery and rhythms of daily life but going beyond these by invoking a religious benediction. She vows that the clean bill of health is "a gift, a grace— / period to count my blessings, start afresh" (*Her Place* 67). The dash signals that the gratitude may be short-lived, but a subsequent line relates, "I've made it back into my life, this once." Her provisional tone simultaneously captures the metaphor of the journey through space and the religiously tinged allusions to mortality, the afterlife, and resurrection. The vertiginous nature of this reprieve evokes thoughts of self-help books devoted to near-death experiences, angelic helpers and spirit guides, and other forms of alternative spirituality meant to shed light on the dark cosmos of our unknowing. Such esoteric avenues may not command much respect among empiricists, especially physicians, but they still prove comforting to those facing the cataclysmic lifestyle changes brought on by illness and other health-related insecurities.

Espaillat synthesizes all of these contrasting perspectives—medical and nonmedical, human and more than human, known and unknown—to underscore the necessary work of thanatopsis at a time of greater and more widespread aging among the US population. As Gawande explains, "In 1950, children under the age of five were eleven percent of the U.S. population, adults aged forty-five to forty-nine were six percent, and those over eighty were one percent. Today, we have as many fifty-year-olds as five-year-olds. In thirty years, there will be as many people over eighty as there are under five" (Gawande, "Way"). Given the concomitant imperative and expectations of better healthcare and longer lifespans, it may be myopic to rely solely on scientific perspectives as chief determiners of the course and quality of our lives.

Bearing witness to Dulce María's painful decline and an increasing sensitivity to her own body's chronological changes have made Espaillat a strong advocate for intergenerational awareness as well as openmindedness amid the limitations posed by failing health. She remains cautious of the epistemological authority represented by such physician-writers as Nuland who insist on speaking about the body's collision with death in unequivocal, "truthful" terms. This direct approach has power, utility, and legitimacy in a professional framework, but the poet also seeks a space of uncertainty, one aligned with the "metaphysical theme" that Sacks understood as requisite to any scenario related to the infirm. This desire is not so much a form of what sociologists call "information aversion" (that is, seeking to avoid facts for fear of what they will reveal) as a predilection for choosing among alternatives, provided that such alternatives exist (Vedantam). Like Archilochus's fox, Espaillat argues that the body's map cannot be navigated as one path only, and that unknowing may be a corollary of hope and faith as much as despair and foreboding. This paradigm is what may be termed *thanatoptic fulfillment*, a paradox of welcome uncertainty about our certain deaths. Amid the emotional ruin represented by her mother's blank demeanor, the poem "Alzheimer's" asks readers to "listen: in this wreckage, even now, / a bird alive somewhere, trying—but how / where nothing else endures?—to be, to sing" (*Shadow* 19). The resilient imagery, combined with the interruptions posed by the em dash, echo Emily Dickinson's "'Hope' is the thing with feathers" where hope "never stops—at all—" (Dickinson, "Hope"). Perhaps the latently singing bird has more in common with the plaque-plagued Alzheimer's brain or the seemingly flatlined electrocardiogram than we think.

7 | TOWARD A CRITICAL CONSENSUS

LITERARY PRESTIGE REGAINED

Considering Espaillat's relatively late incursion into the publication of book-length volumes, the critical response to her work has grown at a brisk pace. By the time her second collection, *Where Horizons Go* (1998), won the T. S. Eliot Poetry Prize, she had accrued a significant number of awards from poetry journals, magazines, institutions, and various poetry contests dating back to the mid-1980s. Since the appearance of her single-authored collections, the honors have continued to multiply. The bibliography on her work now includes substantial commentary, including scholarly appraisals, appreciation essays, critical assessments, book reviews of various lengths, and endorsements of individual works. This body of evaluations has been written first and foremost by poets, as well as by scholars, editors, and literary critics. The predominance of her peers among the appraisers of Espaillat's oeuvre accords with her 2006 receipt of the May Sarton Award, a prize designated specifically to acknowledge poets who have had a significant impact on others in the field.

Indeed, Espaillat's standing in the eyes of her peers is corroborated even further when one finds her invoked as a standard by which to measure other poets. We witness, for instance, R. S. Gwynn's comparative appraisal of the poetry collection *Zero Meridian* (2003), an award-winning first book by Deborah Warren, an artist nearing "sixty, an age when most poets are given to retrospection" (Gwynn 680). Effusive in his praise of Warren's "formal proficiency" and the freshness of her outlook ("a poet on the cusp of senior citizenship still looking ahead to the next spinning of the wheel"), Gwynn concludes that given the high caliber of her two books "published in a two-year span, Warren promises to be as brilliant a late-bloomer as her neighbor on the Merrimack, Rhina P. Espaillat" (680). Though a great admirer of her artistry, Gwynn became aware of Espaillat as a poet only in her second phase, when she "returned" to the poetry scene, hence his forgivable use of the epithet "late-bloomer" to refer to her.

These endorsements of Espaillat's books warrant consideration as a viable critical corpus, as they generally come from notable practitioners of the craft who boast the capacity to assess the formal and conceptual characteristics that make any peer distinct. The endorsements in the form of blurbs appearing on the back covers of her books constitute a veritable compendium of views from many of the country's finest poets from across the generational spectrum. *Where Horizons Go* features comments by fellow poets X. J. Kennedy, Dana Gioia, and Samuel Maio. Kennedy underlines the formal and emotional virtues of the volume; Gioia stresses the "strong," "individual," and "often ingenious" quality of the poems that "add up into something unforgettably personal and personable"; Maio highlights the volume's "highly stylized and clearly direct" language as well as its "tender" sensibilities and "firm convictions." Maio likewise declares Espaillat "a poet of true experience," inviting readers to her work so that they may "know that poetry matters."

Similarly, in his back-cover endorsement of *Rehearsing Absence* (2001), the volume that won Espaillat the Richard Wilbur Award, British poet and translator Dick Davis gestures to her ability to engage large subjects in a quiet voice that "wholly commands the reader's attention and assent." He further praises the "limpid clarity, delicacy, and precision" of her language and "humane vision," characterizing the poems in the collection as "gorgeously crafted" with "unobtrusive skill." Referring to the same volume, the poet and translator Rachel Hadas commends Espaillat's "wonderful sonnets," each piece "sculpted with a particularly canny sense of line," and which "keep their feet on the ground while their spirited thoughts range all over creation." Bruce Bennett, cofounder and editor of the journals *Field: Contemporary Poetry and Poetics* and *Ploughshares*, finds Espaillat's "seemingly effortless command of form" to be "breathtaking," pointing out that "what might have proved limiting or constricting in other hands, reveals modulations and subtleties that constitute a new music." Bennett describes his fellow poet's accomplishment in *Rehearsing Absence* as follows: "Even-paced, precise, utterly self-possessed, her wise woman's voice plays over, and plays with, contingencies, continuities, and contrarieties, illuminating them with a steady light of intelligence. Her habit of—and flair with—metaphor, her probing of close mysteries, her examination of the here and now against the backdrop of an unyielding universe may evoke Frost, but ultimately she is like no one else. Rhina P. Espaillat has become an essential poet."

Playing at Stillness (2005) earned the applause of fiction writer and poet Julia Alvarez, who, in her blurb, commends Espaillat's formal "range—from exquisitely executed formal verse to wonderfully fluid and appealing free verse poems." Poet Tim Murphy holds Espaillat up against her contemporaries Sylvia Plath and Anne Sexton, whom he regards as "her inferiors" when it comes to philosophical outlook. He declares "For My Son on His Wedding Day," featured in the collection, as "the best poem for a son's wedding that I have ever read," and "even better" than another on the same subject by Wilbur. Espaillat's "immaculate voice" makes, in Murphy's view, for "a bemused melancholy and serenity that are precious hard to find in American letters." In his cover endorsement, poet Robert (Bob) Mezey attests to the sheer pleasure he derives from reading Espaillat's work: "I can think of few contemporary poems as thrilling as 'Vandalism,' 'Instruction,' 'When We Sold the Tent,' 'November Music,' 'Cousin,' and 'Old House,'" among others in *Playing at Stillness*. He closes by commending the writer as someone who, in "a dark age . . . gives off light. She is one of our finest poets."

In turn, the back-cover assessment by poet, fiction writer, and teacher Lewis Turco affirms the "true pleasure" of reading Espaillat. He declares her the author of "beautiful" lines that morph "into beautiful poems" as exemplified by "Queen Anne's Lace." Turco considers Espaillat's *Her Place in These Designs* (2008) to be "a wonderful and a wonderfully readable book from cover to cover." He praises her as "the Complete Poet," wielder of a "pitch-perfect" lyricism "in two languages," and generator of a profound "understanding of life." Finally, California poet John M. Ridland declares Espaillat's poems "built to last" and celebrates her "masterful ease" with traditional forms. He even credits the free verse piece "Purim Parade" in the same collection as "one of the most all-American poems" he has ever encountered. While not always considered first among forms of critical evaluation, the cover blurbs testify to the reach that Espaillat has among the poetic community, essentially a jury of her peers.

EXEMPLARY STATUS

While briefly excerpted, the foregoing critical praise becomes especially significant in light of the consistency with which it matches the evaluative consensus among the published reviews of Espaillat's collections. Extant book reviews speak as if with one voice. Simply put, her work enjoys a near unanimous acclaim. The two most notable exceptions seem to confirm this pattern nearly to the point of disbelief.

Joseph S. Salemi, himself an accomplished formalist, faults Espaillat for what he regards as a "nicey-nice" outlook in *Rehearsing Absence* that keeps her from coming to terms with the "unalloyed evil" lodged snugly in human nature (Salemi, "Poetry"). But the reviewer takes exception to that aspect only after referring to one of the book's poems as "an absolutely knockout piece" and to a triptych of Shakespearean sonnets in the volume as "powerful, hallucinatory poems, harrowing in their closeness to the threat of personal annihilation." Furthermore, Salemi says that he harbors "no doubt that she deserves her acclaim: her skill, talent, and experience with language are unquestioned." By the time Salemi gets to his rebuke, the reader has come to recognize it as perhaps the grudging commentary of an otherwise admiring junior colleague afflicted with momentary dissatisfaction about an elder's perceived failure. Fellow poet and critic David Berman immediately stepped up to refute the charges leveled by Salemi against Espaillat's worldview, proceeding to rectify what he understood as the reviewer's exceedingly rapid reading of *Rehearsing Absence* (Berman). But, on closer inspection, the "defense" was less urgently required than Berman may have thought, especially as it became clear that Salemi had merely availed himself of the forum that the book review afforded him to air his unhappiness about what he saw as a relaxing of the borders separating New Formalists from their free verse "adversaries," a case that he had made plain in a previous piece (Salemi, "Typographical Tics"). Because of Espaillat's position at the forefront of the "movement that she never had to 'join,'" Salemi latched onto the occasion of the review as a platform to voice his disagreement with a trend within New Formalism to make unwarranted concessions to the "free verse Establishment."

Similarly, the other dissenting reviewer, the poet Dan Chiasson, uses Espaillat's *Playing at Stillness* as a platform to publicize his aesthetic differences with fellow poet Tim Murphy, a staunch admirer of her work. Chiasson sets out to refute Murphy's memorable pronouncement of Espaillat's superiority to Plath and Sexton. Bothered by such praise, Chiasson concentrates on two pieces in the volume, attempting to challenge the greatness attributed to its author. He quotes Espaillat's "Queen Anne's Lace" in full, but limits his argument to claiming that the poet therein demonstrates "the hazards of ignoring modernity," a conclusion he makes from the piece's lack of engagement with a previous poem on the same subject by William Carlos Williams. He opines, "That an American poet can write a poem about Queen Anne's lace without some acknowledgement, at some level of syntax, diction, tone, rhetoric, or form that William Carlos Williams also wrote such a poem, and further that this short poem is one of the seminal short lyrics of Modernism—this seems to me very peculiar" (Chiasson 150–51).

Chiasson's perception of a lack of allusiveness (read: deference) to the prior piece by Williams suffices for him, lack of analytical support notwithstanding, to describe Espaillat's piece as a poem that goes "bicycling blindly into the wind" (151). The reviewer disdains *Playing at Stillness* as a volume filled with "angelic" flowers and "prayerful wings," granting merely that the poet "seems like a delightful person, and her book full of small kindnesses" (151). With a stance worthy of an aesthetic border patrol officer empowered with the authority to monitor the poet's modernist credentials before granting her permission to enter the fold, Chiasson relies exclusively on disapproval as the critical tool with which to approach Espaillat's "Answering to Rilke." Equally unencumbered by the generally accepted practice of evidentiary support via textual analysis, he simply quotes Espaillat's closing stanza, following which he proceeds to mock her practice thus: "One can imagine an entire series of these poems: humble 'answers' to manifestos, fit to be carved in driftwood. (I've just thought this one up: 'Make it new,' says Mr. Pound. And I say, 'thank you, no!' You like?)" (152).

Apart from these two reproaches, however, a chorus of poetic and critical voices has pronounced Espaillat's work to be exemplary and a model for the defense of the art and its continuing relevance to everyday life. Arguing for the capacity of received forms to transcend particularities of regional speech patterns, literary scholar James Matthew Wilson cites her, a "Merrimack poet," as hard evidence: "I would draw attention to Rhina P. Espaillat, whose books during the past two decades have shown that an often harsh northeastern colloquial dialect can converge well with controlled and elegant verse forms" (Wilson 58). Similarly, in a piece aimed at positing the necessity of rhyme even at a time when some might view it as "out of fashion," former Wisconsin poet laureate Marilyn Taylor offers three examples to sustain her case. First, she cites "Lawyer's Office," a piece by Wisconsin poet Robin Chapman in which, Taylor argues, free verse appears to be the best choice, lest the attempt to render it rhymed should "destroy all of the tumult, most of the fun," and thus spell "artistic disaster" (Taylor, "Reason" 15). Second, she points to the ways in which the inexact rhyming pairs of the slant rhyme seem uniquely suited for Emily Dickinson in "The Soul Selects her Own Society" to explore the private emotional decisions "sometimes irrational, often inexplicable" that we consistently need to make (16). Finally, she turns to Espaillat's reflections in the poem "Snow" to illustrate situations when rhyme seems not only necessary but indeed the artistically superior choice:

> Deception underfoot
> deception on the bough:
> it covers bud and root
> to state the naked now
> as the full-flowered tree
> would charm this out of mind.
> All presence seems to be
> deception of a kind.

Commenting on these lines, Taylor notes that the rhyme is more than just "aesthetically pleasing"; its use appears "downright inevitable." She quotes the closing stanza as "proof positive" of her impression: "Deception underfoot, / deception on the branch: / it covers trunk and leaf / to hide the naked truth" (16). She then pinpoints the "extraordinarily difficult feat" that the poet accomplishes through "true rhymes" (those in which the final vowel sounds are identical), without any of them striking the ear as "trite," "corny," "clichéd," or "overdone" (16). More recently, Taylor has situated Espaillat among a choice list of twentieth- and twenty-first century poets, including such names as Plath, Wilbur, Edna St. Vincent Millay, Ted Hughes, and Donald Justice, who have engaged traditional forms while tackling "wrenching" material in a novel way (Taylor, "How to Write" 17).

For his part, poet Robert Mezey is similarly quick to mention Espaillat, along with Charles Martin and Joseph Harrison, as part of "a small minority" of poets who have asserted themselves in a time when aspiring poets tend almost invariably to "subscribe to the dominant and ignorant current prejudices against rhyme and meter" (McGuire 233–34). The poet and columnist Kay Day embeds Espaillat at the center of an essay displaying how poets create real people in their verse, using as illustration the "powerful" character-driven poem "For Evan, Who Says I Am Too Tidy" (Day 20). Day refers to the piece in *Where Horizons Go* that features a grandmother mulling over the charge of unseemly tidiness by her grandson. The accusation matters to the speaker because neatness is seldom associated with brilliance or creative imagination, qualities typical of those defiant of the established order. In the closing stanza, the elder reasons with Evan that while "tidy seldom goes where genius goes," perhaps tidiness and its opposite both have use for each other, if merely as foils (Espaillat, *Where Horizons Go* 29).

Alfred Dorn, who followed Espaillat's work since he first encountered it during the 1940s at the Poetry Society of America, delighted in the capacity of her verse to heighten the expressive power of classical prosody. In reviewing *Where Horizons Go*, Dorn evokes her "admirable deftness" in handling Shakespearean sonnets, pointing to rhymes that "are neither forced nor trite" and "function effectively as words." He uses her opening poem, "If You Ask Me," as a vehicle demonstrating how rhyme plays a "role that goes beyond a purely phonic one. Since rhymed words stand out more prominently than unrhymed ones, they contribute substantially to the mood and meaning of the poem," a subtler function that "hack" rhymesters fail to understand (Dorn, "Questioning" 109).

While stressing Espaillat's formal dexterity, Dorn places equal importance on the intellectual and spiritual complexity he discerns in the volume. He points out that while "a believer in life," she remains "too skeptical to embrace any credo without reservations." He characterizes her outlook as being marked by "a troubled optimism and a reluctant pessimism." Given this paradoxical positioning, she constantly asks questions even though "she knows in her bones, [they] simply have no answers" (109). Regarding "Falling," which he deems "one of the darkest poems in the book," Dorn weighs in on the bond between the negativity of the piece and the formal elements that come to the fore. The poem tackles the inadequacy of being and the inherent oddity of existence. The first line ("Whatever is, harbors its own unease") announces its central theme, and the last two lines of the second stanza discourage us from seeking consolation in religion: "In the light-spangled solitude of heaven / God reels away from God." In its intimation of a dissonance between ourselves and the world, the closing stanza deals a deadly blow to any redeeming sliver of hope: "And in the heart, born single as a kiss / Broods the sad other—learner, yearner, dier— / That knows, uncomforted, its one desire / Was not for this" (Espaillat, *Where Horizons Go* 22). Dorn deems the "minor key" of the poem's music as one "befitting a somber message," which "depends on rhythm and other phonic elements to achieve its full impact." Abounding throughout her book, such "rhythmic modulations" place in stark relief how Espaillat proves herself "the master rather than the slave of traditional poetic technique" (110).

Just as Espaillat exhibits formal range in *Where Horizons Go*, Dorn recognizes her concomitant emotional and philosophical range, keenly visible in the poem "In Absentia," which uses the technique of apostrophe to resurrect the poet's never-born brother. This loss, incurred while Espaillat was still a young girl, broaches a troubling subject by means of "stage terminology," a semiotic field rife with metaphors for the drama of our existence. The poem, *in toto*, reads:

> Blue-penciled from our script, my stillborn brother,
> have you found room in some congenial stage
> less brutal than live flesh, or do you hover
> above each page
>
> as I grind through commitments on my tour?
> I play to scant applause, and think of you
> sometimes, who in your one brief scene stayed pure
> but missed your cue.
>
> Good to a fault, unflawed as any naught,
> you are the unheard melody, the light
> too far to work by where we shadows squat
> in our cave night.
>
> Type-cast and contract-bound to this one face
> I speak my lines through, whether right or wrong,
> I've envied you your place.
> But not for long. (*Where Horizons Go* 5)

As a "meditation on life's tragicomedy," the text arrives at an affirmation of life as the speaker declares a preference for flawed existence over nonexistence (Dorn, "Questioning" 111). The poem's final lines strike a chord of sad, poignant, but resolute acceptance. On the whole, Dorn regards the accomplishment of the volume as one that places Espaillat firmly "as a compelling voice in the poetry of our time" (114).

MYRIAD USES: RECEPTION BY ANTHOLOGISTS AND CRITICS

When her poems "In My Still Woods," "City Summer," "Spearbearer," and "You Call Me by Old Names" appeared in the 1953 collection *Riverside Poetry*, edited by W. H. Auden, Marianne Moore, and Karl Shapiro, Espaillat enjoyed the distinction of having the most poems featured in the volume, an honor shared with only one other poet among the twenty-four in total. The brief foreword by J. Gordon Chamberlain, the dean of Manhattan's Riverside Church, explains that the editors had judged "nearly two hundred" poems submitted by graduate and undergraduate students from colleges and universities throughout the New York area, and that out of such a substantial number of submissions they picked forty poems that they felt "merited publication" (Chamberlain, Foreword n.p.). One wonders whether Espaillat felt proud about the preferential treatment her work had received from the distinguished editors.

Stanley Romaine Hopper, the respected scholar who wrote the introduction to the collection, also highlighted her contribution in a special way. Only two others among the young poets in the collection received comparable attention. He developed a sustained meditation on the relationship between poetry and religion in the contemporary moment, which he punctuated with references to the devotional elements of Eliot's verse. Stressing his view of the poet's predisposition to be wounded by history, hence the inexorability of poetry's role as a kind of nervous center for the psychological upheavals of humankind, Hopper cites philosopher Jacques Maritain's claim that "the miracle of poetry" lies in its capacity to encapsulate the "creative innocences" of the entire human race. "There are signs of this miracle in this little book," observes Hopper, who then proceeds to quote from the final stanza of Espaillat's "City Summer" to complete his thought about collective trauma and its likely remedy: "There are no tell-tale marks / Upon the hands or feet / Of people in the street; / But on their brows, wan traces of the thorn / So native to the flesh of all things born" (18). Hopper points further to the contemporary poet's "plucking at the conventional givens" of his or her relationship with religion, noting that "decades of plucking at the surface had to precede the present earnestness, which proposes to take its realism to the root of the human condition" (13). He corroborates this point by quoting the middle stanza from Espaillat's "Spearbearer": "For we, with feet unsure, traverse a planet / Grown strange and hostile, and each man is lonely / With but himself to measure by, asserting / Manhood, not godhead" (13).

In 1986 Espaillat's work appeared in another commemorative collection, an anthology marking the twenty-year lifespan of a seminal literary venue, *Encore! A Quarterly of Verse and Poetic Arts*. As the project's finale, the editor selected nearly one hundred out of some three thousand poems that had appeared in the journal during the two decades of its existence. Among them was Espaillat's poem "Dreaming Water." The piece features a speaker whose mind is transported to the reflective, colorful corridors of the famed Italian island-city on the Adriatic:

> I woke up this damp day
> thinking of Venice:
> how lapping water
> smoothed into grace a garment
> of old stones, put on tangled reflections.
>
> Bridges curved like the small of
> the spine arched over
> whispering water
> that gilded their knees with quick
> coins of shifting light.
>
> My bones dreamt water:
> and I thought of green-dappled
> ceilings glimpsed from our
> gondola, the sea
> domestic in its stone gloves. (Briley 58)

Espaillat's verse and her views on poetic language have also earned commendation for their potential as an empowering resource for young learners to enhance their expressive self-confidence. That is the case with an article coauthored by Margo Figgins, a professor of English education who headed the University of Virginia Writer's Workshop for teenagers, and Jenny Johnson, a poet and longtime staff member at the workshop. Figgins and Johnson provide teachers with tips for designing a classroom environment suitable for "wordplay," which amplifies students' abilities to see language as a site for creativity. They make the case for fostering conditions that encourage experimentation, thereby generating greater enthusiasm for language arts. They suggest strategies such as "the use of eponyms, word invention, surrealist activities, and a word lottery" to release students from the "real or imaginary" constraints that expectations of correctness or academic usage may have on their expressiveness (Figgins and Johnson 29). Proposing wordplay as a sort of second language because of its resemblance to poetic practice, which never subscribes to restrictions of "any single dialect," Figgins and Johnson utilize Espaillat's views to accentuate the importance of stimulating students to draw on all the linguistic resources available to them. They quote her remarks about the inherent bilingualism of poetry: "There is a sense in which every poet is bilingual, and those of us who are more overtly so are only living metaphors for the condition that applies to us all. We use a language that seems deceptively like the language of the people around us, but isn't quite. The words are the same, but the weight we give them, the criteria we use to choose this one rather than that one, are our own" (300).

Applying Espaillat's work in a way comparable to that of Figgins and Johnson, philosophy scholar Haim Gordon found aspects to fuel his critique of views on poetry articulated by Martin Heidegger (1889–1976), the influential German philosopher associated with existentialism and phenomenology. Gordon discerns in Espaillat's poem "Bra" the basis for illustrating problems stemming from the relationship between evil and love. He points to the dramatic situation in the "thought-provoking" text and the dilemma that troubles the speaker, an American woman of Hispanic descent ("I count in Spanish"). She identifies with workers' rights ("Union forever . . . committed to US labor"), but in the unspectacular act of shopping for a brassiere, finds herself liking one whose "label says Honduras." The problem of choice for the customer acquires a moral weight no lighter than that of the titular character in Sophocles' *Antigone* at the moment of choosing whether to obey the law of the state, which forbids the burial of her brother, or a higher, unwritten mandate that would condemn her leaving a kinsman unburied. Viewing Espaillat's text against the backdrop of ethical quandaries that a simple visit to the lingerie section can elicit, Gordon finds an illustration of the sort of complexity that escaped the view of poetry advanced by Heidegger, who seemed insufficiently concerned with examining the extent to which "a happening of truth concerning evil can emerge in simple events in which one must make choices" (Gordon 96).

Gordon's evocation of Espaillat's "Bra" as a means by which to highlight a deficiency in the philosopher's thinking on poetry also reveals something about the versatile, cross-disciplinary relevance of this poet's oeuvre. "Bra" likewise appealed to the award-winning poets Robert McGovern and Stephen Haven, both of Ashland University, who included it in an anthology aiming to capture the climate of American poetry at the end of the twentieth century. As their prefatory commentary indicates, the coeditors assembled the collection (which includes notable poets Kennedy, Turco, and Hayden Carruth) from "1200 submissions from across the United States to create a phantasmagoria of experiences with a world of pain, joy, fear, and astonishment during the 1990s." They were also in search of "new perspectives" from preceding decades that offered glimpses of life in "anticipation of the new millennium" (McGovern and Haven, Front Matter).

While McGovern and Haven could identify in Espaillat's verse concerns resonant with the late twentieth-century US literary zeitgeist, poets Robert Mezey and David Mason, as well as nonfiction writer Kristin Bierfelt and scholar James Fowler, have approached her work with an eye on what might be termed a kind of regional hermeneutics. Mezey includes Espaillat's poem "When We Sold the Tent" in an anthology consisting of work by major contemporary poets who have evoked the American West in their writing. The poem offers a poignant portrait that fuses geography with history, permeated, as its four stanzas are, with a deep sense of the extreme human experiences to which the region has served as both backdrop and participant. One cannot read the text without recognizing, with induced empathy, the plight of the indigenous inhabitants who no longer hold sway over sites like "the Grand Canyon / with its shawl of pines," the "parched white moonscapes of Utah," or "Colorado's / magnificat of flowers." The evocation of the land and its miracles, as well as the threnodic beauty of the song, are mediated by the contemplative "we" that fuses both the vanished lives that inhabited the regions and the sober observer gazing at them today. Readers are confronted with the loss and absence that continue to mark these sites:

> When we sold the tent
> we threw in the Grand Canyon
> with its shawl of pines,
> lap full of cones and chipmunks
> and crooked seams of river.
>
> We let them have the
> parched white moonscapes of Utah,
> and Colorado's
> magnificat of flowers
> sunbursting hill after hill.

Long gentle stretches
of Wyoming, rain outside
some sad Idaho
town where the children, giddy
with strange places, clowned all night.

Eyes like small veiled moons
circling our single light, sleek
shadows with pawprints,
all went with the outfit; and
youth, a river of campfires. (Mezey 166)

Published originally in *Merrimack* (Aponick, Brox, and Marion 1992), another anthology with a title allusive to region, though Northeastern rather than Western, "When We Sold the Tent" would find its way into Espaillat's book *Playing at Stillness* (2005). Nor would its dissemination stop there. On September 2, 2008, it became the object of a live national broadcast on the program *The Writer's Almanac*, hosted by the popular radio producer Garrison Keillor (Keillor). Additionally, prompted by the precedent of Mezey's anthology, Mason quotes the final stanza of "When We Sold the Tent" as the epigraph to a section of his nonfiction work *Two Minds of a Western Poet: Essays* (2011), in which he reminisces about his state of mind at age eighteen, the moment when the restlessness of youth had spurred him to leave the region of his birth in search of life as he imagined it in other geographic spaces (Mason 12).

Espaillat's work has appeared in many explicitly regional contexts, including those that link her existentially to the geography she has inhabited since she left New York City for Newburyport. One could speculate about a connection between the lure of spatial realities in her work and her own lived experience as someone who has planted meaningful roots in the various locations that she has called home. The appeal of Espaillat's verse to regionally, geographically, and environmentally minded writers clearly stems from its keen belief in landscapes as habitats of the living—all species included. These are zones harboring stories of beings grounded in or passing through the physicality of the natural world. Espaillat's "Winter Walk," a poem published originally in *Manhattan Poetry Review* (Jul. 1987, no. 9), is a nature poem with a difference. The speaker's affinity and respect for living things allows for a simple walk through snowy woods to reiterate the inexorable reality that death is all around, even in an enthralling landscape.

We followed paw prints like cuneiform:
tracks that said "possum" on the page of snow.
I pictured finding something curled up warm
wherever such things go,

but at trail's turning, came upon no burrow
cradling our quarry in the crystal field,
but something smaller, torn beyond all sorrow,
That mercy could not shield.

The tracks we followed on a winter day
for pleasure, for delight in all that moves,
ticked on alone. We took another way.
Blood settled in the grooves. (*Lapsing* 9)

With his inclusion of "Winter Walk" in *Heartbeat of New England* (2000), editor James Fowler selected a text that not only suggested "nature poetry" of the kind often inspired by the New England habitat, but also illustrated Espaillat's engagement with those organisms whose existence (and the loss thereof) might typically be shrugged off as evidence of the cycle of life. Similarly, in writing about Espaillat as a voice representing the city of Newburyport, Kristin Bierfelt inscribes the elder poet's work within the literary geography of eastern Massachusetts's North Shore, thereby enhancing the map that she herself sets out to trace in her 2009 book *The North Shore Literary Trail* (Bierfelt).

Broadly, Espaillat's poetry tackles the perennial theme of resilient humanity in a world governed by greed, conflict, desolation, uncertainty, tragedy, and the indomitable yearning to bond and belong. Amid all the pessimism, however, hope, possibility, imagination, joy, and love coexist. As a result, anthologists seeking to assemble thematic collections have found a wealth of suitable material in her oeuvre. By the same token, the Icelandic poet, visual artist, politician, and activist Birgitta Jónsdóttir included Espaillat's verse in her two anthologies of poetry and art that feature work by contributors—per the editor's call—from "the world community." These volumes, both published the year after the devastating September 11, 2001 terrorist attacks in New York, express the artists' collective sorrow and unwavering hopes for peace in the wake of these cataclysmic events. *The Book of Hope* includes Espaillat's poems "Invitation" and "Bread" (9, 86); the other, *The World Healing Book*, features "On Schedule" and "Morning

Prayer" (16, 124). The immediacy of the unifying vision, that artists of the word and image would actively and unequivocally express their solidarity with the overall human species, must have struck a powerful chord with Espaillat, who has long been convinced of the potential for art to offer an antidote to long-held antipathies and ongoing strife.

Espaillat's involvement in projects like these two international collections affirm the draw of her work for editors interested in lyrically conveying views of civic participation through literature. Thus, Adam Davis more recently included her verse in his collection *Taking Action: Readings for Civic Reflection* (2012). Activating the metaphor of exile to express the disenfranchisement of women in a still largely patriarchal world, poets Deborah Keenan and Roseann Lloyd organized an anthology of work by US women poets with ancestral links to other lands by birth or ancestry. They wished for the grouping of texts to capture the drama of "lost identities that must be found again, languages that fall into the pidgin pool," and those that enunciate "suspended hopes for freedom" (Keenan and Lloyd). Consistent with the aspiration to amass and curate work that bears witness to the exilic condition of women who have endured various forms of displacement and resettlement, the editors found in Espaillat's "You Call Me by Old Names" the voice of a speaker who unabashedly asserts her foreign birth. When she perceives slights against her humanity on account of her background and national difference, she resolves the discomfort through ownership of the journey from immigrant nobody to self-certain, critically informed, and vocal somebody.

BY DESIGN OR DESIGNATION: GAUGING WOMEN'S PLACES IN VERSE

Given the humane vision that informs her poetic praxis, the reception of the more recent collection *Her Place in These Designs* (2008) illuminates the success of Espaillat's verse at communicating with readers across the widest range of poetic and cultural literacies. A brief review by the poet Paul Lake uses the event of the book's publication to draw attention to Espaillat's "remarkably large and distinguished body of work" that places "her among the best poets of the last half-century." He argues that to match the achievement of her "meticulously crafted formal poems" in "their variegated diction, range of subjects, and depth of thought and feeling, one must turn to her slightly elder peers, Richard Wilbur and the late Anthony Hecht, for comparison" (Lake 59). Lake identifies Espaillat's output as modern in its intellectual skepticism and religious uncertainty without succumbing "to despair or moral relativism," as laid bare in her explorations of racism in "Replay" and "Grainy Bits" (59). He reads her as a "religious skeptic, aware of contingencies of chance and fate" who employs "the language of religion" to express yearning for the sort of human community that invites and yet supersedes the need for an overseeing God (59).

Poet Julie Stoner's review of the book makes a convincing case for the ability of Espaillat's work to interest young people in a manner that raises questions and piques their critical awareness. She uses as example the impact *Her Place in These Designs* had on her two daughters—one ten, the other twelve—in whose company she read the volume before writing her appraisal. Stoner's review evolves as a rendition of their exchange. At home working on a craft project when their mother sat nearby reading Espaillat's collection, the girls first reacted to its "weird cover," referring to the photograph of *Nude Woman*, a sculpture of a plaster lady, her head bent pensively forward and her body placed at the very center of the page. This is a piece by Alfred Moskowitz, Espaillat's husband, as captured by the camera of Philip Moskowitz, one of their sons; the image portrays a woman deep in thought, enigmatically grounded in a center that she has assumed to be (or taken as) her place. The serenity and firmness of her pose as well as the implications of claiming and inhabiting a space *and* place permeate the photo. After offering the girls some background about this paratextual element, Stoner entertained their request to sample a bit of Espaillat's work. At first she hesitated to oblige, doubting that she would find "poems for kids" in the volume, but settled for one that on the surface seemed safe enough, a piece about a missing hermit crab.

Stoner observes, "Not far into reading 'Crab Poem' aloud, my heart sinks as I realize what a dark and complicated sonnet this really is. Far too dark and complicated for a fifth-grader and an eighth" (Stoner). She recalls avoiding the final stanza's "uncomfortable theological implications," and assuming that the silence of the girls after hearing the poem meant she had made a poor choice. Then, the reactions emerged, with the ten-year-old commenting on Espaillat's "funny" comparison of the crab's walk to "tapdancing." She conceded that it "does kind of sound that way when they're on a table, or something hard." For her part, the twelve-year-old zeroed in on the way the speaker in the poem went from being on her knees looking for the crustacean—albeit unsuccessfully—to "maybe praying on her knees for stuff, and not getting that either." While unsure about "liking" the composition, she admitted that "it makes you think." The younger sister likewise found it "kind of brave talking about God like that in a poem," meditating upon the "kind of stuff" that comes to mind "when bad things happen."

The conversation graduated to the girls grappling with Espaillat's choice to involve heaven in human affairs at so quotidian a level as searching for an ambulant crab. The younger girl pointed out that the poet "knows that if God can do *anything*, then big disasters and little disasters are really the same, to Him" (Stoner). At this point the sisters requested other "animal poems" in the volume, which led to their consideration of the sonnet "Woodchuck." At one point, they worried whether the gun evoked in the text was real, fearful lest the speaker dispatch the furry beast with it, but felt relief upon knowing she was only imagining the gun, not wielding it. They then consumed the poem "Squirrel," which describes "those smallest fingers clasp[ed] together" as if in prayer; this image of rodent piety begged the question "whether or not heaven is fair, / entirely deaf or not to such small prayer." "Parable" was deemed to be enticingly "creepy" given that the speaker exists simultaneously as the bear, the animal keeper, and the speaker-spectator in the audience. The girls kept their mother "reading for nearly an hour, requesting encores of the poems they particularly like[d]."

Clearly, Stoner's review is unusual for its use of dramatic technique, recreating dialogues about the book with her preteen daughters instead of merely evaluating it on her own. The implicit approbation of Espaillat's collection surfaces through its unexpected appeal to these young critics. Such an audience would probably take to her verse on the basis of its sonic qualities and visual concreteness, less so for its metaphysical nuances and eminently human concerns such as religious doubts and the limits of hope amid tragedy and death. Stoner's intergenerational experience lays bare the versatile appeal of Espaillat's volume, and by extension, her inclusive worldview.

A review of *Her Place in These Designs* by Alfred Nicol focuses on Espaillat's "meditation on the related polarities of obedience and defiance, custom and departure," which the reviewer perceives as particularly pervasive (Nicol, "Lately"). His piece undertakes a sustained analytical assessment, seeking out a kind of conceptual core to the volume. He reads her poem "Lares et Penates," a two-sonnet sequence on disposing of her parents' belongings after their deaths (in particular, her mother's porcelain and her father's books) as a way of pitting the urge to discard and move on against the will "to conserve, to bring back." These valences dramatize "the contradictions of the heart." Nicol finds that Espaillat outlines "her defining polarities, her dear contradictions" in an unpretentious way, hybridizing "memory, dream and everyday occurrences" so as to locate, by "every avenue," a difficult place of existential belonging. This conflicted position, simultaneously restful and restive, defines "her place in these designs." Likewise, Nicol reads Espaillat's "On Re-Reading a Sonnet Written in 1951," a poem in which the speaker revisits thoughts expressed in her youth, as "a catalyst to writing the introspective and retrospective collection of poems" ("Lately"). The critic's hypothesis about the introspection-retrospection dyad proves enormously helpful in a broad evaluation of the collection.

In his review, Nicol also considers the poem "Clara, My Unconceived," whose speaker converses with a beloved doll—"a hostage from the past"—resting "on dusty shelves." In so doing, the gently philosophical voice tackles the coexistence of absence and presence. Looking at her "childhood's last- / and-never daughter," the speaker muses about what it would have been like to have raised a little girl, something that is virtually impossible now given her advanced age. She also ponders "loves that keep themselves safe, out of time," since the doll is no longer animated by the same imaginative fuel that ignites a child's mind and affections. The speaker relates the toy's perpetual stillness to "Sister Ada's rendering of the soul, / whose vacancy, she said, was all its task. / She did not tell us why. We didn't ask" (*Her Place* 20–21). The poem's turn from "a pleasant stroll down memory lane" into an eerie peering "into the Abyss" begs the question of what "vacancy" it is we are consistently trying to fill, whether with material objects or people. In Nicol's view, this juxtaposition of a joyful moment with a poignant or otherwise painful alternative typifies Espaillat's capacity to be a "poet of friendly surfaces and terrible depths"—a quality, he argues, that she shares with her much-admired predecessor Robert Frost ("Lately").

"Triptych," a piece comprising three thematically linked sonnets, each describing a woman at a point of momentous decision making, stands out as another core text in Nicol's reading of *Her Place in These Designs*. The larger philosophical theme touches upon our relative ability (or lack thereof) to escape our given circumstances. Sonnet I ("Departures") opens thus: "A woman grips her ticket; gate fourteen; / lines lumbering to board." It is a scene of separation from the parental home. Having recently married, "she tries to understand why she is vexed" (*Her Place* 53). Sonnet II ("Suppose") begins with the quatrain "A woman with a suitcase boards a bus. / She has shrugged off her life like a worn dress, / stepped clear of it, packed nothing to discuss / or mourn for; to be glad of, even less." Signaling a break with a former role and assumed status, the final three lines point to her sense of a new beginning: "There in the suitcase tucked between her knees/ (still tagged with names she will not wear again) / nothing but a blank notebook and a pen." Sonnet III ("Roadmap") situates the action at a moment when the protagonist breaks away from an incompatible relationship: "A woman spreads a road map on the seat, / fevered with purpose, bruised by what he said, / by what she shouted back. The mapled street / unspools behind her" (54).

According to Nicol, the scene of this impassioned woman "driving an automobile, running away from a destructive relationship" harnesses the raw and profound ambivalence of emotional uncoupling ("Lately"). The poem describes "hands trembling on the wheel, stricken, sweat cold / with fear of what she craves—foresees return" (*Her Place* 54). Amid her precipitous departure, the subject remains aware of the wretched likelihood that she has not quite severed all ties. "She will 'learn her name again,'" notes Nicol, pointing to her premonition as yet another instance of recognition of "her place in these designs." Instead of offering a glib and happy ending, Espaillat aims to "shock" the reader with this indeterminacy, studying the "kind of entrapment" characterizing a troubled relationship and, by extension, a life that "one cannot step clear of" ("Lately"). The reviewer points out that while the author herself does not match the profile of the woman in the car, she does represent the character at a metaphorical level given her "abiding concern" throughout the volume about how we cannot sidestep "the essential life, the life that defines [us]." Taking "nothing for granted," raising doubts and questions, and going forward without "complacent nostalgia," Espaillat "turns over in her mind and closely examines what she values most."

The pattern of contradictions that so intrigues Nicol obtains in Espaillat's vision where "love itself can set in motion the engines of cruelty." This irony manifests itself in "On the Power of Love to Ennoble the Spirit," which takes as its subject the Indian monarch Shah Jahan, who had the Taj Mahal built for the queen he adored, but did so amid great abuse of the workers. The emperor chose to honor the memory of his beloved by ensuring that a similar feat of art and engineering could not be replicated; she alone would be so honored. Thus, out of love for his departed wife, he had the hands of the industrious workers severed and the architects decapitated. Unwilling to "accept anything on good authority," including love, hate, and all that lies between, the poet perseveres in the quest for meaning amid such brutalities. She does so while making room for the possibility that in the end, all of the zeal we have in life for attaining emotional satisfaction, resolution, and even some measure of peace may not matter. The sonnet "Contingencies," for instance, reminds us that sometimes we must proceed as if it did (Nicol, "Lately").

In the poem "Guidelines," Nicol finds "the finest didactic poem anyone has written in some time," and provides a sampling of the first stanzas: "Here's what you need to do, since time began: / find something—diamond rare or carbon-cheap, / it's all the same—and love it all you can" (*Her Place* 36). Nicol offers as key to the aesthetic and moral success of the piece the fact that "it avoids sounding like unsolicited parental advice," conveying rather the sense of the speaker "talking to herself through her own confusion" ("Lately"). That is, indeed, the constructive spirit pervading the fourth and fifth stanzas:

> It's going to hurt. That was the risk you ran
> with your first breath; you knew the price was steep,
> that loss is what there is, since time began
>
> subtracting from your balance. That's the plan,
> too late to quibble now, you're in too deep.
> Just love what you still have, while you still can. (*Her Place* 36)

Nicol concludes his explication of *Her Place in These Designs* with a brief statement on Espaillat's "delightfully self-effacing" sonnet "Lately I've Wondered," a piece whose speaker tries to imagine herself being judged by others after death. She ruminates over a variety of possible scenarios, including who will remember her and how. In the end, she comes to terms with the fruitlessness of such a morbidly fascinating exercise. The speaker "shrugs her shoulders and tells herself 'it's no use,' it's 'not mine to know'" (Nicol, "Lately"). In this poem, we can detect a subtle desire on the part of the artist to distance herself from the narcissism of fellow artists confident of their place in posterity, famously illustrated by the closing couplet of Shakespeare's Sonnet 18. There, the speaker proclaims the immortality of his beloved by virtue of her association with the poem he has just written for her: "So long as men can breathe, or eyes can see, / So long lives this, and this gives life to thee" (Shakespeare, *Complete Works* 1693). Espaillat may be questioning the braggadocio of the poet as artistic entrepreneur, just as she seems to question so many "givens" in this volume as in the preceding ones. Irrespective of whether, as in the case of Shakespeare, poets hit the mark when predicting the longevity of their legacies, Espaillat steers clear of literary egomania; there are just more productive uses of one's time. One such endeavor would be casting what might be called the *stuff of life* in a manner that even ten- and twelve-year-old readers, such as Stoner's intrepid daughters, could profitably engage with and enjoy.

SCHOLARLY APPRAISALS

Apart from his study of *Her Place in These Designs*, Nicol also contributed a comprehensive essay on Espaillat's literary trajectory that appeared as a chapter in Supplement XXI of the reference series *American Writers: A Collection of Literary Biographies*, edited by Jay Parini (Nicol, "Rhina P. Espaillat"). Nicol's critical effort here expands on the overviews of the poet's life and works previously undertaken by fellow poet Len Krisak ("Rhina P. Espaillat") and literary scholar Silvio Torres-Saillant ("Formalismo"). Krisak, a close collaborator with Espaillat in the Powow River Poets, along with Dorn, helped to make her work visible to the New Formalist crowd. He played a key role in facilitating what would become her productive collaboration with the West Chester Poetry Conference and Center. Accordingly, his overview establishes Espaillat's credentials as a New Formalist *avant la lettre*, in that she had mastered traditional prosody on her own since the 1940s (78). Krisak observes that she followed a route comparable to that of her slightly elder contemporaries Wilbur, Hecht, Kennedy, Justice, and James Merrill, who, like her, form part of the pantheon of poets associated with New Formalism. Krisak tells us further of the renewal of "her engagement with verse" as she assumed a leadership role in the creation of the Fresh Meadows Poets, the publication of books beginning in 1992, the numerous awards that have materialized, her key participation in the Powow River Poets, and her "influential" involvement as part of the West Chester University Poetry Conference faculty, a position that endeared her to that community of poets who group themselves under the aesthetic banner of "the New Formalism" (82).

Subsequently, the overview by Torres-Saillant appeared as the introduction to *Agua de dos ríos*, a bilingual compilation of poetry and prose by Espaillat published by the Ministry of Culture of the Dominican Republic. The volume is one of a series of honors conferred by the government of her birth country. Torres-Saillant's essay seeks to familiarize a target audience comprised primarily of US Dominicans as well as other Spanish-speaking readers with Espaillat's background and career path. Her rise to prominence had, after all, occurred among predominantly white practitioners and audiences in the mainstream of

American verse production. On the whole, the piece covers the poet's beginnings, her return to literary visibility postretirement in the early 1990s, the fame and critical accolades her work has earned, her aesthetic creed, her inclusive and empathic worldview, and her commitment to community as reflected in her leadership work with local projects spearheaded by Dominican immigrant poets in Lawrence, Massachusetts.

Covering a larger expanse, Nicol has produced a first-rate, comprehensive account of Espaillat's life and works. Despite its relative brevity at seventeen pages, his overview manages to encompass Espaillat's oeuvre with sound attention to the poet's biography, historical context, and literary career; as such, it is an invaluable critical resource. Nicol's essay takes an in-depth look at Espaillat's thought process, her existential disposition, and the conceptual engagement discernible in her verse, supplementing the preceding approaches to her work. Nicol grapples with the difficult theology and the potentially "dark" outlooks haunting some of Espaillat's poetry, while simultaneously recognizing its "graciousness and warmth of humanity" (Nicol, "Rhina P. Espaillat" 97). At the formal level, he characterizes her work's "seamless match of conversational tone and meter" as the accomplished feat of "a contemporary master of traditionalist poetics" (97). The critic argues that in poetry as in the fractious realm of contemporary social relations, Espaillat's "major literary concerns are centered on the idea of inclusiveness" (97). Her tendency to promote this orientation and social value becomes evident at the artistic level in her trying her hand at genres that have fallen out of fashion with contemporary poets, such as the didactic poem, as well as in her steering clear of "opaque or hermetic" expressions in her verse broadly.

Nicol also bears witness to her willingness to foster literary border crossing by encouraging intermingling between the Spanish-speaking events of the Pedro Mir Reading Circle (Tertulia Pedro Mir) in Lawrence and its Anglophone counterpart in Newburyport. By the same token, she has imported Spanish forms (*ovillejo*, *glosa*, and *décima*) into Anglophone American verse, translated Spanish-language verse into English and vice versa, and recruited classical guitarist John Tavano and Nicol himself to bring the melopoeia performance (poetry recited to musical accompaniment) to New England (Nicol, "Rhina P. Espaillat" 99). She thus publicized, especially to audiences "north of Boston," an art form that she first encountered during her Dominican childhood. It was a means of delighting people with the promotion of "a new way of hearing poetry" (99–100). Espaillat's manner of handling meter and rhyme reproduces the ethos of expansiveness discerned by Nicol insofar as she manipulates the so-called rigidity of classical prosody in a way that allows readers to consume forms that might otherwise have appeared intimidating. In keeping with Frost's model, she lays "the rhythms of common speech over a grid of iambic pentameter, bending without breaking the meter; often she uses enjambment to half-muffle end rhyme." Espaillat thereby produces an art that conceals its artifice, letting us see merely "the tip of the iceberg" (100).

To Nicol, the villanelle "Highway Apple Trees," featured first in Espaillat's debut collection *Lapsing to Grace*, serves as a quintessential example of the poet's rendering traditional prosodic structures in an accessible form. The poem, in short, celebrates the haphazard triumph of a "harvest" that "just grows" despite the lack of anyone actively tending to it. This small miracle suggests "the disorderly way life has of coming alive" in the most unlikely or inhospitable of circumstances. The first two stanzas encapsulate the spirit of the poem:

> Nobody seeds this harvest, it just grows,
> miraculous, above old caps and cans.
> These apples may be sweet. Nobody knows
>
> If they were meant to ripen under those
> slow summer clouds, cooled by their small green fans.
> Nobody seeds this harvest, it just grows. (*Lapsing* 1)

Nicol's close reading of the poem, with particular attention to form, evinces "the syncopated rhythm" to which the lines dance, creating the effect of "improvisation, as it should be in a poem whose theme is the provisional, make-do nature of existence, where there is no hierarchical imposition of relevance or irrelevance" (101). In a passage devoted to a metrical analysis of lines two and three of the first stanza, Nicol excavates the poem's meaning: "Though every line is of course made of five iambic feet, the caesuras fall in different places, so that the ear hears phrases of different lengths. A caesura separates the second line into two parts, of two feet and of three feet. The opposite occurs in the third line, where the three-foot section comes first, after which the lines are enjambed so that there is no natural stop till the comma creates a caesura in line five" (101). Nicol likens the verbal performance here, namely Espaillat's use of "punctuation as an indication of where to draw in new breath," to that of a saxophonist (101).

The critic proceeds to shed light on different aspects of Espaillat's poetic practice as they relate to the phenomena that have shaped her vision, including bilingualism, domesticity, and artistic communities. He also comments upon her engagement with the divine order, devoting an entire section to Espaillat's "quarrel with God" by investigating several facets of her difficult theology, one in which she challenges the divinity to do right by humanity. More heretical than truly atheistic, Espaillat puts divinity to the test. God figures as a constant in her poems, faith in Him showing up not as "a given but something desirable placed just beyond the poet's reach" (109). Nicol offers the sonnet "You Who Sleep Soundly through Our Bleakest Hour" as perhaps Espaillat's "most passionate outburst in her quarrel with God" (110). Published originally in *Sparrow* and collected in her Stanzas Prize–winning volume *The Shadow I Dress In* (2003), the sonnet reads:

> You who sleep soundly through our bleakest hour,
> who hear the meekest cry, and turn away,
> who ride the river, blessing it with power
> to cancel what we've made day by slow day;
> You whom we cannot know nor flee, who hide
> behind your countless aliases, who bear
> the weapon of your absence like a tide
> against our helplessness, and fail to care;
> You who stand by while madness picks the lock,
> stroke cuts the wires, tumor rigs the mine:
> Look how we scour the earth to find—in rock,
> in fire, in word—your signature, some sign
> of you in thought that quarrels with your will,
> and as it quarrels, hungers for you still. (*Shadow* 71)

By having the speaker of this Elizabethan sonnet directly address the deity, charged here as being "indifferent, hostile in his absence, complicit," Espaillat seems less interested in dismissing the existence of the Almighty than in demanding that He live up to the image of caring parent that the catechism of her childhood presented as truth.

This request, according to Nicol, lays bare how her "work does not so much deny spiritual truths as weigh them against the experience of mortal men and women in an attempt to bring the two sides of the scale into balance" ("Rhina P. Espaillat" 111). But in addition to what the critic unearths here, the poet could also be reopening the age-old conversation between the creature and its creator dramatized in the Book of Job (38:4–31). The Hebrew deity has little patience for Job, a mortal who comes to Him with plaints about unearned misfortunes that he, a pious and fearful believer, has endured. The Lord responds with a volley of rhetorical questions that leave the man contrite and remorseful, as well as aware of his insignificance. The divinity terminates the conversation with such retorts as, "Where were you when I laid the foundation of the earth? . . . Have you commanded the morning since your days began?" as well as "Can you bind the chains of the Pleiades, or loose the cords of Orion?" (*Bible* 650–51). The Lord condemns Job's complaints as impudent and asserts his prerogative as supreme architect of Creation, remaining aloof to human misery and dismissing the need for explanations. Espaillat may be hinting that the conversation should not have ended there, that perhaps Job's meek acceptance of the Almighty's inscrutability lets Him off the hook a bit too easily. Ultimately, though, what emerges is a voice self-assured of its moral right to demand goodness from the Maker, the demand put forward, in Nicol's words, by "the maker of poems," thereby staging a sort of clash of creative titans (Nicol, "Rhina P. Espaillat" 112).

Like Nicol, poet Leslie Monsour has funneled considerable energy into Espaillat's work. *Rhina Espaillat: A Critical Introduction* (2013) is a slim volume intended to make the older poet's verse conceptually available to the general reader. In it, Monsour identifies Espaillat's lost brother as a subtext for "Their Only Child," the opening piece in the collection *Rehearsing Absence*:

> I am the one that doesn't get away.
> Their blood tumbles with promise, teeming
> quicksilver too luminous to stay;
> I am the whole catch, landed and streaming
> rainbows. Those others they dream of
> circle the wormed hook, but sensing harm,
> slide on forever. I am the one
> trailing their bait through the film of the ideal,
> rising to this flawed light. No more, no less
> than actual, like a death, I am the real
> one, the waking, the caress. (*Rehearsing* 3)

The controlling metaphor of "Their Only Child" captures the drama of the fish seeking to escape the "wormed hook" of the expectant fisherman and "slide on forever." The speaker, her parents' only living child, exists because she bit the "bait," unlike her younger brother; while she managed to rise "to this flawed light," he slipped away. The darkness of the tone, reflected in the representation of life to the nonliving as a "flawed light" and the experience of survival as little more than an ordinary task to undertake, matches the metrical structure of the three quatrains that constitute the piece. The irregularity of these lines adds to the matter-of-fact tone which belies the heavy themes, including the trauma of premature death and the humbling sadness of meditating upon that which never was.

Monsour has identified Espaillat's utterances as being typically characterized by an attraction to "paradox and contradictions as vehicles for exploring and understanding the links and tensions that exist between opposites" (Monsour, *Rhina P. Espaillat* 35–36). Her dualistic themes bring to mind the poets of the Spanish Golden Age and the English Metaphysical poets, especially Herbert and Donne, who favored "paradox, oxymoron, and conceit as inventions of wit" (36). From "Being the Ant," which revisits Aesop's ancient fable of "The Ant and the Grasshopper," to "Impasse: Glose," which tackles the age-old battle between reason and emotion, to the signature poem about translated lives, "Bilingual/Bilingüe," Monsour elevates the poet's quest to resolve oppositional tensions without granting victory to any one side. "In Espaillat's universe," the critic proposes, "when different worlds mingle, both sides retain their integrity, largely because the striving toward understanding and the desire to communicate it are never abandoned in the work" (46).

A LATINO/A READING

One of the most sustained critical assessments of Espaillat's oeuvre prior to the present study comes from literary scholar Frederick Luis Aldama, who has scrutinized her verse along with that of Julia Alvarez, the Cuban American medical doctor Rafael Campo, and C. Dale Young, the physician son of an Asian-Latino father and an Anglo mother. Aldama's *Formal Matters in Contemporary Latino Poetry* (2013) surveys the skillful engagement with prosody and unique artistry of American poets of Hispanic descent. The volume devotes a chapter and an interview to each of the poets under consideration. The scholar stresses the element of creation in each body of writing, identifying the disposition to "bring a new reality into the world" rather than merely produce a replica of concrete reality or regurgitate preexisting versions. He delineates the "willful application (or the will to style)" of these poetic practitioners that gives "shape, meaning, and vitality" to their respective verse (Aldama 136). Particularly in relation to Espaillat's verse, Aldama highlights the "nonmimetic impulse" (131) in her aesthetic practice as well as the eminently sensorial quality of her poems. He engages the poet's meditation on "the seeming impossibilities of the transmutation of one sense into another" (132) as posited in the lines, "Touch / and color into sound, sound into sign, / sign into sense again and back," from the poem "On the Impossibility of Translation," the sonnet that closes Espaillat's *Her Place in These Designs*.

"On the Impossibility of Translation" expands upon the challenge of transferring poetic meaning from one language to another, a topic that the poet wrestles with in "Translating," featured in the same volume. Taken together, the two pieces revolve around "an art difficult as marriage, whose medium is the stony grit of language" (*Her Place* 79). These texts incite an overarching meditation on language, craft, and the parameters fostering or inhibiting genuine communication. Aldama emphasizes Espaillat's view of the "limitations to our mental faculties—limits to our capacity for synesthesia as well as the conversion of acoustic stimuli into phonemes that form words that point to things in the world (signs)" (Aldama 132). In the closing lines of "On the Impossibility of Translation," the speaker reviews for the presumed listener the observable reality of transmuted meanings: "You've heard, / fitful above the fields, the summer sung / in high, cascading turns of fluent Bird, / and seen, in shallow pools in every town, / how rain translates the sky and writes it down" (*Her Place* 88). Aldama characterizes the terminal moment in the poem as an "alchemical performance" wherein the text translates "the commonplace into the abstract," all the while deploying classical prosody "to create heightened tensions and satisfying resolutions" (133). He identifies a tendency to "abstract the commonplace" as a dominant feature of Espaillat's poetic praxis (113).

The scholar finds this feature a consistent quality of her verse going back to her first book, *Lapsing to Grace*. Here, in the poem "Unison," a scene following a rain shower serves as the speaker's vehicle to venture into deep introspection, while in "September" she meditates on both seasonal shifts and the 1929 stock market crash. In "Tapping the Glass," a visit to the snake den at the zoo triggers the speaker's identification with the captured reptiles. She comes to recognize herself not only as the one seeing but also as the object of the animals' perception. Their mutualistic relationship emerges in the cross-rhymed quatrain in iambic tetrameters, which yields a rhythm common to hymns (Aldama 115–16). With hymns standing as songs of communion and fellowship, this feature subtly encourages readers to intuit a connection between these often-maligned, cold-blooded animals and their human counterparts, all creatures caught in the wide net of interconnected life.

Aldama's *Formal Matters* applauds Espaillat's capacity to converse with artists throughout the ages as well as with individuals who have defied daunting odds. Her work champions the individual spirit, especially when eroded by bitter circumstances and outrageous fortune. "Reading Vermeer," from *Where Horizons Go*, takes issue with a poet who defines his own literary endeavors by unduly focusing upon the loneliness of artistry and the "risk" it involves. As suggested by the poem's title, the speaker, shunning exceptionalism or pretense, instead identifies with a definition of the artist's craft discernible in the work of seventeenth-century Dutch painter Johannes Vermeer Van Delft (1632–1675). The speaker prefers the serene world depicted on a painter's canvas, where "people, drenched in light, like honey, wear / the blessing of the hive" (Espaillat, *Where Horizons Go* 56). Scenes of ordinary life prevail over abstract affectation, as when a "woman reads a letter: nothing new" (56). Aldama refers to the aesthetic stance conveyed by the speaker's musings in the poem as a predilection for "the commonplace" (119). The speaker also displays a propensity to self-conscious "metacritical" commentary, granting that her impression of the woman and her maid in the painting "could be wrong," or even a mere figment of a poet's imagination: "and mine the only poem in these pages / to celebrate a life that slows to song" (Aldama 119; Espaillat, *Where Horizons Go* 56).

In his examination of this poem, Aldama accentuates the ekphrastic conceit, a kind of intertextuality wherein writers engage the works of artists produced in other art forms or media. It is a recurring feature in Espaillat's writing. Coined originally by Roman rhetoricians of the first century AD out of the Greek prefix *ek-* (out) and the verb *phrassein* (to tell), *ekphrasis* initially referred to digressions in oratory, but by the fourth century AD its primary meaning had shifted to denote the literary representation of visual art. The memorable description of the shield of Achilles in the *Iliad* of Homer is often seen as the "earliest known example" of the technique (Ellis 616). Espaillat's references to people "drenched in light" and to the woman "framed by her room" reading a letter may provide the necessary visual clues for the reader familiar with Vermeer's work to recognize the painting in question.

By highlighting Espaillat's penchant for ekphrasis as a tool to explore subjects that are dear to her, Aldama makes a contribution to the scholarship on her work whose significance becomes more apparent as one considers it beyond the coverage that the modest length of his chapter permitted him. *Her Place in These Designs* abounds in poems that showcase ekphrastic relations with paintings from across the centuries. One example is "Leonardo's Metaphor," a sonnet that develops the idea of the body as "an organ on which the soul played" (*Her Place* 68). Another sonnet, "On the Ambivalence of Angels: *Expulsion from Paradise*, Giovanni di Paolo," evokes Adam and Eve's departure from Eden as depicted by the fifteenth-century Italian painter. Here the speaker imputes a certain ambivalence to the angel assigned the task of escorting "our youthful parents" out of the Garden: "See how the angel seems to yearn / after them, as if eager to come too" (69).

The piece titled "Pentimento," also a sonnet, takes its subject from another painting by Vermeer. Prefaced by an epigraph by Sir Herbert Read (1893–1968), the text sheds light on the "traces" of a figure that the artist had "attempted to paint out" yet remain discernible "beside the two women chatting in the foreground" (72). As might be expected of Espaillat's democratic eye, the text concentrates not on the two women most prominent to the viewer but on the barely visible figure, the one that would have existed had the painter not changed his mind. After all, the word *pentimento* is derived from the Italian verb *pentirsi*, meaning "to repent." Like the tempter snake or her lost brother, Espaillat gives a platform for the thoughts and words of the figure that did not materialize, the one relegated to mere palimpsestic "traces." This (un)forgotten presence is a "curious absence that your eye / can almost see through, here and yet not here" (72). Serving as the speaker in the poem, the barely visible figure simply tries to comprehend why the painter "first made, then banished me away," a question that might resonate with any number of scenarios, lived or imagined, in which one godlike agent bears a disproportionate amount of power over another (72).

No less engaging is "Paul Helleu Sketching with His Wife," a sonnet that deals with the titular painting by American artist John Singer Sargent (1856–1925), who spent much time overseas imbibing the French arts scene. Sargent's work captures the painter Paul César Helleu (1859–1927) working on a grassy riverbank, a little boat to his right and, on the left, his wife peering, as Espaillat's poem notes, "beyond the canvas" (73). The speaker in the poem uses the third-person point of view to flesh out the character of Madame Helleu, reconstructing her state of mind in light of the couple's relationship, all of which is extrapolated from this pictorial representation. Likewise, the Elizabethan sonnet "Portrait of Don Manuel Osorio de Zúñiga" meditates in the third person about the power relations captured in the painting of the same name by Spanish artist Francisco de Goya (1746–1828). Goya's piece depicts a child of nobility, Don Manuel (1784–1792), the short-lived son of the Count of Altamira who availed himself of the services of the artist, officially the king's painter at the time. The child, hardly older than five, is outfitted in splendid red velvet and holds a pet magpie by a string. In the jaunty bird's beak may be found the painter's calling card. At the boy's feet, three hypnotically staring cats crouch to the right and more birds occupy a cage to his left. The portrait suggests to the speaker something of the political economy of the world Goya inhabited: "A string / links child and bird and painter's signature, / as if to say that genius, claw and wing / must share alike the favor of the small / red velvet connoisseur who owns them all" (*Her Place* 74).

Aldama explicates the sonnet "Nothing New," in which the speaker assumes the defense of *Souvenir de Mortefontaine*, a piece that "enshrines the landscape, yes, but tells the truth" (75). This 1864 work by French landscape and portrait painter Jean-Baptiste-Camille Corot (1796–1875) earned the dismissal of at least one notable colleague. The poem's epigraph consists of a comment made on August 22, 1865, by Jean-François Millet (1814–1875). A French realist painter associated with the Barbizon school, Millet in his comment dismissed Corot's works on the grounds that, though "beautiful," they "reveal nothing new" (75). Aldama contends that by taking sides with Corot against Millet, Espaillat asserts the inherent value of a painter's memory as captured on the canvas, a brief flash of human experience. Espaillat thus enters the fray of aesthetic mediation between two tendencies in nineteenth-century French art, and she settles for a nonmimetic practice that privileges the interpretation of lived experience (Aldama 130–31). This inclination is visible in the last of the ekphrastic poems in *Her Place in These Designs*, one that reflects on *The Bath*, an intimate piece by American painter and printmaker Mary Cassatt (1844–1926). This artist's work was often exhibited alongside that of the European Impressionists, and she counted the French artist Edgar Degas (1834–1917) among her close friends (Strasnick). Espaillat's sonnet comments lyrically on Cassatt's depiction of a mother tenderly bathing her small daughter, closing with a tantalizing question about the painter's own relationship to maternity: "One wonders what the eye / of the skilled artist made of this other life, / she who was never mother, never wife" (*Her Place* 78).

Aldama is quick to identify how the speakers in Espaillat's verse often walk a fine line as a result of the poet's habit of entering characters' heads and recreating their reactions to various phenomena regardless of their respective moral compasses. The sonnet "Six of One"—the title most likely an abbreviated version of the idiomatic expression "six of one and a half dozen of the other," meaning, "it's all the same"—evokes the problematic figure of the Genoese sailor and icon of New World exploration Christopher Columbus (1451–1506). The speaker addresses the mariner who would later gain the rank of Admiral of the Ocean Sea, pointing to his erroneous itinerary, which earns him a mocking comparison with American aviator Douglas Corrigan (1907–1995), who, in 1938, departed from Brooklyn with Long Beach, California, as his intended destination. He landed in Ireland instead. The poem evokes the difficulty of Columbus's passage, especially with his "crew hysteric," and his finally coming through to "hail Columbia by a name mistaken / and dub her people 'Indians.'" Eventually, he travels home, forsaken by his sponsors, "to die a poor man's death" (*Where Horizons Go* 23). The poem manages thus to imagine the story of the explorer from the perspective of an individual choosing among the options for self-advancement available to him.

This look at the Columbian enterprise prior to the horrors that it would subsequently unleash gives the speaker the liberty to consider the question of whether the adventurer did right or wrong in following his impulse: "So all roads lead to Rome, / but Rome's not always where our purpose wends. / Should you regret the trip? Well, that depends" (23). No doubt, here, especially with the sardonic tone, Espaillat's pen bears an "ironic edge," to use Aldama's phrase, which would seem acceptable if one managed to place oneself in the sailor's situation before his arrival in the Americas (Aldama 119). If hindsight were to creep in and the reader harbor any empathy for the indigenous populations that bore the brunt of the colonial transaction, it would be hard to remain neutral to Columbus's decision-making process and the motivations informing it.

Perhaps Espaillat's decision to phrase the response to whether or not Columbus should regret his actions through a conditional ("that depends") stems from a willingness to consider the speculative nature of all of these queries. Most of us are unaware of the consequences of our actions in the long run, let alone those that result from following our ambitions. Nor is it always auspicious when our dreams come true. In act 2, scene 1, of Oscar Wilde's 1895 play *An Ideal Husband*, the Undersecretary of Foreign Affairs Sir Robert Chiltern must confront the morally flawed decisions that had brought about his wealth. As events seem to be coming to a head, potentially ruining his personal life, Chiltern remembers "having read somewhere, in some strange book, that when the gods wish to punish us they answer our prayers" (Wilde 55). In more recent times, J. Robert Oppenheimer (1904–1967) felt no joy on July 16, 1945, when the fruits of his labor as director of the Manhattan Project proved successful and he witnessed the atomic bomb detonate in Alamogordo, New Mexico. As the smoke, fire, dust, light, and darkness mushroomed into the immense cloud of destruction, Oppenheimer recalled the haunting words of Vishnu from Hinduism's ancient scripture the *Bhagavad Gita*: "Now I am become Death, the destroyer of worlds." The compulsion to be remarkable and accomplish great feats (in short, the quest for glory in any number of fields and endeavors) can ironically manifest itself in the most grievous ways.

Nicol's aforementioned discussion of Espaillat's poem "On the Power of Love to Ennoble the Spirit" points to her caution even when the motivating force behind the quest may be explained as love. The poem "The Master Explains" delves into the perverse motivation of the obstetrician who cut his signature into his patient's belly after successfully delivering her new baby—as a way, perhaps, to claim credit for his accomplishment. In Aldama's view, the poet "takes the reader into the reasoning of a mind that we certainly don't recognize as healthy" (122). But what if the pathology involved can be construed as excessive artistic pride? The poem leads one to wonder whether any creator or, in this case, practitioner of a craft that facilitates creation, runs the risk of indulging in boastfulness as unhealthy as that of the hubristic obstetrician.

Aldama has paid close attention to the facets of Espaillat's works that address novel forms of perception and communication. "Tooth Poem," a piece in *The Shadow I Dress In* (2004) that returns to the harrowing subject of Dulce María's Alzheimer's disease, points to a progressive loss of sensory acuity as one of the unsettling characteristics of that debilitating illness (Aldama 122). Similarly, the poem "Translation," from the same volume, narrates the extent to which language and cultural differences hinder our respectful perception of others, causing us to misrecognize the aspects of their humanity that we take for granted in ourselves (123). The sonnet "Easy Words," spoken in the staccato rhythm of monosyllabic lines, reflects upon the efficacy and lasting effects of words wielded as weapons. Many times, we miscalculate the pain we can cause through careless or barbed utterances (126).

Espaillat also interrogates perception itself as the faculty whereby we discern everyday phenomena in the physical world. For instance, "Refraction" deals with a wave's change in direction as a result of its interaction with a medium. In terms of optics, refraction accounts for "the tardy manifestation of existence in the form of light," which has an impact on how we create and subsequently access memories (Aldama 124). "Eyes," from *Playing at Stillness*, dramatizes the speaker's envy for a fly's 360-degree access to its surroundings thanks to its compound eyes. The piece launches into what Aldama terms "an epistemology of vision" (127). Here, we might recall Espaillat's powerful attraction to Edna St. Vincent Millay's poem "Renascence," whose "poetic eye" is akin to the impressive spectrum offered by the fly's aggregate point of view. Early in her artistic upbringing, the possibilities, both seen and unseen, in "Renascence" compelled the young Espaillat to think of such figurations as perhaps "what consciousness is for" (NK/STS). As time has passed, the collection of lenses comprising the fly's field of view still aptly symbolizes the mature poet's desire to behold the world from various perspectives, humble as well as grandiose, simultaneously grounded in the concrete world while borne aloft by the abstract and the invisible.

8 | EVER-WIDENING CIRCLES
A POETICS OF INCLUSION

WORLDVIEW AND POETIC PRAXIS

The history of English prosody has been an ongoing negotiation between tradition and change, the change not infrequently achieved by means of the reclamation of diction, styles, and structures formerly deemed antiquated or no longer trendy. From the Old English hemistich to early Middle English accentual verse, and then on to accentual syllabic verse, alliterative long lines, iambic pentameter, and all that has followed from the fifteenth through to the twenty-first century, poets have sought to assert themselves by altering the technical and conceptual inheritance received from their predecessors. The Shakespearean scholar George T. Wright offers an astute summary of prosodic disputes in the history of verse production in English:

> Analysis of poetic modes comes generally after the fact, but in every period prosodic criticism has a moralistic flavor. Adherents of quantitative verse in the Renaissance condemn the inexpressive native iambic verse, with its meager and invariable two syllables to a foot. . . . Theorists of the 18th century scourge the

intrusion of anapestic or trochaic variation into the steady iambic current as har-
bingers of revolutionary anarchy. Many 19th-century poets (e.g., Keats, Arnold)
disdain their Augustan precursors as writers of mere prose. 20th-century propo-
nents of free verse are excoriated by defenders of older forms but in turn con-
demn the rigid pentameter of tradition. Among some late-century poets, how-
ever, strict forms have come again into vogue. (Wright 358)

By the time Espaillat published her first book-length collection, the poetic
scene had morphed into a site of much contestation, with the field fractured
along sharply delineated aesthetic lines. The matter of form produced the clear-
est partitioning of the field into distinct camps. Advocates of free verse and pro-
ponents of classical English prosody stood out as the most recognizable flanks.
One could contend that Espaillat herself was recruited by one of the sides given
her long and productive collaboration with individuals and institutions tied to
New Formalism.

What poets and critics refer to as New Formalism emerged in the United
States during the 1980s, when a meaningful cohort of poets began to preach the
gospel of meter and rhyme (Caplan 2012). Bruce Meyer and Jonathan N. Barron
provide a sound overview of the resurgence of classical prosody in the United
States for the introduction to their coedited volume *New Formalist Poets*, which
appeared as No. 282 in the *Dictionary of Literary Biography Series* (Meyer and Bar-
ron xvii–xxii). We can summarize briefly by pointing out that, imbued with the
sense of rebellion against the "free verse Establishment," the proponents of tra-
ditional prosody promoted their cause by means of several key documents and
initiatives that evinced the spirit of their movement. Among them, *The Direction
of Poetry* (1988), edited by Robert Richman, gathered poems by seventy-six prac-
titioners of "rhymed and metered verse . . . since 1975," as if wishing to assert the
resilience of the fixed forms and display strength in the number of those writ-
ing them even at a time when free verse predominated in literary circles. Tim-
othy Steele's *Missing Measures: Modern Poetry and the Revolt against Meter* (1990)
offered, in the words of Richard Wilbur's endorsement, "not a formalist mani-
festo but an even-handed scholarly account of the whole background of 'free
verse' poetics." Gioia's *Can Poetry Matter?: Essays on Poetry and American Culture*
(1992) went public in defense of classical prosody, going as far as proposing that
even the best-loved work of the poets associated with the "free verse" school,
including William Carlos Williams, often partook of the formal resources that
we associate with meter and rhyme. At the start of the 1990s Gioia paired up with

Michael Peich in leading the effort that produced the West Chester University Poetry Conference as a locus devoted to exploring formal and narrative verse.

In 1990 a feisty critical essay by poet and scholar Ira Sadoff shook up the sector of the American poetry scene that had publicly articulated a preference for traditional prosody. Written in response to the claims and the formalist ideology of *The Direction of Poetry*, the essay refuted the interpretation by the anthologist and some favorable reviewers of the book that poetry had lost its relevance in the lives of the American people, and that renewing the former currency of the fixed forms would remedy that situation. While conceding that poetry matters less in the contemporary moment than it did in earlier times, Sadoff contested the idea that the advent of free verse as the mode of choice for poets of more recent generations was the cause of the decline. Rather, he urged readers to consider whether the poets *themselves* might not be the source of the problem. American poets, he argued, had allowed their work to slide into banality due to their own lack of serious engagement with the world, socially speaking. He contended further that the desire to recover the fixed forms emanates from an ideologically fraught and "dangerous nostalgia" of the "neo-formalists" for a kind of literary ancien régime in which poets, operating as "purveyors of taste," held a position of greater prestige and significance in the overall society than laypeople (Sadoff, "Neo-Formalism" 7). He warned the advocates of a "return to form" that they might inadvertently be yearning for the return to the exclusionary ideologies of class, gender, race, and culture that informed the status quo during the times when poetry mattered more to the public than it does now. The artistic philosophy advocated by Richman's anthology, in Sadoff's view, represented the yearning of "conservative" poets "to restore art to the nostalgic ideals of fixed harmonies, of pure beauty and grace, to restore the 'essential values' of 'Western civilization'" (8). Sadoff maintained that formal choices in and of themselves would not rescue poetry from the social apathy that afflicts it in contemporary times. Rather, the poets ought to examine themselves with the aim of infusing their art with much greater substance than their work had generally demonstrated in the decades leading up to the publication of *The Direction of Poetry*.

Sadoff's rebuke to his peers in the art world may strike readers as a bit cantankerous, but the spirit that moved it remains compelling to this day, especially as he does not equate the use of traditional prosody with what he regards as insufficient substance in contemporary American poetry. Nor does he characterize the use of free verse as automatically conferring weight. Although often read as a flat-out attack on New Formalism, Sadoff's piece simply argued against the expectation that form, in and of itself, would transform poetry's relationship with the American public. His essay declares, for instance, that "the best poets of our age, and of any age, use all the vehicles of craft to create a dramatized, inclusive experience. And that inclusiveness, which makes simultaneous and integrated the pleasures of language and culture . . . is a far better measure than meter for poetic talent." The author goes on to contend that "poets must recognize the dialectical relationship between the word and the world. Poets must strive for integration of sight and sense; we must value context, the way in which discourse dramatizes perception" (10).

Given Espaillat's poetic praxis, she too would oppose the adoption of classical prosody if it entailed a poetic outcome devoid of contact with the yearnings of our fellow human beings. She would most likely find it hard to speak favorably of any artistic production that excludes others or does not strive to touch them in some way. Although she loves traditional prosody, which allows her the artistically joyful tension of operating at the intersection of restriction and freedom—a challenge that she has termed "dancing in a box"—she would certainly oppose a "return to form" that allows no room for the "form" of free verse poetry to have its say or sway. Similarly, she would concur with the caveat formulated by scholar Derek Attridge, who warns proponents of a "return" to classical prosody about the need to avoid "backlash formalism," by which he means one that fails to take into account the situatedness of writers and readers and treats literature as self-sufficient on grounds of a supposed ethical or political neutrality (Attridge 567).

A look at the age brackets of the poets anthologized by Mark Jarman and David Mason in *Rebel Angels: 25 Poets of the New Formalism* (1996), which brought together an impressive array of authors identifying themselves as wielders of classical prosody, conveys something about Espaillat's "old" formalism. Of the twenty-five writers classed as "Poets of the New Formalism" in the collection, only two—Frederick Feirstein (1940–) and Thomas M. Disch (1940–2008)— were born before Espaillat had started composing formal poems in English. This temporality perhaps explains her location as an ally of the New Formalists who has steered clear of any prosodic militancy or disparagement of free verse "adversaries" (to use the language of Joseph Salemi). Because she had had occasion to practice her "old" formalism prior to the rise of the antagonistic context that accompanied the "new" formalism, she did not seem to regard herself as inhabiting a given side among the poetic schools then in apparent opposition. Undoubtedly, she must have welcomed the embrace of the New Formalists when she ended up in their midst, especially given their shared enjoyment of seeking self-expression within formally rigid structures. But her trajectory had left her devoid of the compulsion to voice impassioned rebukes such as those ventilated across the aesthetic divide from the mid-1980s through the 1990s.

An enthusiastic practitioner of traditional prosody, Espaillat has remained eminently open to experimenting with any and all techniques that strike her as appropriate to the art. She reiterates that she "hated the poetry wars" largely because she found them pointless, contending that no particular style will guarantee the quality that poets should strive for in their work. Irrespective of formal preferences or levels of expertise, poets all have to face their own challenges. No one facing the entire spectrum of technical options will be free from the pitfalls of the craft: the free verse artist might succumb to "sloppiness and prosiness" just as the formalist "can fall into sing-song and monotony and forced rhymes" in addition to "unwarranted repetition simply to pad out the line." She acknowledges that poets face the imperative of taking the craft seriously "no matter how you write" (Scheele 42). Ideally, each poem attempts to engage readers at a profound level of human connection on its own terms regardless of its stylistic credentials, and poets may avail themselves of any of the resources that the various literary traditions have on offer.

Before Sadoff's indictment of neoformalist "nostalgia," Diane Wakoski (1937–), an avant-garde poet affiliated with the Beat Generation and the Confessional School, had issued her own acerbic condemnation of the movement. She characterized it as aesthetically and politically reactionary (Wakoski 3). For her, it reflected the country's "growing conservatism," just like the outcry of "the new batch of Republicans, including all those college kids who helped Ronald Reagan into a second term in the White House, that we need to return to old values" (3). Contrary to the neoformalists who griped about their marginality vis-à-vis the "free verse Establishment," Wakoski, in effect, regarded formal verse as having the upper hand in influencing the mores of the nation at the time. She pointed to the recent publication of collected poems by Allen Ginsberg (1926–1997) and Robert Creeley (1926–2005), neither receiving "a Pulitzer Prize or other major award for those collections" (3). Her repudiation came out of her feelings of being attacked by a prominent voice of the neoformalist creed, namely John Hollander, whose talk she had attended at the Modern Languages Association Convention in December 1985. She felt she had "heard the devil" when Hollander took the liberty of "denouncing, basically the free verse revolution, fulfillment of the Whitman heritage, making defensive jokes about the ill-educated slovenly writers of poetry who have been teaching college poetry classes for the past decade, allowing their students to go out into the world, illiterate of poetry" (3).

It seems clear in hindsight that over the course of the poetry wars, both sides overstated their case, the harshness of their rhetoric generally exceeding the degree of their aesthetic difference vis-à-vis the other side. Even Wakoski, despite her mordant antitraditionalist rhetoric, could still approvingly invoke the achievements of formal poets. She valued practitioners with "the celestial ear of a Wilbur or an Auden," two artists known for their superior handling of classical prosody (3). Overall, it seems that even the most resolute proponents of one poetic mode over another have found it hard to remain completely loyal to the tenets of the aesthetic dogma they preach. The biographical and critical note on Amy Lowell (1874–1925) written by Louis Untermeyer for the 1942 anthology that Espaillat has cherished for decades may bear this out. Observing that Lowell took the Imagist movement away from Pound, Untermeyer's note affirms that she "reorganized the group, made it a fighting word, and stormed up and down the country on a crusade of furious emancipation. . . . The air seethed with loud efforts to 'free' poetry from the shackles of rhyme, regular rhythm, and other traditional assets" (Untermeyer, *Treasury* 1078). "Yet," the anthologist concludes, "she tried every poetic device and brilliantly violated the Imagist 'manifesto'" (1078).

Untermeyer had previously devoted a meaningful entry to "free verse" in his reference work *The Forms of Poetry* (1926), in which he defined the genre without a hint of prejudice, as being "based upon a broad (and often irregular) movement rather than on a fixed pattern; it might be said to be founded on a general rhythm rather than on a precise meter" (17). Untermeyer's entry attributes to Lowell, in his view "a pioneer and one of the greatest modern exponents of this form," the statement that "verse can never be free," and recalls that she had proposed to call it "cadenced verse" instead (17). Apart from this homage to Lowell, the entry points readers to the ancient and distinguished credentials of free verse. In particular, the Book of Job, the Song of Solomon, and the Psalms count among "the greatest free verse ever written." Untermeyer characterizes ancient Hebrew poetry as generally "built on balance: instead of rhyme, it uses similar consonants (alliteration); instead of a set meter, it employs the 'strophic' measure" (18).

Coauthoring the entry on free verse for a more recent reference source, Donald Wesling and Enikö Bollobás also acknowledge the longevity of the free verse tradition, dating back "to the oral roots of poetry, to the period preceding the development of regular metricity. Sumerian, Akkadian, Egyptian, Sanskrit, and Hebrew poetries all share one characteristic: in their texts, repetition and parallelism create prosodic regularity, while meter in all of its types does not regulate the verse" (Wesling and Bollobás 425). David Caplan has quite soundly characterized the tenor of the condemnations aimed at neoformalist aesthetics as more polemical than analytical (Caplan 19). Perhaps neither of the opposing flanks could be expected to make convincing cases because both have tended to exaggerate their claims of difference from one another, as well as overestimate the quotient of newness boasted by their side compared to that of the other.

In the final analysis, no poetic fundamentalism can sustain itself with pretensions of purity. After all, art is known for its defiance of stasis. A venerated ancestor figure to many free-verse practitioners in the twentieth century, Pound invigorated his Imagist revolution by drawing from the highly stylized poetic achievements of medieval Florentine poets Dante Alighieri (1265–1321) and Guido Cavalcanti (1255–1300), as well as the traditional verse of the French troubadours, particularly the twelfth-century bard Arnaut Daniel. When Pound sought to assemble the contents of *Des Imagistes* (1914), the anthology whereby he set out to announce a new era for poetic expression, he did not shun the formal verse contribution by James Joyce (1882–1941) in his predominantly free verse volume. Nor did Pound's aesthetic offensive target only the classical prosodic establishment represented by the Romantic and Victorian poets still influential in England and the United States at the start of the twentieth century. He also battled Walt Whitman (1819–1892), the compatriot who reigned supreme as founding father of American free verse. Pound's "A Pact," a moving piece he published in the July 1913 issue of *Poetry*, lyrically evokes a moment in his maturity when he no longer felt bent on committing poetic patricide, understanding that there can be "commerce" across the aesthetic divide:

> I make a pact with you, Walt Whitman—
> I have detested you long enough.
> I come to you as a grown child
> Who has had a pig-headed father;
> I am old enough now to make friends.
> It was you that broke the new wood,
> Now is a time for carving.
> We have one sap and one root—
> Let there be commerce between us. (Pound, *Personae* 89)

During our January 2013 interview at her Newburyport home, Espaillat expressed satisfaction at what she perceived as a greater degree of acceptance and respect among poets across the entire spectrum of practitioners. She caught a glimpse of that atmosphere some years ago from the general tenor of the statements made by the poets invited by Annie Finch to speak on form, narrative, and tradition for the collection of essays titled *After New Formalism* (1999). The contributors revisit many of the totalizing claims about the virtues for which the movement was celebrated, as well as the sins for which it was attacked. African American poets Marilyn Nelson (1947–) and Carolyn Beard Whitlow (1945–) refute the oft-heard charge that women, African-descended peoples, and other minorities "have no place" in what some have viewed as an inherently exclusionary "tradition." In response, they affirm the propensity of artists in those nondominant populations to create by means of a fusion of forms (Nelson 13; Whitlow 66). Adrienne Rich likewise articulated an argument for the innovative coexistence of forms in the creativity of emerging or historically underrepresented groups (Rich 7). Finch, in her introduction, seems to encourage restraint from the spokespersons of New Formalism, especially in light of the temptation to boast of greater goods than can actually be delivered.

As to the need for "formalism," the American British poet Anne Stevenson, who is Espaillat's junior by only one year, attempts to resolve the question of poetic mode with striking openness. Stevenson's words bear an uncanny resemblance to the versatile outlook of her Caribbean-born sister in the craft. Outlining the ultimate test that all verse must pass, she explains, "The case for formalism is won with every good poem that is written—and then sensitively read by readers who can judge for themselves whether it is worth re-reading" (Stevenson 221). The idea that the prosodic choices a poet makes will only find justification in the outcome, namely the extent to which the resulting text will matter to readers or listeners when it reaches their eyes or ears, identifies a crucial core value of Espaillat's oeuvre and the poetics that inform it.

FOR THE AGES: VERSE AS INVITATION

Any student of Espaillat's work will recognize a complementary relationship between the elements that scholars, critics, and reviewers find in her oeuvre and those features that she herself admires in the works of other poets. Surveying her formal and informal literary criticism, that is, her writings on the subject and the views she has expressed in response to interview questions, we can derive a sound idea of her poetics, or the conceptual basis of her artistic praxis as a verse maker. Here, we look at what she endorses and impugns in the writing of poets throughout the ages and her sustained critical appreciation of a few select poets whom she regards as essential. For instance, Espaillat has, for many decades, extolled the legacies of such women predecessors as Edna St. Vincent Millay, Elizabeth Barrett Browning, and Sara Teasdale, admiring the musicality, keen observation, and emotional force of their verse, in addition to their evocative fusions of sound and sense. Negative comments do not come easily to Espaillat when judging the work of artists whom she admires less, but when she does decry a particular poetic tendency or choice, she offers grounds for her assessment. We devote the next section of the discussion to her self-analysis, or those instances when she judges her own levels of mastery of the craft.

What matters in poetry, Espaillat insists, "is writing something genuine that is true for you now, that you really mean now, and that you care enough to share it with other people now. If it lasts, wonderful, so much the better." While declaring her commitment to reach people, she does not see herself as "writing for the ages." Surveying the European tradition, she places John Milton among the poets for the ages, while conceding that his poetry is less easy to adore than Frost's given its comparatively ornate style. She views Emily Dickinson as a poet for the ages who "fools people in different ways." On the one hand, "she says, 'I'm an old crackpot, I'm just an old maid,' and then she just gives it to you. And it hurts. When poetry is for the ages, when it's really genuine, at some level, it hurts, because it reminds you of all the things that we're going to lose." Espaillat is not oblivious to those critics and reviewers of her work who identify in it precisely those characteristics that she views as marks of greatness in these admired predecessors. She shrugs off any similarities, declaring herself too biased to judge: "I don't trust any judgment of my own on any poem because I'm prejudiced. It's mine, so I like it. . . . I'm trying very hard not to expect too much [from others]" (NK/STS).

The imprint needed for a poet to last, a "quality of greatness" that Espaillat sees embodied in the work of Frost, is a nebulous one. She defines it as the ability to speak the truth in an accessible way: "Things he says about people remain true. The terrible things and the good things he says about people remain true." She predicts that five centuries from now, people might still be reading his work and acknowledging, "I have an uncle like that." She does not have a similar opinion about the Prairie Poets, who are "good . . . but not great." Although she enjoys the work of Carl Sandburg, whom she regards as deserving of celebrity, she believes he will "eventually disappear." She likewise includes Wallace Stevens among those who will "eventually disappear" (NK/STS).

Espaillat speaks self-effacingly about her contribution to the field. As such, she harbors few illusions about earning a place in posterity, other than the humble expression of it that she terms "personal posterity," the kind that involves "doing something for somebody that's going to have consequences." She feels that "if you've touched any life—you may have that posterity" (NK/STS). She therefore trusts that she may have touched many among the thousands of students she taught in New York City classrooms. When asked to comment on the continued prestige of Frost, she answers categorically, "He was very good," while at the same time doubting that her work will last the way his has. Likewise, she regards Wilbur as a poet "for the ages," while "most of us are not," a thought that explains her declaration that "frankly" she would feel lucky to be remembered by her great-grandchildren's generation.

Amid her consistently low-key demeanor, Espaillat has ways of verifying whether or not her poetry reaches readers: she receives her validation when welcoming letters, calls, and emails from those who have read her work. Many of these informal reviews attest to the joy, pain, satisfaction, and identification elicited by the reading experience. "When something that I've written makes someone else feel less alone because the experience is the same or similar, then I feel good," she confesses, adding conclusively: "That, for me, is a poem that works" (Kang 192). Espaillat's reliance on the reaction of readers partially explains her continued participation in workshops and her membership in poetry groups, an enthusiasm she has maintained since her early days. She explains that her interaction with peers in such communities remains key to her evolving practice: "I need the readers, the input. I need the eyes that are not mine, like everybody else. The peers, the workshop" (NK/STS). While she accepts the notion that poetic creation can emanate from the sparks that fly from solitary musings, she views that stage as a kind of initiation, a moment of genesis: "The poem does happen that way, but that's the first draft. After that, you need reality, and reality means that you have to have other people say, 'Stanza 2 doesn't work.'" Espaillat likewise treasures her collaboration with younger New England poets such as Alfred Nicol and Len Krisak. She speaks fondly of a fellow poet, the late David Berman, who was a lawyer and highly intelligent man "so finicky with himself that . . . he [threw] out stuff that the rest of us would kill to have written." This self-scrutiny characterizes the seriousness of the West Chester University Conference crowd as she came to know it. She values that poetry community for its role in making formal verse less peculiar in American letters than it was for the preceding generations. She remarks, "The whole spectrum has gained respectability, and everyone is being more civil with people all along the spectrum. I'm very happy about that because I hated the poetry wars" (NK/STS).

Given how much Espaillat has meditated on the work, process, and community building required for her craft, we imagine she must have had occasion to formulate a profile of the poet she does *not* wish to resemble. We therefore spent a portion of our extended conversations eliciting from her a sense of what constitutes a "bad poet," as well as bad poetry. We found her refreshingly willing to speak of those whose work she does not admire, with one important caveat: she refused to offer negative commentary about the poetry of individuals who are still alive so as to avoid the possibility of offense. She quickly dismisses those poets, living or deceased, who seem to delight in the opacity of their work, who deny cognitive access to readers and listeners not already initiated in the arcane particularities of their distinct style or subject matter. She also distinguishes the "great" poets from those with occasional "sparks" of genius. She points to the "sparks" in "Thirteen Ways of Looking at a Blackbird," an experimental triumph by Stevens, as well as "The Snow Man" and "Anecdote of the Jar." Espaillat does not hold a high opinion of the legacy of William Carlos Williams, to whom she attributes the "foolish" affirmation that "if you've read one sonnet, you've read them all." She rebukes his attitude as unduly "dismissive" and insists upon the counterproductivity of such a trait: "I don't dismiss free verse at all. I write it, but I'm not good at it. I love reading it when it's done well." Characterizing Williams as a "prosodic ideologue," she claims that "he had it in for people who did not write the way he did." This intractability placed him among the leading instigators of the so-called poetry wars. Distancing herself from any aesthetic orthodoxy, she explains her own judgment of poems to be holistic: a piece's success comes "not by the way it was done but by the results: does it reach me, does it reach anybody, does it communicate?" (NK/STS).

In a similar vein, her contemporary Amiri Baraka (1934–2014) strikes Espaillat as "more politician than poet," a talented writer whose "politics went overboard and forgot to be poetry." She also admits reservations about a "great deal of violence and prejudice" that marred his oeuvre; here, she gestures specifically to his well-known anti-Semitic pronouncements. T. S. Eliot's anti-Semitism, on the other hand, she finds more marginal to the core of his artistic production. She finds fine poetry in his "Ash Wednesday" and describes his take on old age in "Gerontion" as "fluid," "evocative," and "musical." She praises the handling of time in *Four Quartets* (1943) as well, though she resists "forgiving" him entirely for his prejudice. Instead, she reasons that his verse "would have been even better without it," but that he "was a good enough poet to have written a lot of very good work despite it." The key freedom of the critical reader, she reasons, is the capacity to indict the negative while acknowledging the beauty that can coexist. She quips, "I just eat my way around the brown spots in the apple" (NK/STS).

Espaillat charges Whitman with writing "too much," contending that if he "had written about a fourth of what he wrote, he would have been a much better poet," but she does not begrudge his work its undeniable renown. His poems reach people and resonate with them, largely because of his "insistence on addressing the individual human being." Whitman's ongoing appeal, she maintains, lies in his success at convincing the reader that he is speaking directly to him or her. She acknowledges "Crossing Brooklyn Ferry" as a text whose passion influenced her powerfully, prompting her to write her sonnet "For My Great-Great Grandson, the Space Pioneer," in which she ventures to address "a listener in the future." She finds impressive the mesmerizing rhythm of Whitman's free verse composition, relying as it does on anaphoric lines that reproduce the movement of the ferry. With recurring patterns of syntax, repetition of diction, phrases, and structures such as the incantatory imperatives of the final stanza, "Crossing Brooklyn Ferry" exemplifies the marriage of sound and sense that in Espaillat's view enables a poet to touch another human being. The dialogic features that she extols so warmly in "Crossing the Brooklyn Ferry" emerge more plainly in the poem that immediately precedes it in Whitman's *Leaves of Grass*, namely "Song of the Open Road." Here, the speaker invites the listener along a journey oriented by "the efflux of the soul" (Whitman 153). The final stanza extends to the reader an offer that amounts to a bargain of human solidarity and companionship: "Camerado, I give you my hand! / I give you my love more precious than money, / I give you myself before preaching or law; Will you give me yourself? / will you come travel with me? / Shall we stick by each other as long as we live?" (159).

Similarly, Espaillat's assessment of poetry by feminist icon Adrienne Rich (1929–2012) reveals a general admiration of her capacity to yield harmonious sound and sense connections. She also discerns an appropriate balance between the ideas communicated and the artistic resources employed to ensure nuance and verve. Espaillat notes that Rich's work "started out very powerful, very moving," but laments that as the writer grew older and more politically entrenched, her ideological investments tended to monopolize her voice, often at the expense of artistry. Espaillat comments that "sometimes the 'what' takes over so much that the 'how' disappears. I think poetry works best when the 'what' and the 'how' are indistinguishable, keeping such a good balance that you don't feel you're being preached at" (NK/STS).

In contrast, she has much praise to shower on the poetry of Brooklyn-born Martín Espada for his success at forging compelling verse out of "all that political, social passion" that underlies his work. She points to his poem titled "In Praise of Local 100" as a model for the match between "the container and the contained" (Kang 181). The text opens with a dedication: "For the 43 members of Hotel Employees and Restaurant Employees Local 100, working at the Windows on the World restaurant, who lost their lives in the attack on the World Trade Center" (Espada, *Alabanza* 231). We deduce from the second stanza that the deceased workers traced their origins back to Puerto Rico, Ecuador, Mexico, Haiti, the Dominican Republic, Yemen, Ghana, and Bangladesh. The opening lines suggest the tenor of Espada's dirge for the workers being commemorated: "*Alabanza*. Praise the cook with the shaven head / and a tattoo on his shoulder that said *Oye*, / a blue-eyed Puerto Rican with people from Fajardo, / the harbor of pirates centuries ago. / Praise the lighthouse in Fajardo, candle / glimmering white to worship the dark saint of the sea" (231). Espaillat applauds the poem's capacity to speak tenderly yet without sentimentality, and to evolve the tragic scope of September 11 both within and beyond the specificities (including particular victims' names) that the work seeks to honor. Espada renders the event comparable to other world tragedies, expanding the horizon of human empathy and exemplifying the kind of word-art "that makes rings around experience, that keeps going" as it spreads from one perceptual field, time frame, hurt soul, and seeking mind to another (NK/STS).

To her credit, Espaillat applies rigorous standards to the work of even some of the best-known English-language poets. She ranks Elinor Wylie (1885–1928), who in the 1920s and 1930s enjoyed considerable prestige, among those American poets who deserve to be remembered, while viewing Archibald MacLeish (1892–1982), whom readers remember primarily for his award-winning verses (among them, "Ars Poetica"), as "a better playwright than he was a poet." She expresses little enthusiasm for the British American poet Denise Levertov (1923–1997), whose civic and political engagement she admires but whose verse she finds "overrated." She characterizes the work of Hart Crane (1889–1932) as "incomprehensible" but with a "hypnotic quality" that renders it alluring as well. She adds that he had "a musician's ear for language. You can't take him in long stretches, not big helpings, but in small helpings he is delicious." Espaillat speaks approvingly of the "highly intellectual" nature of the work of Louise Bogan

(1897–1970) as well as the "extremely moving" verse of Langston Hughes (1902–1967), a poet "who really got the pulse of his time." She holds in high esteem the work of famed British American W. H. Auden (1907–1973), a poet, "of course, for the ages," whose evocative piece "The Shield of Achilles" she has often returned to when pondering issues relating to the dangers of surrendering an individual ethical will to the dictates of political and religious creeds.

She has nothing but praise for the works of the late Theodore Roethke (1908–1963) and the prominent activist-educator Nikki Giovanni (1943–). A poet less well known than Roethke or Giovanni, Baltimore-born Afaa Michael Weaver (1951–) earns Espaillat's applause as well. Weaver made a living in factory work before teaching overseas in Taiwan. His linguistic compass points east and west, with fluency in both Chinese and English. Espaillat gestures to poems like "A Ship's Log," based on the preserved records from a vessel used to transport enslaved Africans—specifically children—from their original homes to the sites of their literal or social death in the Americas. The piece concentrates on family separation, the children who traveled without parental protection, the preserved traces of their original names, and the plight of the mothers mourning their lost generations. After reading aloud the list of names floating at the center of the work, which proves to be a kind of incantatory memorial to the watery dead, she declares, "Now that's what I call a poem" (NK/STS).

Kenneth Koch (1925–2002) likewise merits a place of distinction in Espaillat's pantheon, both for the high caliber of his verse and for his service to poetry. Instrumental "in drawing children to the art," Koch worked against the pedagogical inclination that gained much traction during the twentieth century: presenting the work of poets "as if it was philosophy." Teachers, Espaillat recalls, might typically ask students to compose a poem on such vaunted themes as "liberty" or "goodness," but the young people would "see through it" and offer anemic responses based on what was expected of them rather than what really triggered their imagination. As Espaillat sees it, Koch "gave us permission to do 'crazy' things," such as asking students to write a poem about mundane realities, including quotidian objects like "a tree," "an old hat," or a "red squirrel." The habitual and rote became new. Such an upending of expectations about acceptable topics for poetry, because these simple topics are "humorous in a delightful way," worked to "draw a lot of kids back to poetry" (NK/STS).

Espaillat also harbors great admiration for the "wonderful formalist poet" Howard Nemerov (1920–1991), who "really knew what to do with language, how to carve it." It honors her immensely to have twice received the sonnet prize named after him under the auspices of the *Formalist*. She won it first in 1998 for the sonnet "Contingencies," with John Frederick Nims (1913–1999) serving as final judge; the second time, she received the award for "Discovery," in 2003, with Gioia as the final judge. Espaillat was also honored with the T. S. Eliot Poetry Prize, judged by X. J. Kennedy, who in her view, "should have been poet laureate years ago." A "profound" artist, the author of "absolutely first-rate" verse, Kennedy does not get his due, Espaillat conjectures, because he also pens "light poetry," even though the work is never trivial. She values him as "a great educator" who, as editor of dozens of anthologies, "has brought a great many young people to poetry." Espaillat also greatly admires Natasha Trethewey (1966–), the former US poet laureate (2012–2014), for her capacity to revivify and collectivize a painful family history: "She brings her biography into the poetry but she manages to make it matter to others."

Espaillat wishes that Edgar Bowers (1924–2000) had written more than he did. She acknowledges John Hollander (1929–2013) and John Ciardi (1916–1986) as the authors of "very good" poems. As for James Merrill (1926–1995), she accepts the judgment of many who pronounce him great, but she confesses to a certain inability to "get into" his work despite his craftsmanship and precision: "Every poem is finished like jewelry, but there is a distance to it, a coolness that I can't get past." She finds it wanting in playfulness. Ultimately, her dissatisfaction may stem from the perception that the poetry has so concerned itself with technical perfection that it loses touch with the equally important goal of engaging readers or listeners at the level of human intimacy. Merrill's verse, then, like that of Baraka, fails to attend to the need for a balance between the how and the what, the container and the contained.

When judging poets from the past, her contemporaries who remain active practitioners, and younger writers who have achieved distinction or are still in the apprenticeship stage, Espaillat generally parts ways with individual poets or schools that fail to attain what she calls "genuine communication." This singular effect, she claims, tends to be compromised when too much attention is paid to trendiness, with the intent being to write for the people "in the know" rather than to attract a wider cross-section of readers. "They leave me cold," she confesses, "and I get the feeling when I read their material that they're more intent on being remarkable than on really communicating." It matters little to her whether "poetry is remarkable or not provided that it communicates. What I want from poems is for them to draw me into another life, another experience I have not had." She recalls the poetry of her late friend Yala Korwin (1933–2014), with whom she cofounded the Fresh Meadows Poets, for its capacity to "make me live the Holocaust. She put me through the experience of the death camps." Korwin's poetry does not achieve its depth of communication "by explaining [the event] in academic terms or being smart about it, but by making it so visceral that I can't stay out" (NK/STS).

Espaillat is not unaware of the intellectual currency of discourses that problematize the concept of communication in poetry. She herself has persuasively argued that poets do not speak in the same language used by their fellow human beings. "The words are the same," she observes, "but the weight we give them, the criteria we use to choose this one rather than that one, are our own" (Espaillat, *Where Horizons Go* 69). Many scholars and poets have made solid cases for the uses of opacity and ambiguity in the literary creation of meaning. The poet Daniel Tiffany, a native of Akron, Ohio, traces to the earliest poetry in English "an affinity for objects whose rarity and eccentricity were signaled by a peculiar verbal identity," suggesting that "lyric poetry first emerged in English as the enigmatic voice of certain highly wrought objects" (Tiffany 73). Tiffany outlines what could be construed as an intellectual history of obscurity in English-language poetry; he draws primarily on speculative thought from a number of major European thinkers whose views subscribe to philosophical materialism (75). He finds in the works of Jorie Graham (1950–), the Pulitzer Prize–winning author of such collections as *The Dream of the Unified Field* (1995), *Materialism* (1993), and *Erosion* (1983), an "ambitious and programmatic" engagement with the "iconography of materialism" articulated via lyric verse heavily conversant with philosophy and history (87). Thus, Graham's poetry juxtaposes "meditations on the mysterious texture of things" alongside "translations and 'adaptations'" of texts mostly by philosophers who have had "something interesting to say about the nature of materiality" (87–88). This configuration appears intellectually rigorous, but is it accessible?

Cognizant of arguments legitimizing the various traditions relating to poetic obscurity and their more contemporary manifestations, Espaillat does not see herself as a proponent of abstruse textuality. She participates in an entirely different conversation about meaning, one that does not regard poetic communication as a primary portal to rigorous philosophical debate. Communication, as Espaillat understands it, has no other test to pass than the kind of rapport it fosters among people in the realm of everyday social relations. As we might gather from the comments above about Merrill's work, she asks of each poem she encounters, "Does it touch anybody, does it resonate?"

The poetry of tragic artist Sylvia Plath (1932–1963), which Espaillat confesses she "can't enjoy," presents her with the need to articulate her own emotional and ethical demands. Though Espaillat regards Plath as an "extremely gifted" practitioner whose command of poetic form was "absolutely tip-top," she faults the latter for failing to harness feelings and talents toward the creation of what Espaillat terms "humane poetry." She explains how Plath's iconic poem "Daddy" is a "hymn to hate, or at least to ambivalence, the ambivalence perhaps so great that the hate takes over." Espaillat contends that the text of the poem does not offer any evidence that the father, whom the speaker characterizes with terms attributable to Nazis, deserves the kind of treatment that he receives from his daughter in the lyrical work. She does not, however, dismiss the significance of the state of mind of the speaker, the poet, or the emotional turmoil unleashed by Otto Plath's death. Grief-stricken by his passing, Plath did have a nervous breakdown. Espaillat surmises that "the ambivalence was extreme," leading to the escalation of the young woman's emotional turmoil and struggle with mental illness, all of which were laid bare on the page more often than not.

In characterizing the management of emotions in this poem as "unreasonable," Espaillat opens herself up to the charge of wishing to legislate sentiment in the text and denying room for the irrational in poetry. She responds to this challenge by arguing that "poetry should be as irrational or rational as you are. It should mirror the poet." However, she claims not to feel at all "drawn into poetry that is irrational to the point of losing contact with the rest of us." She finds a failure of communication resulting not from the complex psychopathology enacted in "Daddy," but from "the extreme nature of the poetry, its violence and total inwardness, the total looking toward the self" (NK/STS). Self-referential poetry that communicates democratically usually comes from a poet who looks through windows. Being made of glass, a window lets us behold our reflection in it, but we also see through the reflection to the outside world, a reality perceptible beyond the limited immediacy of our face and body. Plath, Espaillat muses, inhabits a room made of mirrors, not windows. As a result, everything she sees there reflects her own life, her own situation, her own psychosis—which no one can blame her for, given her mental condition. The poem, then, corresponds genuinely to the situation whence it came, but it lacks the necessary capacity to trigger empathy, since a reader cannot unilaterally climb into that mirrored, windowless room. When the self does not look outside to other selves, it fails to invite the reader—or readers in the widest sense—in at all.

The image of the speaker in Plath's "Daddy" inhabiting a windowless room made of mirrors articulates, for Espaillat, an instance of suffering that offers abstractions of horror instead of explanations. She likewise frowns upon the work of several poets, especially from the twentieth century, that harbor the same tendency to shut all but a few readers out. Some artists assume that a text's reticence to engage will serve as a draw for those seeking an interpretive challenge; others may not even bother to put themselves to the test. Espaillat refuses to compromise in her demand that poetry "at least attempt to speak to somebody outside of it." She immediately dispels any notion that she might be disavowing the self: "We all use the self—it's all we have. But you use the self as a kind of tube through which you talk. You can't close it up at the other end. You use your own life, your prejudices, your passions, and your feelings as a tube, but it should get out there to somewhere or someone else" (NK/STS). Nor does she wish to censor violence as poetic material, provided that it aims to provoke important insights about human motivation and behavior rather than simply offer gratuitous spectacle. A recognition of violence must necessarily figure as a counterpoint to love, for we cannot ignore pain, conflict, and horror and still claim to be representing the full spectrum of lived or imagined experiences. Espaillat encapsulates her ideal poetic disposition in her characterization of Stanley Kunitz (1905–2006): he imbued his work with "total humanity" and a "compassion and love for all things without sentimentality."

As Nicol has pointed out, Espaillat is not averse to human ugliness and the frustrations that mar everyday life. In her foreword to *Lines of Flight: Poems* (2011), a collection by award-winning American poet Catherine Chandler, she first emphasizes the book's achievements at the level of form, imagery, and thought. In particular, she applauds its finesse at incorporating the dark side of life, marveling at the "great deal of damage" recorded by Chandler's poems, including "the personal losses, political, inevitable, and accidental 'disappearances,' the scars left by history under the green fields of home, the carnage to which the Vietnam Memorial, among so many, bears witness" (Espaillat, Foreword x). Espaillat relishes these "dark, intelligent observations of human experience," which reveal "the inexorable slaughter that underlies life." Chandler's success, the foreword tells us, resides in her capacity to offer counterbalancing ideas that force a sort of equilibrium even if "only haphazardly." That eloquence in accounting for contending forces in our existence resounds throughout Chandler's evocative poem "Lost and Found," whose four two-line stanzas Espaillat quotes in toto:

A key, a button, a leather glove.
First love.

A friend to cancer, a voice to grief.
An old belief.

An arrowhead, a perfect shell.
The first bluebell.

The river's source, a taste for ink:
Hope, I think. (ix)

In her conclusion, Espaillat points to "Henslow's Sparrow," praising its lines for offering "a possibility that almost heals the ache they create." This rhetorical prowess is a quality that she feels encompasses the whole volume, a book that she pledges "to return to again and again—for both the possibility and the ache" (xii).

It is Espaillat's belief, then, that enunciating personal pain does not, in and of itself, suffice to touch others and catalyze their empathic investment. The poetry of the grieving self that hoards painful feelings and fails to extend an invitation—however reluctant—to the reader by means of accessible communication will work at cross-purposes with itself. In contrast, the poetry of Anthony Hecht (1923–2004) earns Espaillat's praise for its success at managing the burden of grief. She has examined his legacy in an essay titled "Pious Simplicities and Complex Realities," which she wrote for a still-unpublished volume of critical studies on this well-loved American bard, edited by the poet Ernest Hilbert. "Pious Simplicities" highlights Hecht's achievement in terms of managing traumas as well as the manner in which we, as readers, find ourselves not only coming to terms with those suffering great wrongs but also gauging our own potential for perpetrating them. An in-depth critical consideration sustained by insightful exegeses of several representative pieces from Hecht's repertoire, Espaillat's essay ponders the reader's reception—aesthetic and moral—of the "magnificent" poem "More Light! More Light!" which evokes the suffocating drama of two Jews buried alive by a Polish prisoner upon the command of a soldier represented "only by his weapon." The Luger seems to act "eerily under its own power" as death links these figures in the Nazi death camp. The soldier appears, represented "by the riding boot that 'packed down the earth' over the still-living Jews, just before the Luger shoots the Pole in the belly" (Espaillat, "Pious Simplicities" 3). Espail-

lat speaks of "the initial shock" prompted by the poem's "three opening stan-
zas, all the more troubling for the restraint, precision and detachment of their
language" (1).

She observes that Hecht's poem promotes a multiply pronged approach to
the tragedy, centered not only upon the obvious victims but also on the Ger-
man soldier who wields fatal power over others as decreed by higher authori-
ties. We gather that he has lost moral individuality, hence his capacity to resist
the otherwise reasonable tendency toward human compassion. Most likely for
the sake of defending "the glory of his people, or the purity of his race, or some
other abstraction he has been taught to deem valuable above all else, including
the living bodies of others," the soldier is also dead (3). Hecht's poetry, Espaillat
insists, advises us against the morally calamitous presumption that we can ever
regard the body as "an entity lesser in value than some other perceived good, or
in defense of some ostensibly nobler, purer, intangible element of our nature"
without the chance of grave consequences (3). After her sensitive explication
of many individual poems, Espaillat concludes with a summation that merits
reproduction in its entirety:

> No poem or prose, however good, is going to bring about a change in human
> nature that will do away with injustice, cruelty, or cynicism, whatever their
> source. But excellent writing can sharpen the senses, challenge the intellect,
> kindle the imagination and encourage the reader to generous thought. And great
> writing—like that of Hecht, which so qualifies on all counts, aesthetic, moral
> and intellectual—can do more. It can teach us to confess doubt, to acknowledge
> the moral ambiguities inherent in every human impulse, and to guard against
> self-satisfied overconfidence in ourselves and in those institutions we have cre-
> ated in our own image. (10)

ESPAILLAT ON ESPAILLAT

While by no means comparable in length or depth to the critical acumen she
has devoted to the work of other poets, Espaillat has long been open to critiqu-
ing features of her own work. Her self-reflective commentary may be found in
the numerous interviews she has granted since she regained her literary visibil-
ity beginning in the early 1990s. She took a gamble in 2003 when she selected

twelve poems from her oeuvre as the ones that would outlive her "in the unlikely event that anyone will be reading any poem of mine after my lifetime" (Espaillat, *Greatest Hits* 11). These were published in *Greatest Hits: 1942–2001* (2003), a chapbook featured in a series by Pudding House Publications whose editors adhere to rather strict guidelines, as they set forth on the copyright page: "The series is invitational only; queries or submissions could disqualify a poet for the following three years" (n.p.).

Espaillat's first selection, "Calculus" is a favorite of hers because of the affectionate situation that inspired it, namely an intimate late-night conversation with one of her physicist sons. Her rationale for the second poem in the selection, "A Love Poem, Off Center," dealing, as it does, with imperfections and failings that love somehow circumvents, is its effective illustration of some of her most prevalent themes: "the gap between the ideal and the real, our abstract expectations, and life as we live it" (8). "Learning Bones" memorializes the poet's "old school" father who preferred the Latin names for taxonomic systems in science. The poem salutes the "sheer value" of the father-daughter relationship, regardless of their differences in generation and opinion. The fourth poem, "Workshop," constitutes a manifesto of one aspect of Espaillat's poetics, namely her harmonious vision of the relationship between an artistic calling and the demands of material existence. "People in Home Movies" uses the metaphor of film "to imagine time slowed down, speeded up, and even reversed, before returning to the reality that must be accepted" (9). It relies on what the poet calls "the obsessive, repetitive sestina" to imitate the compulsive anxiety and aching nostalgia with which we often replay scenes of the past.

The sixth lyric Espaillat selected for the collection, "Minefields," explores her husband Alfred's memories as an infantryman at the Battle of the Bulge during World War II. She reconstructs his emotional turmoil as a survivor who must periodically "confront the absence—the lost future" of those among his peers who perished in action (9). The villanelle "Song," a poem she designates "as a cry of grief" over her mother's deteriorating memory and selfhood, follows. Written in 1992, two years before Dulce María succumbed to the ravages of Alzheimer's disease, the poem dramatizes her mother's vain attempt to retain words she knew. It relies largely on alliteration and other sound-centered devices. The irony of the "highly musical, playful villanelle as a form" persuades us that art can triumph over the grief it initially sets out to represent by deliberately transforming it into beauty.

The eighth poem, "Almost," celebrates the small joys of daily existence by means of "a parking-lot near-encounter" of the poet with her firstborn. The subsequent piece, "Bra," surprised Espaillat, who admits that she rarely writes "with political or social issues as subjects." While shopping, she found herself suddenly attuned to all that is at stake, politically and morally, in the purchase of a rather unremarkable consumer item. The "duality of its diction and the circularity of its total form" accords with the ambivalence underlying the deceptively simple choice (10). The next piece, "Bilingual/Bilingüe," pays tribute to the family drama, the conflicts, and the happy outcome of the language policy instituted at home by the poet's father. The eleventh poem, "Contingencies," explores the nature of chance and its eerie impact on our lives, while the final work, "Retriever," dramatizes the affectionate and philosophically dense rapport between a dog and its owner.

This last piece illuminates how love can (and perhaps must) prevail, even across the divide of species. "The dog's joy in particular," Espaillat explains, "aroused my curiosity: What did the animal make of all the repeated strenuous effort? How did he see his own role in the life of his master, whom he clearly adored?" (11). She herself endeavors to cross into the nonhuman realm through the imagination, working to reconstruct a sense of canine perception and upending the assumption that a human's point of view must necessarily take precedence over that of a nonhuman. The imaginative crossings in the poem recall the intricate empathic maneuvers undertaken by the poet in "Andante con moto," a piece omitted from the *Greatest Hits* collection but very similar to "Retriever" and thus worth mentioning here. Published alongside "Stumbling" and "Suncatcher" in the *Texas Poetry Journal*, "Andante con moto" was inspired by the solemn processional in the second movement of Symphony no. 4 in A Major, op. 90, by the nineteenth-century German composer Felix Mendelssohn (1809–1847). Mendelssohn apparently conceived of this composition after having viewed a religious procession in the streets of Naples in 1830 (Halpern). Espaillat's imagination traverses the realm of sound to sight, leaping from the musical expression of the pertinent part of the symphony to reconstruct the funeral cortège that the twenty-one-year-old Mendelssohn had so avidly witnessed. She transports herself liminally from her location in contemporary New England to inhabit Naples in the first half of the nineteenth century, sliding from the realm of the living to that of the dead, and drifting from her perspective to that of the intrigued young composer. She penetrates the mind of the deceased as well, his body "borne in state" (Espaillat, "Andante" 23). The speaker in her poem, the dead man himself, enunciates the fragility of life and the ephemeral nature of what lingers behind after we have departed from this earthly realm for the next.

It might appear dissonant to some critics that Espaillat should choose to condense her considerable output to a mere dozen poems in *Greatest Hits: 1942–2001*. No doubt, another anthologist could formulate an alternative list illustrating still more facets of her breadth of vision and complexity of artistic registers. The competing anthologist would probably select pieces that stress the primacy of love in its capacity to overcome problematic differences; explore the puzzling nature of perception; struggle with the contrastive demands of passion and reason; ponder the contingent, perhaps chaotic, and often senseless nature of existence; meditate on the problematic relationship we humans have with the divine; or ruminate on the limitations of time, the body, and art itself. The *Greatest Hits* selection carries indisputable weight as a composite *ars poetica*, a sort of artistic self-portrait that we must not ignore when forwarding any claims about her aesthetic worldview. The poems and the glosses that she provides point to several other elements that we can independently recognize as constituents of her literary philosophy and artistic praxis: Espaillat's insistence on the necessary balance between the "container and the contained" or "the how and the what"; the primacy of communication as an indispensable characteristic of the most effective poetic art; the role of music and sound as key conveyors of meaning; and her aversion to aesthetic ideologies that close ranks too tightly around particular dogmas, especially pertaining to art's role or place in society.

A clear consistency between theory and practice emerges as we read the work of Espaillat, who writes poems that stylistically and thematically live up to the creed that she articulates in her opinions about the craft. Her oeuvre abounds in poems such as "Metrics," which illustrates sonically why she needs sound to match her sense; "Why Publish," which advances her lyrical thesis about the relationship between the creative artist and the public; and "Warning," a piece whose speaker dissuades readers from coming to poetry looking for something that the art cannot likely give them. Frederick Aldama points to Espaillat's construction of the poet as globally minded dumpster diver, a scavenger invested in making meaning out of the "discarded heaps of debris found in the world" (Aldama 127). While far from the most glamorous figuration, this scrappy model captures the poet's disposition to draw on the whole mess of human endeavor as raw material. Here we might think of an oft-quoted remark from the start of act 1 in the play *Heauton Timoroumenos* (*The Self-Tormentor*, 163 BC), by the Roman dramatist Terence (ca. 190–159 BC). The character Chremes, an elder of Attica, offers unsolicited advice to his neighbor Menedemus, whom he wishes to dissuade from the self-inflicted torment of working himself to exhaustion as a means of coping with a personal problem. Apparently not used to having a neighbor thus meddle in his affairs, Menedemus requests an explanation. Chremes responds that because he is a man (and thus human), anything that happens to other people matters to him: "Homo sum: humani nihil a me alienum puto" (Terence 186–87). Espaillat upholds this humane vision and supplements it with her own ingredients: an affective rapport with the earth and an eye for its nonhuman and even its more-than-human inhabitants.

As we hope the preceding pages have demonstrated, Espaillat's prolific body of verse has long adhered to the vision she articulated through evocative metaphors in the afterword to *Where Horizons Go*. Here, she sets forth two ways of practicing the art of poetry: in one, the writing draws "very small circles around itself," its speaker standing "as a member of a narrowly delineated group and looking at 'outsiders' with eyes that discern less and less detail as distance increases" (70). In the other, the writing aims for "very large circles" that "draw in rather than exclude" (70). Espaillat reinforces the metaphor of the circles that extend or limit access to those not already inside by allowing a poetic voice from generations past to speak on her behalf. The afterword closes with a brief poem, a quatrain by Oregonian Edwin Markham (1852–1940), a bard who enjoyed much prestige in his time as we gather from the words of fellow poet Ella Wheeler Wilcox (1850–1919), who declared him to be "the greatest poet of the century" (Markham 191). Titled "Outwitted," the four-line poem by Markham sets forth the following scenario: "He drew a circle that shut me out— / Heretic, rebel, a thing to flout. / But Love and I had the wit to win: / We drew a circle that shut him in" (1). Markham's speaker, clearly someone who has endured exclusion for his religious beliefs, political leanings, or other reasons at the hands of a "he" with the power and authority to condemn the nonconformist, chooses to refrain from retaliation. Instead, the speaker allies with "Love" to "win" the quarrel at the affective level by weaponizing empathy. This strategy responds to the small, exclusionary circle that the adversary ("he") originally drew to shut the speaker out. The latter draws a bigger, inclusive one that has the capacity to "shut him in." The resolve of Markham's speaker to fight exclusion with inclusion resonates with the core of Espaillat's expansive poetic philosophy and worldview.

In 1998, on the occasion of publishing what was only her second book-length collection, Espaillat chose these aforementioned lines by a poet from the past to convey the tenets that have consistently sustained her approach to the craft. Over two decades and numerous volumes—her own verse and her translations of other poets' works—have transpired since then. At this writing, her collection of poems *And After All* is forthcoming from Able Muse Press, and she has assembled the manuscript for another volume, titled *The Field*, which she is preparing to submit to potential publishers. Meanwhile, she has continued to rely on periodicals to disseminate a number of her unpublished poems, chiefly *Think*, *Rattle*, and *The Hudson Review*, among others. She has taken no break from writing, translating, lecturing, and helping to build literary communities. As a result, reams of her work still await public view either through publication in periodicals or in anthologies. The greater bulk of her poems published in journals, magazines, and anthologies, in addition to the sizable corpus of her published translations, remain uncollected. This veritable goldmine exists for literary scholars interested in excavating its many untapped riches.

With the considerable, progressive growth of her visibility and prestige, Espaillat finds herself at age eighty-six pressed for time to accept all the invitations to lecture, read, and conduct workshops that keep coming. Given all that she has weathered and accomplished along her literary trajectory since *Where Horizons Go*, we feel comfortable letting the metaphor of the widening circles have the last word in this study. In light of the productive tension between the small circles that seem to shut others out and the large circles that seek to draw them in, it is the latter impulse that most decisively encapsulates the enduring vitality and humane ethos of the poetry and poetics of Rhina Polonia Espaillat.

WORKS CITED

Aldama, Frederick Luis. *Formal Matters in Contemporary Latino Poetry*. Palgrave Macmillan, 2013.

Alemán, Manuel, editor. *Las caras del amor: Antología poética contemporánea*. Versal Editorial Group, 1999.

"Alfred Dorn." Obituary. *The New York Times*, 6–7 Jan. 2014.

Alvarez, Julia. *El mejor regalo del mundo: La leyenda de la vieja Belén/The Best Gift of All: The Legend of La Vieja Belén*. Translated by Rhina P. Espaillat, Santillana USA Publishing, 2009.

Alvarez, Julia. "La Ñapa: Mariposas Unite," Nov. 2012, www.juliaalvarez.com/napa/mariposas-unite.php. Accessed 15 Oct. 2013.

Alvarez, Julia. "My English." *Punto 7 Review: A Journal of Marginal Discourse*, vol. 2, no. 2, 1992, pp. 24–29.

Alvarez, Julia. *Something to Declare: Essays*. Algonquin Books of Chapel Hill, 1998.

"Americanization." *Collier's New Encyclopedia* (1921). Wikipedia. en.wikisource.org/wiki/Collier%27s_New_Encyclopedia_(1921)/Americanization. Accessed 30 Dec. 2017.

Anzaldúa, Gloria. *Borderlands/La Frontera: The New Mestiza*. Aunt Lute Books, 1987.

Aponick, Kathleen, Jane Brox, and Paul Marion, editors. *Merrimack: A Poetry Anthology*. Loom Press, 1992.

Attridge, Derek. "A Return to Form?" *Textual Practice*, vol. 22, no. 3, 2008, pp. 563–74.

Auden, W. H., Marianne Moore, and Karl Shapiro, editors. *Riverside Poetry, 1953: Poems by Students in Colleges and Universities in New York City*. Haddan House Book/Association Press, 1953.

Baer, William, editor. *Rhyming Poems: A Contemporary Anthology*. U of Evansville P, 2007.

Baer, William, editor. *Sonnets: 150 Contemporary Sonnets*. U of Evansville P, 2005.

Barbato, Joseph. Preface. Sklar and Barbato, pp. 9–10.

Bartky, Sandra Lee. "Foucault, Femininity, and the Modernization of Patriarchal Power." *Theorizing Feminisms: A Reader*, edited by Elizabeth Hackett and Sally Haslanger, Oxford UP, 2006, pp. 277–92.

Bate, Walter Jackson. *John Keats*. Belknap Press of Harvard UP, 1963.

Bates, Karen Grigsby. "History Makes Hiring Household Help a Complex Choice." *All Things Considered*, from NPR, 24 May 2013, www.npr.org/blogs/codeswitch/2013/05/24/185508615/going-to-meet-the-ma-am.

Baugh, Albert C., editor. *A Literary History of England*. 2nd ed. Prentice-Hall, Inc., 1948.

Baxter, Cindy. "Koch Industries: Still Fueling Climate Denial." *Greenpeace.org*, 6 May 2011, www.greenpeace.org/usa/koch-industries-still-fueling-climate-denial/. Accessed 16 May 2014.

Benedict, Kate. "Cheat Sheet of Repeating Forms." *Tilt-a-Whirl*, www.katebenedict.com/Tilt-a-Whirl/Whirl-About/CheatSheetofRepeatingForm.html. Accessed 15 Aug. 2014.

Benét, William Rose. "A Master Collects the Masters." *The Saturday Review*, 24 Oct. 1942.

Berlin, Isaiah. *The Hedgehog and the Fox: An Essay on Tolstoy's View of History*. 2nd ed., Princeton UP, 2013.

Berman, David. "A Review of Joseph Salemi's Review of Rhina Espaillat's *Rehearsing Absence*." *Able Muse*, 8 Mar. 2002. Accessed 20 Jan. 2016.

The Bible. Oxford Annotated Version, Revised Standard Edition. Edited by Herbert G. May and Bruce M. Metzger, Oxford UP, 1962.

Bierfelt, Kristin. *The North Shore Literary Trail: From Bradstreet's Andover to Hawthorne's Salem*. History Press, 2009.

Bloom, Bernard S., Nathalie de Pouvourville, and Walter L. Straus. "Cost of Illness of Alzheimer's Disease: How Useful Are Current Estimates?" *The Gerontologist*, vol. 43, no. 3, 2003, pp. 158–64.

Blunt, Alison, and Robyn Dowling. "Setting Up Home: An Introduction." *Home*, edited by Blunt and Dowling, Routledge, 2006, pp. 1–31.

Bottum, Joseph. "Rhyme & Reason." *First Things*, Apr. 2010, pp. 59–61.

Bourne, Randolph. "Trans-National America." *The Radical Will: Selected Writings, 1911–1918*, edited by Olaf Hansen, U of California P, 1992, pp. 248–64.

Braziel, Jana Evans, and Anita Mannur, editors. *Theorizing Diaspora: A Reader*. Blackwell Publishing, 2003.

Brecht, Bertolt. *Poems: 1913–1956*. Edited by John Willett and Ralph Manheim with Erich Fried, Methuen, 1979.

Briley, Alice, editor. *Second Encore!: Selections from the Magazine* Encore. 20th anniversary limited ed., Allegheny Press, 1986.

Bryant, William Cullen. "Thanatopsis." *The Norton Anthology of American Literature*, vol. 1, edited by Ronald Gottesman et al., W. W. Norton, 1979, pp. 673–75.

Buell, Lawrence. "The Ecocritical Insurgency." *New Literary History*, vol. 30, no. 3, summer 1999, pp. 699–712.

Buell, Lawrence. *The Environmental Imagination: Thoreau, Nature Writing, and the Formation of American Culture*. Belknap Press of Harvard UP, 1995.

Buell, Lawrence. *Writing for an Endangered World: Literature, Culture, and Environment in the U.S. and Beyond*. Belknap Press of Harvard UP, 2001.

Candelario, Ginetta E. B. "Voices from Hispaniola: A *Meridians* Roundtable with Edwidge Danticat, Loida Maritza Pérez, Myriam J. A. Chancy, and Nelly Rosario." *Meridians: Feminism, Race, Transnationalism*, vol. 5, no. 1, 2004, pp. 69–91.

Cane, Melville, John Farrar, and Louise Townsend Nicholl, editors. *The Golden Year: The Poetry Society of America Anthology (1910–1960)*. Fine Editions Press, 1960.

Caplan, David. "What Was New Formalism?" *A Companion to Poetic Genre*, edited by Erik Martiny, Wiley-Blackwell, 2012, pp. 17–33.

Cárdenas, José A. *All Pianos Have Keys and Other Stories*. Intercultural Development Research Association, 1994.

Cavalli-Sforza, Luigi Luca, Paolo Menozzi, and Alberto Piazza. *The History and Geography of Human Genes*. Princeton UP, 1994.

Chamberlain, J. Gordon. Foreword. Auden, Moore, and Shapiro, n.p.

Chancy, Myriam J. A. "The Heart of Home: Loida Maritza Pérez in Dialogue." *MaComère*, no. 5, 2002, pp. 6–18.

Chen, Pauline W. "The Doctor as Poet." *New York Times*, 1 Dec. 2011, well.blogs.nytimes.com/2011/12/01/the-doctor-as-poet/?. Accessed 6 June 2014.

Chen, Pauline W. "Resurrectionist." *Writer, MD: The Best Contemporary Fiction and Nonfiction by Doctors*, edited by Leah Kaminsky, Vintage, 2012, pp. 19–49.

Chiasson, Dan. Review of *Playing at Stillness* by Rhina P. Espaillat. *Poetry*, vol. 187, no. 2, Nov. 2005, pp. 150–52.

Chocano, José Santos. *Alma América*. Edited by Francisco Bendezú, Serie Escritores de Lima. Editoral Nuevos Rumbos, 1958.

Christophersen, Bill. "Spruce but Loose: Formalism in the Nineties." *Poetry*, vol. 174, no. 6, 1999, pp. 345–51.

Clifford, James. "Diasporas." *Cultural Anthropology*, vol. 9, no. 3, 1994, pp. 302–38.

Coghill, Sheila, and Thom Tammaro, editors. *Visiting Frost: Poems Inspired by the Life and Works of Robert Frost*. U of Iowa P, 2005.

Cohen, Robin. "The Diaspora of a Diaspora: The Case of the Caribbean." *Social Science Information*, vol. 31, no. 1, 1992, pp. 159–69.

Cohen, Robin. *Global Diasporas: An Introduction*. U of Washington P, 1997.

"Contributors." *Poetry*, vol. 158, no. 5, Aug. 1991, pp. 296–98.

Corrigan, Maureen. "'Lean In': Not Much of a Manifesto but Still a Win for Women." Rev. of *Lean In: Women, Work, and the Will to Lead*. By Sheryl Sandberg. *NPR Fresh Air* from WHYY, 12 Mar. 2013, www.npr.org/2013/03/12/174016175/lean-in-not-much-of-a-manifesto-but-still-a-win-for-women. Accessed 13 Mar. 2013.

Cruz-Hacker, Alba. "Dominican-Americans from Here and There: Articulations of Exile and Dual Identity." Unpublished manuscript, pp. 1–32.

Davis, Adam, editor. *Taking Action: Readings for Civic Reflection*. Great Books Foundation/Center for Civic Reflection, 2012.

Day, Kay. "Characters in Poetry." *The Writer*, vol. 117, no. 6, June 2004, pp. 20–21.

De Beauvoir, Simone. 1949. *The Second Sex*. Translated by H. M. Parshley, Vintage, 1989.

Decker, Clarence R. Foreword. Cane, Farrar, and Nicholl, pp. vii–ix.

Deitz, Paula, editor. *Poets Translate Poets: A* Hudson Review *Anthology*. Syracuse UP, 2013.

Delbanco, Nicolas, and Alan Cheuse, editors. *Literature: Craft and Voice*. McGraw-Hill, 2010.

Del Castillo, Adelaida R. "Mexican Gender Ideology." Delgado and Stefancic, pp. 499–500.

Delgado, Richard, and Jean Stefanic, editors. *The Latino/a Condition: A Critical Reader*. New York UP, 1998.

Dicker, Susan. *Languages in America: A Pluralist View*. Multilingual Matters, 1996.

Dickinson, Emily. *The Complete Poems of Emily Dickinson*. Edited by Thomas H. Johnson, Little, Brown and Co., 1960.

Dickinson, Emily. "'Hope' is the thing with feathers." *The Complete Poems of Emily Dickinson*, edited by Thomas H. Johnson. Back Bay Books, 1976, p. 254.

Diplomatic List. United States Department of State. Washington, DC, Nov. 1935.

Docker-Marcus, Amy. "A Doctor Explains the Healing Power of Poetry." *The Wall Street Journal*, 17 Apr. 2017, www.wsj.com/articles/a-doctor-explains-the-healing-power-of-poetry-1491908401.

Dorn, Alfred. Letter to Rhina Espaillat, 3 May 1983. Author's papers.

Dorn, Alfred. Letter to Rhina Espaillat, 15 Sept. 1991. Author's papers.

Dorn, Alfred. "A Questioning Muse." *Iambs and Trochees*, vol. 1, no. 2, fall/winter 2002, pp. 108–14.

Dufoix, Stéphane. *Diasporas*. Translated by William Rodarmor, U of California P, 2008.

Ellis, Jonathan. "Ekphrastic Poetry in and out of the Museum." *A Companion to Poetic Genre*, edited by Erik Martiny, Blackwell, 2012, pp. 614–26.

Espada, Martín. *Alabanza: New and Selected Poems, 1982–2002*. W. W. Norton, 2003.

Espada, Martín. "Coca-Cola and Coco Frio." *Paper Dance: 55 Latino Poets*, edited by Victor Hernández Cruz, Leroy V. Quintana, and Virgil Suarez, Persea Books, 1995, pp. 44–45.

Espaillat, Rhina P. "À Minuit." *Ladies' Home Journal*, Aug. 1948, p. 48.

Espaillat, Rhina P. *Agua de dos ríos: Poemas, prosa y traducciones—una colección bilingüe*. Secretaría de Estado de Cultura, Editora Nacional, 2006.

Espaillat, Rhina P. "Andante con moto." *Texas Poetry Journal*, vol.1, no. 1, spring 2006, p. 23.

Espaillat, Rhina P. "Answer." *Ladies' Home Journal*, Nov. 1947, p. 298.

Espaillat, Rhina P. "Changeling." *Poetry*, vol. 158, no. 5, Aug. 1991, p. 255.

Espaillat, Rhina P. "Comments on the Translation of Robert Frost Poems." Frost, *Algo hay*, pp. 14–25.

"Rhina P. Espaillat." *Contemporary Authors Online*, Gale, 2003. *Contemporary Authors Online*, link.galegroup.com/apps/doc/H1000128957/CA?u=nysl_ce_syr&sid=CA&xid=48b8ddff. Accessed 2 Jan. 2018.

Espaillat, Rhina P. "Cutting Bait" *Poetry*, vol. 158, no. 5, Aug. 1991, pp. 255–56.

Espaillat, Rhina P. *El olor de la memoria:cuentos/The Scent of Memory: Short Stories*. Ediciones CEDIBIL, 2007.

Espaillat, Rhina P. Foreword. *Lines of Flight: Poems*, by Catherine Chandler, Able Muse Press, 2011, ix–xii.

Espaillat, Rhina P. *Her Place in These Designs*. Truman State UP, 2008.

Espaillat, Rhina P., translator. *The Hudson Review*, the Spanish Issue, vol. 64, no. 1, 2011, pp. 90–94, 102–04, 124.

Espaillat, Rhina P. *Lapsing to Grace: Poems and Drawings*. Bennett and Kitchel, 1992.

Espaillat, Rhina P. Letter to Silvio Torres-Saillant, 17 Feb. 2000.

Espaillat, Rhina P. "Migration, Identity, Belonging." Biennial Dominican Studies Association Conference, Hostos Community College, CUNY, Bronx, New York, 6 May 2006. Keynote Address.

Espaillat, Rhina P. *Mundo y palabra/The World and the Word*. Oyster River Press, 2001.

Espaillat, Rhina P. "On Waiting." *Ladies' Home Journal*, Nov. 1947, p. 298.

Espaillat, Rhina P. "Pious Simplicities and Complex Realities: Anthony Hecht and the Religious Impulse." Manuscript, 10 pp., single-spaced, Times New Roman font, 8 1/2 x 11 paper.

Espaillat, Rhina P. *Playing at Stillness*. Truman State UP, 2005.

Espaillat, Rhina P. "Poems by Rhina P. Espaillat." *Review: Literature and Arts of the Americas*, vol. 40, no. 1, 2007, pp. 126–27.

Espaillat, Rhina P. "Re: Biographical Details." Received by Silvio Torres-Saillant, 17 Feb. 2000.

Espaillat, Rhina P. "Re: Buenas Noticias!" Received by Silvio Torres-Saillant, 28 Jan. 2013.

Espaillat, Rhina P. "Re: Following Up on Our Previous Conversation." Received by Silvio Torres-Saillant, 27 June 2014.

Espaillat, Rhina P. "Re: Greetings!" Received by Silvio Torres-Saillant, 16 Aug. 2006.

Espaillat, Rhina P. "Re: Some Answers to Your Questions." Received by Silvio Torres-Saillant, 4 Aug. 2014.

Espaillat, Rhina P. *Rehearsing Absence*. U of Evansville P, 2001.

Espaillat, Rhina P. "Read between the Lines." Our Poetry Corner. *Lethbridge Herald*, June 1948, n.p.

Espaillat, Rhina P. *Rhina P. Espaillat: Greatest Hits: 1942–2001*. Pudding House Publications, 2003.

Espaillat, Rhina P. *The Shadow I Dress In*. David Robert Books, 2004.

Espaillat, Rhina P., translator. "Spanish and Latin American Devotional Poetry." *Sewanee Theological Review*, vol. 56, no. 1, Christmas 2012, pp. 11–70.

Espaillat, Rhina P. *The Story-Teller's Hour*. Scienter Press, 2004.

Espaillat, Rhina P. "There is Nothing of You Not Worshiped." *Ladies' Home Journal*, Nov. 1947, p. 298.

Espaillat, Rhina P. "Two Cameos." Guest Folio. *Post Road Magazine*, issue 23, 2012, n.p.

Espaillat, Rhina P. *Where Horizons Go*. New Odyssey Press, 1998.

Espaillat, Rhina P. "Why I Like to Dance in a Box." Finch, *Formal Feeling*, 64–65.

Espaillat, Rhina P., and Sarah Aponte, editors. *Juan Pablo Duarte, the Humanist: A Bilingual Selection of His Writings*. Biblioteca Nacional Pedro Henríquez Ureña/CUNY Dominican Studies Institute, 2015.

Fernández, Roberta, editor. *In Other Words: Literature by Latinas of the United States*. Arte Público Press, 1994.

Field, Eugene. *A Little Book of Western Verse*. The Works of Eugene Field. Vol. 1. Charles Scribner's Sons, 1896.

Figgins, Margo A., and Jenny Johnson. "Wordplay: The Poem's Second Language." *English Journal*, vol. 96, no. 3, Jan. 2007, pp. 29–34.

Finch, Annie, editor. *After New Formalism: Poets on Form, Narrative, and Tradition*. Story Line Press, 1999.

Finch, Annie, editor. *A Formal Feeling Comes: Poems in Form by Contemporary Women*. Story Line Press, 1994.

Finch, Annie, and Marie-Elizabeth Mali, editors. *Villanelles*. Alfred A. Knopf, 2012.

Fowler, James, editor. *Heartbeat of New England: Anthology of Contemporary Nature Poetry.* Tiger Moon, 2000.

Fox, Alan. "Conversation between Rhina P. Espaillat and Alan Fox in Brentwood, California, February 6, 2012." *Rattle*, vol. 18, no. 2, winter 2012, pp. 131–47.

Frost, Robert. *Algo hay que no es amigo de los muros: cuarenta poemas/Something There Is That Doesn't Love a Wall: Forty Poems.* Translated by Rhina P. Espaillat, Ediciones El Tucán de Virginia, 2014.

Frost, Robert. *Selected Letters of Robert Frost.* Edited by Lawrance Thompson, Holt, Rinehart and Winston, 1964.

Frost, Robert. *Selected Poems of Robert Frost.* Introduction by Robert Graves, Holt, Rinehart and Winston, 1966.

Gawande, Atul. *Better: A Surgeon's Notes on Performance.* Picador, 2007.

Gawande, Atul. *Being Mortal: Medicine and What Matters in the End.* Metropolitan Books, 2014.

Gawande, Atul. "The Way We Age Now." *The New Yorker*, 30 Apr. 2007, www.newyorker.com/magazine/2007/04/30/the-way-we-age-now.

Gilman, Charlotte Perkins. "An Extinct Angel." 1891. *The Yellow Wall-Paper and Other Stories.* Edited by Robert Shulman, Oxford UP, 1995, pp. 48–50.

Gioia, Dana, editor. *100 Great Poets of the English Language.* Penguin Academics/Pearson Longman, 2005.

Gioia, Dana. *Can Poetry Matter? Essays on Poetry and American Culture.* Graywolf Press, 1992.

Gioia, Dana, and David Mason, editors. *Twentieth-Century American Poetry.* McGraw-Hill, 2003.

Gioia, Dana, David Mason, and Meg Schoerke, editors. *Twentieth-Century American Poetics: Poets on the Art of Poetry.* McGraw-Hill, 2003.

Gordon, Haim. *Dwelling Poetically: Educational Challenges in Heidegger's Thinking on Poetry.* Rodopi, 2000.

Gorenstein, Dan. "How Doctors Die: Showing Others the Way." *The New York Times*, 19 Nov. 2013, www.nytimes.com/2013/11/20/your-money/how-doctors-die.html?. Accessed 11 July 2014.

Gray, John, Carol L. Meyers, and David Wolpe. "Commentaries." *Biography: Adam and Eve—Lost Innocence*, aired 12 Feb. 1996. *Netflix*. Accessed 11 Apr. 2013.

Gross, Jill Oestreicher. "Local Poets Ready to Wow the Nation." *Newburyport Current* [MA], 17 Mar. 2006, pp. 17–18.

Guynn, Jessica. "Yahoo CEO Marissa Mayer Causes Uproar with Telecommuting Ban." *Los Angeles Times*, 26 Feb. 2013, articles.latimes.com/2013/feb/26/business/la-fi-yahoo-telecommuting-20130226. Accessed 19 Mar. 2013.

Gwynn, R. S. "Histories and Mysteries." *The Hudson Review*, vol. 58, no. 4, winter 2006, pp. 675–80.

Halberstam, Judith [Jack]. *Female Masculinity*. Duke UP, 1998.

Halpern, Susan. "Program Notes: Mendelsohn, 'Symphony No. 4,'" www.halpernprogram notes.com. Accessed 30 Mar. 2015.

Harris, Gardiner, and Mark Landler. "Obama Tells Mourning Dallas, 'We Are Not as Divided as We Seem.'" *The New York Times*, 11 July 2016.

Hernández-Truyol, Berta Esperanza. "Culture and Economic Violence." Delgado and Stefancic, pp. 536–38.

Hollander, John. *Rhyme's Reason: A Guide to English Verse*. Yale UP, 1981.

Hollinger, David A. *Postethnic America: Beyond Multiculturalism*. Basic Books, 1995.

Homer. *The Iliad*. Translated by Richard Lattimore, U of Chicago P, 1962.

hooks, bell. "Dig Deep: Beyond *Lean In*." *The Feminist Wire*, 28 Oct., 2013, thefeministwire .com/2013/10/17973/?fb_source=pubv1. Accessed 29 Oct. 2013.

hooks, bell. *Yearning: Race, Gender, and Cultural Politics*. South End Press, 1990.

Hopkins, Gerard Manley. "The Child Is Father to the Man." *Gerard Manley Hopkins: The Complete Poems*. Edited by Robert Bridges, Lexicos Publishing, 2012. Kindle edition.

Hopper, Stanley Romaine. Introduction. Auden, Moore, and Shapiro, pp. 9–18.

Hua, Anh. "Diaspora and Cultural Memory." *Diaspora, Memory, and Identity: A Search for Home*, edited by Vijay Agnew, U of Toronto P, 2005, pp. 191–208.

Hughes, Langston. "The Negro Artist and the Racial Mountain." *The Black Aesthetic*, edited by Addison Gayle, Jr., Doubleday, 1971, pp. 175–81.

Iglesias, Elizabeth M. "Maternal Power and the Deconstruction of Male Supremacy." Delgado and Stefancic, pp. 175–81.

Jarman, Mark, and David Mason, editors. *Rebel Angels: 25 Poets of the New Formalism*. Story Line Press, 1996.

John of the Cross, Saint. *St. John of the Cross (San Juan de la Cruz), Alchemist of the Soul: His Life, His Poetry (Bilingual), His Prose*. Edited and translated by Antonio T. de Nicolás, Paragon House, 1989.

Johnson, Greg, Thomas Arp, and Laurence Perrine. *Perrine's Sound and Sense: An Introduction to Poetry*. Cengage Learning, 2014.

Jónsdóttir, Birgitta, editor. *The Book of Hope*. Lorenzo Press, 2002.

Jónsdóttir, Birgitta, editor. *The World Healing Book*. Lorenzo Press, 2002.

Jordan, June. "Where Is the Love?" *African American Literature*, edited by Keith Gilyard and Anissa Wardi, Pearson, 2004, pp. 1193–98.

"Julia Richman Senior Already a Published Poet." *New York Herald Tribune*, 1949, p. 12.

K., Sylvia. "Doctor/Writer: Richard Selzer." *Teen Ink*, www.teenink.com/fiction/author_inter views/article/5434/DoctorWriter-Richard-Selzer/. Accessed 24 May 2014.

Kang, Nancy. "'Truth Is Always Both': An Interview with Rhina P. Espaillat." *MELUS*, vol. 40, no. 1, spring 2015, pp. 177–94.

Kang, Nancy, and Silvio Torres-Saillant. "Dancing in a Box: A Look2 Essay on Rhina P. Espaillat." *Ploughshares*, vol. 40, no. 4, winter 2014–15, pp. 181–94.

Keenan, Deborah, and Roseann Lloyd, editors. *Looking for Home: Women Writing about Exile*. Milkweed Editions, 1990.

Keillor, Garrison. *The Writer's Almanac*. Radio broadcast, Minnesota Public Radio. 2 Sept. 2008. www.mpr.org.

Kendall, Tim. *The Art of Robert Frost*. Yale UP, 2012.

Kennedy, X. J. Introduction. *The Powow River Anthology*, edited by Alfred Nicol, Ocean Publishing, 2006, pp. xi–xv.

Kennedy, X. J., and Dana Gioia, editors. *An Introduction to Poetry*. 13th ed. Longman, 2010.

Killing Us Softly 4: Advertising's Image of Women. Directed by Sut Jhally. Performance by Jean Kilbourne. Media Education Foundation, 2010, 45 min. DVD.

Kokot, Waltraud, Khachig Tölöyan, and Carolyn Alfonso, editors. *Diaspora, Identity, and Religion: New Directions in Theory and Research*. Routledge, 2004.

Korwin, Yala H. *Crossroads: Poems*. Xlibris Corp, 2011.

Kossman, Nina, editor. *Gods and Mortals: Modern Poems on Classical Myths*, Oxford UP, 2001.

Krisak, Len. "Rhina P. Espaillat." *Dictionary of Literary Biography*, vol. 282: *New Formalist Poets*, edited by Jonathan N. Barron and Bruce Meyer, Bruccoli Clark Layman, Gale Group, 2003, 78–82.

LaFemina, Gerry, editor. *Token Entry: New York City Subway Poems*. Smalls Books, 2012.

Lake, Paul. Review of *Her Place in These Designs*, by Rhina P. Espaillat. *First Things*, June/July 2009, p. 59.

Little, Bliss S., and Benjamin J. Broome. "Diaspora." *Encyclopedia of Identity*, edited by Ronald L. Jackson II, Sage Publications, 2010, pp. 221–26.

Long, Alexander. "The Psychic Landscape." *Smartish Pace*, no. 20, smartishpace.com/essays/the_psychic_landscape/. Accessed 25 Oct. 2013.

Lopez, Barry. "A Dark Light in the West: Racism and Reconciliation." *The Georgia Review*, fall 2010, pp. 365–386.

Lopez, Barry. "A Scary Abundance of Water: Growing Up with the San Fernando Valley." *LA Weekly*, 9 Jan. 2002, www.laweekly.com/news/a-scary-abundance-of-water-2134257. Accessed 23 Jun. 2016.

Makuck, Peter. "Heartlands." *The Hudson Review*, vol. 58, no. 3 autumn 2005, pp. 498–506.

Malory, Thomas. *Malory: Works.* Edited by Eugène Vinaver, Oxford UP, 1954.

Maríñez, Sophie. "Espaillat, Rhina." *The Oxford Encyclopedia of Latinos and Latinas in the United States,* vol. 2, edited by Suzanne Oboler and Deena González, Oxford UP, 2005, pp. 68–69.

Markham, Edwin. *The Shoes of Happiness and Other Poems.* Doubleday, Doran & Co., 1934.

Marzán, Julio. *The Spanish American Roots of William Carlos Williams.* U of Texas P, 1994.

Mason, David. *Two Minds of a Western Poet: Essays.* U of Michigan P, 2011.

Mather, Cotton. *Magnalia Christi Americana: or, the Ecclesiastical History of New England.* Books I and II. Edited by Kenneth B. Murdock and Elizabeth B. Miller, Harvard UP, 1977.

McAlpine, Katherine, and Gail White, editors. *The Muse Strikes Back: A Poetic Response by Women to Men.* Story Line Press, 1997.

McCarthy, Julie. "On India's Trains, Seeking Safety in the Women's Compartment." *Morning Edition,* from NPR, 28 Mar. 2013, www.npr.org/2013/03/28/175471907/on-indias-trains-seeking-safety-in-the-women-s-compartment.

McClymer, John. "The Americanization Movement and the Education of the Foreign-Born Adult." *American Education and the European Immigrant: 1840–1940,* edited by Bernard Weiss, U of Illinois P, 1982.

McGovern, Robert, and Stephen Haven, editors. *And What Rough Beast: Poems at the End of the Century.* Ashland Poetry Press, 1999.

McGuire, Thomas G. "War, Tradition, Iconoclastic Talent: A Conversation with Robert Mezey." *War, Literature & the Arts,* vol. 21, nos. 1–2, 2009, pp. 215–34.

Meyer, Bruce, and Jonathan N. Barron. Introduction. *Dictionary of Literary Biography.* Vol. 282, *New Formalist Poets,* edited by Jonathan N. Barron and Bruce Meyer, Bruccoli Clark Layman/Gale Group, pp. xvii–xxiii.

Mezey, Robert, editor. *Poems of the American West.* Alfred A. Knopf, 2002.

Millay, Edna St. Vincent. *Renascence and Other Poems.* Harper & Brothers Publishers, 1917.

Mishra, Sudesh. *Diaspora Criticism.* Edinburgh UP, 2006.

Monsour, Leslie. "Introduction to the Life and Poetry of Richard Wilbur." Wilbur, *Oscura fruta,* pp. 12–29.

Monsour, Leslie. *Rhina Espaillat: A Critical Introduction.* Story Line Press, 2013.

Moore, Robert. *Unexpected Colors: Poems and Songs.* Beech River Books, 2009.

Moskowitz, Alfred. "My Recollections during Battle." *The Bulge Bugle,* vol. 31, no. 2, May 2012, pp. 13–14.

Murphy, Timothy. "Lost in Translation." *Sewanee Theological Review,* vol. 56, no. 1, Christmas 2012, pp. 13–15.

Murray, Ken. "Why Dying is Easier for Doctors." *Time,* 1 Sept. 2014, time.com/3194806/why-dying-is-easier-for-doctors/.

Nelson, Marilyn. "Owning the Masters." Finch, *After New Formalism*, pp. 8–17.

Nestle, Joan, Clare Howell, and Riki Anne Wilchins, editors. *GenderQueer: Voices from Beyond the Sexual Binary*. Alyson Books, 2002.

Nicol, Alfred. "'Lately I've Wondered': A Review of Rhina P. Espaillat's *Her Place in These Designs*." *Per Contra*, Jan. 2011, percontra.net/archive/21nicol.htm.

Nicol, Alfred, editor. *The Powow River Anthology*. Ocean Publishing, 2006.

Nicol, Alfred. "Rhina P. Espaillat." Supplement XXI of *American Writers: A Collection of Literary Biographies*, edited by Jay Parini, Charles Scribner's Sons/Gale Cengage Learning, 2011, pp. 97–114.

Noel, Urayoán. "For a Caribbean American Graininess: William Carlos Williams, Translator." *Small Axe*, no. 42., Nov. 2013, pp. 138–150. doi:10.1215/07990537-2378964.

Nuland, Sherwin B. *How We Die: Reflections on Life's Final Chapter*. Vintage, 1994.

Nuland, Sherwin B. "The Uncertain Art: Writing." *The American Scholar*, vol. 70, no. 1, 2001, pp. 129–32, search.proquest.com/docview/194747161?accountid=14214. Accessed 2 June 2014.

Nuland, Sherwin B. "Up from Hippocrates." Review of *Blood and Guts: A Short History of Medicine*, by Roy Porter. *The New Republic*, 17 Feb. 2013, pp. 31–36.

Oates, Joyce Carol. "Where Are You Going, Where Have You Been?" *Fiction: A Pocket Anthology*, 7th ed., edited by R. S. Gwynn. Pearson, 2012, pp. 292–308.

Oboler, Suzanne. *Ethnic Labels, Latino Lives: Identity and Politics of (Re)Presentation in the United States*. U of Minnesota P, 1995.

Oxford English Dictionary. Oxford UP, 1978.

Ovid. "Perseus Tells the Story of Medusa." *The Metamorphoses*. Translated by Anthony S. Kline. Book 4, pp. 753–803. University of Virginia Library Electronic Text Center. ovid.lib.virginia.edu/trans/Metamorph4.htm#478205208. Accessed 15 Sept. 2017.

Pack, Robert, and Jay Parini, editors. *American Identities: Contemporary Multicultural Voices*. Middlebury College P, 1994.

Paravisini-Gebert, Lizabeth, and Consuelo López Springfield, editors. Special issue of *Callaloo: A Journal of African Diaspora Arts and Letters*, vol. 23, no. 3, 2000.

Parini, Jay. *Robert Frost: A Life*. Henry Holt, 1999.

Payne, Alexander. Interview with Terry Gross. "Alexander Payne, Baby Photos and Ted Williams." *Fresh Air Weekend*, from NPR, 8 Dec. 2013, www.npr.org/2013/12/07/249333050/fresh-air-weekend-alexander-payne-baby-photos-and-ted-williams.

Paz, Octavio. *The Labyrinth of Solitude: Life and Thought in Mexico*. Grove Press, 1961.

Pepple, Alexander, editor. *Able Muse Anthology*. Able Muse Press, 2010.

Petronius and Seneca. *Satyricon. Apocolocyntosis*. Translated by Michael Heseltine and W. H. D. Rouse, revised by E. H. Warmington, *Loeb Classical Library* 15, Harvard UP, 1987.

Pope, Alexander. *Collected Poems*. Edited by Bonamy Dobrée, E. P. Dutton, 1956.

Pound, Ezra, editor. *Des Imagistes: An Anthology*. Albert and Charles Boni, 1914.

Pound, Ezra. *Personae: The Collected Poems of Ezra Pound*. New Directions, 1926.

"Powow River Poets Going Bilingual." *The Daily News* [Newburyport, MA], 9 Nov. 2000, p. B3.

Ramazani, Jahan. "A Transnational Poetics." *American Literary History*, vol. 18, no. 2, 2006, pp. 352–59.

Remnick, David. "Into the Clear." *The New Yorker*, 8 May 2000, pp. 76–89.

Rich, Adrienne. "Format and Form." Finch, *After New Formalism*, pp. 1–7.

Richardson, Joan. *Wallace Stevens: The Later Years, 1923–1955*. Beech Tree, 1988.

Richman, Robert, editor. *The Direction of Poetry: An Anthology of Rhymed and Metered Verse Written in the English Language since 1975*. Houghton Mifflin, 1988.

Rilke, Rainer Maria. *Selected Poems of Rainer Maria Rilke*. Translated by Robert Bly, Harper & Row, 1981.

Rivera, Jenny. "Domestic Violence against Latinas by Latino Males." Delgado and Stefancic, pp. 501–07.

Rizzo, Meredith. "The Poetic Intimacy of Administering Anesthesia." *Shots: Health News*, from *NPR*, 16 Apr. 2017, www.npr.org/sections/health-shots/2017/04/16/523816317/the-poetic-intimacy-of-administering-anesthesia.

Rodriguez, Richard. *Brown: The Last Discovery of America*. Viking, 2002.

Rodríguez-Peralta, Phyllis W. *José Santos Chocano*. Twayne Publishers, 1970.

Rosario Adames, Fausto. "Escritora Rhina Espaillat dice RD se expone al oprobio del mundo entero." *Acento*, 27 Oct. 2013, acento.com.do/2013/actualidad/1130893-escritora-rhina-espaillat-dice-rd-se-expone-al-oprobio-del-mundo-entero/.

Rothstein, Edward. "Connections; Faced with 'Parvenu' or 'Pariah,' Ellison Settled on 'Artist.'" *The New York Times*, 15 May 1999, p. A19.

Sacks, Oliver. Preface to the 1973 edition. *Awakenings*, by Sacks. Harper Perennial, 1990, pp. xvii–xix.

Sadoff, Ira. "'Flat death': Irretrievable Loss in Three Contemporary Poets." *The Kenyon Review*, vol. 31, no. 3, summer 2009, pp. 188–99, www.jstor.org/stable/40600076.

Sadoff, Ira. "Neo-Formalism: A Dangerous Nostalgia." *The American Poetry Review*, vol. 19, no. 2, Jan./Feb. 1990, pp. 7–13.

Safran, William. "Deconstructing and Comparing Diasporas." *Diaspora, Identity, and Religion: New Directions in Theory and Research*, edited by Waltraud Kokot, Khachig Tölöyan, and Carolyn Alfonso, Routledge, 2004, pp. 9–29.

Safran, William. "Diasporas in Modern Societies: Myths of Homeland and Return." *Diaspora*, vol. 1, no. 1, 1991, pp. 83–99.

Salemi, Joseph S. "In Memoriam: Alfred Dorn (1929–2014)." *The Pennsylvania Review*, 7 Jan. 2014, pennreview.com/2014/01/in-memoriam-alfred-dorn-1929-2014/.

Salemi, Joseph S. "The Poetry of Nicey-Nice." Review of *Rehearsing Absence*, by Rhina P. Espaillat. *Expansive Poetry & Music Online Review*, Mar. 2002, expansivepoetryonline. com/journal/rev032002.html.

Salemi, Joseph S. "Typographical Tics: Social Climbing in the New Formalism." *Expansive Poetry & Music Online Review*, Mar. 2000, expansivepoetryonline.com/journal/cult032000.html.

Sánchez Beras, César. *El sapito azul/The Little Blue Frog*. Translated by Rhina P. Espaillat, Grupo Santillana, 2010.

Sánchez Beras, César. *Lawrence City and Other Poems*. Translated by Rhina P. Espaillat, Wellington House Publishing, 2007.

Sánchez Beras, César. *Scar on the Wind: Selected Short Poems/Cicatriz en el viento: selección de poemas breves*. Translated by Rhina P. Espaillat, Obsidiana Press, 2013.

Sánchez Beras, César. *Trovas del mar/Troves of the Sea*. Translated by Rhina P. Espaillat and Len Krisak, Editora Buho, 2002.

Santayana, George. *Poems*. Charles Scribner's Sons, 1923.

Scheele, Roy. "A Conversation with Poet Rhina P. Espaillat." *Texas Journal of Poetry*, vol. 2, no. 1, spring 2006, pp. 24–46.

Schmuller, Angelo Aaron, editor. *Modern Lyrics Anthology*. Parthenon Publishing, 1982.

Schreiber, Jan. "*Rehearsing Absence* by Rhina Espaillat." Review. *The Edge City Review*, vol. 6, no. 1, Sept. 2002, pp. 39–41.

"Secretary of Labor Thomas E. Perez." Office of the Secretary, United States Department of Labor. www.dol.gov. Accessed 26 June 2016.

Sedgwick, Eve Kosofsky. *Epistemology of the Closet*. U of California P, 1990.

Seeley, Virginia, editor. *Latino Caribbean Literature*. Multicultural Literature Collection. Globe Fearon, 1994.

Shakespeare, William. *The Complete Works of William Shakespeare*. Edited by Irving Ribner and George Lyman Kittredge, Xerox College Publishing, 1971.

Share, Don, and Christian Wiman, editors. *The Open Door: One Hundred Poems, One Hundred Years of* Poetry *Magazine*. U of Chicago P, 2012.

Sharp, Judith. "Rhina Espaillat Talks about T. S. Eliot and Reading." *Truman State UP Blogs*, 21 Mar. 2012, www.blogs.truman.edu/tsup/2012/03/21/rhina-espaillat-talks-about-t-s-eliot-and-reading/. Accessed 6 June 2013.

Shaw, Robert B. "Straws in the Wind." Review of *Rehearsing Absence*, by Rhina P. Espaillat. *Poetry*, vol. 180, no. 6, Sept. 2002, pp. 345–54. *Proquest*, Accessed 20 Dec. 2015.

Sheffer, Gabriel. Introduction. *Modern Diasporas in International Politics*, edited by Sheffer, Croom Helm, 1986, pp. 1–15.

Sklar, Morty. Preface. Sklar and Barbato, pp. 5–8.

Sklar, Morty, and Joseph Barbato, editors. *Patchwork of Dreams: Voices from the Heart of the New America*. The Spirit That Moves Us Press, 1996.

Sor Juana Inés de la Cruz. *Poems, Protest, and a Dream*. Edited and translated by Margaret Sayers Peden, Penguin Books, 1997.

Steele, Timothy. *Missing Measures: Modern Poetry and the Revolt against Meter*. U of Arkansas P, 1990.

Stern, Daniel. "One Who Got Away." Review of *Down These Mean Streets*, by Piri Thomas. *The New York Times Book Review*, 21 May 1967, pp. 43–44.

Stevenson, Anne. "The Trouble with a Word like Formalism." Finch, *After New Formalism*, pp. 217–23.

Stoner, Julie. "Book Review of *Her Place in These Designs* by Rhina P. Espaillat." *Able Muse*, Tribute Issue, winter 2009, ablemuse.com/v8/book-review/julie-stoner/her-place-these-designs-espaillat?s=761e3c63439dfef8cf6cd226011b2ea0.

Strasnick, Stephanie. "Degas and Cassatt: The Untold Story of their Artistic Friendship." *Artnews*, 27 Mar. 2014, www.artnews.com/2014/03/27/national-gallery-show-explores-artistic-friendship-of-degas-and-cassatt/.

Taylor, Marilyn. "How to Write the Poem that Scares You." *The Writer*, vol. 125, no. 2, Feb. 2012, p. 17+.

Taylor, Marilyn. "The Reason behind the Rhyme." *The Writer*, vol. 122, no. 2, Feb. 2009, pp. 15–16.

"Teen-age Poet Wins Honors." *New York Sun*, 5 June 1950.

Terence. *The Woman of Andros. The Self-Tormentor. The Eunuch*. Edited and translated by John Barsby, Loeb Classical Library 22, Harvard UP, 2001.

Teresa of Avila, Saint. *The Complete Works of St. Teresa of Jesus*. Vol. 3, edited by Allison Peers, Sheed and Ward, 1946.

Thiel, Diane, editor. *Open Roads: Exercises in Writing Poetry*, Pearson Longman, 2005.

Thiel, Diane, editor. *Winding Roads: Exercises in Writing Creative Nonfiction*. Pearson Longman, 2008.

Tiffany, Daniel. "Lyric Substance: On Riddle, Materialism, and Poetic Obscurity." *Critical Inquiry*, vol. 28, no. 1, 2001, pp. 72–98.

Thompson, William, editor. *Fashioned Pleasures: Twenty-Four Poets Play Bouts-Rimés with a Shakespearean Sonnet*. Parallel Press, 2005.

Toledo-Pereyra, Luis H. "Richard Selzer: Premiere American Surgeon-Writer." *Journal of Investigative Surgery*, vol. 20, no. 6, 2007, pp. 319–23.

Tölölyan, Khachig. "Rethinking *Diaspora(s)*: Stateless Power in the Transnational Moment." *Diaspora*, vol. 5, no. 1, spring 1996, pp. 3–36.

Torres-Saillant, Silvio. *Diasporic Disquisitions: Dominicanists, Transnationalism, and the Community*. Dominican Studies Working Papers 1. CUNY Dominican Studies Institute–City College of New York, 2000.

Torres-Saillant, Silvio. "Dominican-American Literature." *The Routledge Companion to Latino/a Literature*, edited by Suzanne Bost and Frances Aparicio, Routledge, 2013, pp. 423–35.

Torres-Saillant, Silvio. "Espaillat, Rhina P." *Making It in America: A Sourcebook on Eminent Ethnic Americans*, edited by Elliott Robert Barkan, ABC-CLIO, 2001, pp. 115–16.

Torres-Saillant, Silvio. "Formalismo y credo musical: Introducción a la poesía de Rhina P. Espaillat." *Agua de dos ríos: Poemas, prosa, y traducciones, una colección bilingüe*. By Rhina P. Espaillat, Secretaría de Estado de Cultura. Editora Nacional, 2006, pp. 5–31.

Torres-Saillant, Silvio. *An Intellectual History of the Caribbean*. Palgrave Macmillan, 2006.

Torres-Saillant, Silvio, and Ramona Hernández. *The Dominican Americans*. Greenwood Press, 1998.

Torres-Saillant, Silvio, and Ramona Hernández. "Dominicans: Community, Culture, and Collective Identity." *One Out of Three: Immigrant New York in the Twenty-First Century*, edited by Nancy Foner, Columbia UP, 2013, pp. 223–45.

Tsagarousianou, Roza. "Rethinking the Concept of Diaspora: Mobility, Connectivity and Communication in a Globalised World." *Westminster Papers in Communication and Culture*, vol. 1, no. 1, 2004, pp. 52–65.

Turco, Lewis. *The Book of Forms: A Handbook of Poetics*, 3rd ed. UP of New England, 2000.

Untermeyer, Louis C. *The Forms of Poetry: A Pocket Dictionary of Verse*, revised ed. Harcourt, Brace, 1926.

Untermeyer, Louis C., editor. *A Treasury of Great Poems, English and American*. Simon and Schuster, 1942.

US Inflation Calculator. Accessed 14 June 2016. www.usinflationcalculator.com/.

Vartabedian, Sonya. "Bridging Poetry." *The Daily News* [Newburyport, MA], 8 Jan. 2001, p. B1–2.

Vedantam, Shankar. "Why We Think Ignorance Is Bliss, Even When It Hurts Our Health." *Shots: Health News*, from NPR, 28 July 2014, www.npr.org/blogs/health/2014/07/28/3339 45706/why-we-think-ignorance-is-bliss-even-when-it-hurts-our-health.

Vendler, Helen, editor. *Poems, Poets, Poetry: An Introduction and Anthology*, 3rd ed. Bedford Books, 2010.

Wakoski, Diane. "Picketing the Zeitgeist: The New Conservatism in American Poetry." *American Book Review*, vol. 8, no. 4, May/June 1986, p. 3.

Ward, Aileen. *John Keats: The Making of a Poet*. Viking Press, 1963.

Wells, Spencer. *The Journey of Man: A Genetic Odyssey.* Random House, 2003.

Wenkart, Henny, editor. *Sarah's Daughters Sing: A Sampler of Poems by Jewish Women.* Ktav Publishing House, 1990.

Wesling, Donald. *The New Poetries: Poetic Form Since Coleridge and Wordsworth.* Bucknell UP, 1985.

Wesling, Donald, and Enikö Bollobás. "Free Verse." *The New Princeton Encyclopedia of Poetry and Poetics,* edited by Alexander Preminger et al., Princeton UP, 1993, pp. 425–27.

White, Gail, editor. *Landscapes with Women: Four American Poets.* Singular Speech Press, 1999.

Whitlow, Carolyn Beard. "Blues in Black and White." Finch, *After New Formalism,* pp. 63–69.

Whitlow, Carolyn Beard, and Marilyn Krysl, editors. *Obsession: Sestinas in the Twenty-First Century.* Dartmouth College P, 2014.

Whitman, Walt. *Leaves of Grass.* Norton Critical Ed., edited by Sculley Bradley and Harold W. Blodgett, W. W. Norton, 1973.

Wilbur, Richard. *Oscura fruta: cuarenta y dos poemas/Dark Berries: Forty-Two Poems.* Translated by Rhina P. Espaillat, Ediciones El Tucán de Virginia, 2013.

Wilde, Oscar. *An Ideal Husband.* Edited by Russell Jackson, 2nd. ed., New Mermaids Editions A & C Black/W. W. Norton, 1993.

Williams, William Carlos. *The Autobiography of William Carlos Williams.* Random House, 1951.

Williams, William Carlos. *By Word of Mouth: Poems from the Spanish, 1916–1959.* Edited by Jonathan Cohen. New Directions, 2011.

Wilson, James Matthew. "The Intractable 'Poetry' Problem." *Modern Age,* summer 2011, pp. 58–62.

Wolf, Emily, editor. *Fresh: Poetry Collection for Young People.* Fresh Meadows Poets, 1998.

Wordsworth, William. *The Complete Poetical Works of William Wordsworth.* Edited by E. de Selincourt. Clarendon Press, 1944.

Wordsworth, William. *William Wordsworth.* Edited by Stephen Gill and Duncan Wu, Oxford UP, 1994.

Wright, George T. "English Prosody." *The New Princeton Encyclopedia of Poetry and Poetics,* edited by Alexander Preminger et al., Princeton UP, 1993, pp. 354–58.

"Yeats Collection." *Milton McC. Gatch, PhD.* miltongatch.us/yeats_collection.html. Accessed 28 July 2014.

Yellin, Emily. *Our Mothers' War: American Women at Home and at the Front during World War II.* The Free Press, 2004.

Zimmer, Benjamin, "Ma Ferguson, the Apocryphal Know-Nothing." *Language Log,* 29 Apr. 2006.

Zorzi, Rosella Mamori, and Gregory Dowling, editors. *Gondola Signore Gondola: Venice in 20th Century American Poetry.* Supernova Edizioni, 2007.

INDEX

Notes: In this index RE stands for Rhina Espaillat. Book and poem titles without a name in parentheses denote a work by RE.